SUT

HERO OF THE FLEET

This book is dedicated to my dear wife, Lily,
and to my lovely family.

HERO OF THE FLEET

TWO WORLD WARS, ONE EXTRAORDINARY LIFE – THE MEMOIRS OF CENTENARIAN WILLIAM STONE

MAINSTREAM
PUBLISHING

EDINBURGH AND LONDON

First published in Great Britain in 2009 by
MAINSTREAM PUBLISHING COMPANY
(EDINBURGH) LTD
7 Albany Street
Edinburgh EH1 3UG

ISBN 9781845965082

A catalogue record for this book is available
from the British Library

Typeset in Caslon and Requiem

Printed in Great Britain by
Clays Ltd, St Ives plc

Contents

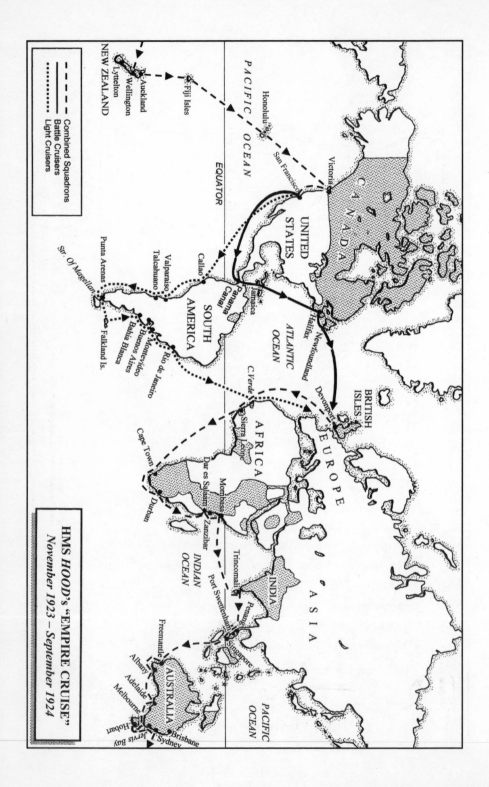

HMS *HOOD*'s "EMPIRE CRUISE"
November 1923 – September 1924

Combined Squadrons
Battle Cruisers
Light Cruisers

NEW ZEALAND
Auckland
Wellington
Lyttelton
Fiji Isles

PACIFIC OCEAN

Honolulu
San Francisco
Victoria
EQUATOR

CANADA

UNITED STATES

Panama Canal
Callao
Jamaica
Halifax
Newfoundland
Devonport

ATLANTIC OCEAN

SOUTH AMERICA

Str. Of Magellan
Punta Arenas
Valparaiso
Talcahuano
Rio de Janeiro
Montevideo
Buenos Aires
Bahia Blanca
Falkland Is.

BRITISH ISLES

EUROPE

C. Verde
Sierra Leone
Cape Town
Dar es Salaam
Mombasa
Zanzibar
Durban

AFRICA

INDIAN OCEAN

ASIA

INDIA

Trincomali
Penang
Port Swettenham
Singapore

PACIFIC OCEAN

AUSTRALIA

Freemantle
Albany
Adelaide
Melbourne
Hobart
Jervis Bay
Sydney
Brisbane

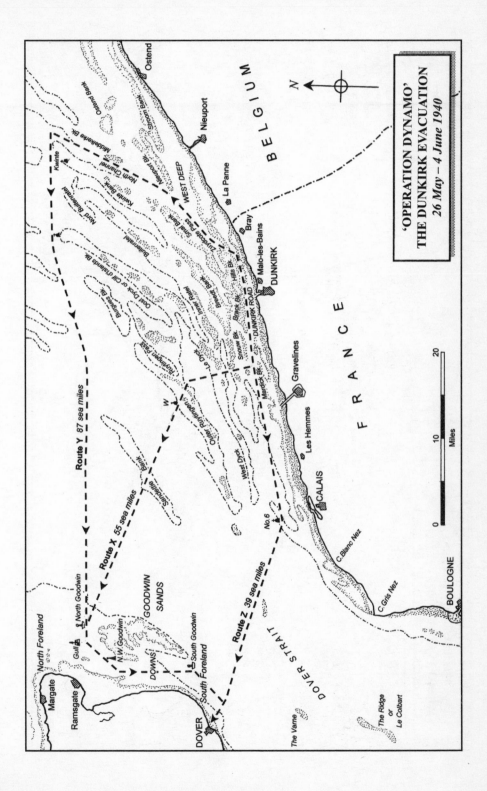

'OPERATION DYNAMO'
THE DUNKIRK EVACUATION
26 May – 4 June 1940

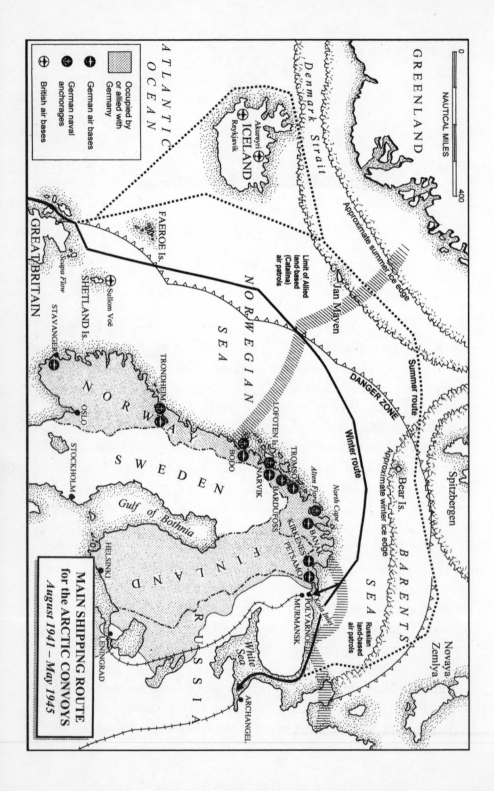

MAIN SHIPPING ROUTE
for the ARCTIC CONVOYS
August 1941 – May 1945

British air bases

German naval
anchorages

German air bases

Occupied by
or allied with
Germany

*ATLANTIC
OCEAN*

GREENLAND

NAUTICAL MILES

0

400

Denmark Strait

Akureyri

ICELAND
Reykjavik

Approximate summer ice edge

Limit of Allied
land-based
(Catalina)
air patrols

Jan Mayen

Summer route

DANGER ZONE

FAEROE Is.

N O R W E G I A N
S E A

GREAT
BRITAIN

Scapa Flow

SHETLAND Is.

Sullom Voe

STAVANGER

NORWAY

OSLO

TRONDHEIM

BODO

LOFOTEN IS.

TROMSO

NARVIK

BARDUFOSS

Alten Fjord

North Cape

Winter route

Bear Is.

Approximate winter ice edge

B A R E N T S

S E A

Spitzbergen

SWEDEN

STOCKHOLM

*Gulf
of
Bothnia*

HELSINKI

FINLAND

BANAK

KIRKENES

PETSAMO

North Cape

Russian
land-based
air patrols

Novaya
Zemlya

LENINGRAD

*White
Sea*

POLYARNOE

Kola Inlet

MURMANSK

ARCHANGEL

R U S S I A

FOREWORD

William Stone was born into a large family in rural Devon in 1900; from an early age he had the desire to enter the Royal Navy. Not surprisingly his father felt that William was too young at 15 years old, and was reluctant to agree to him enlisting in the second year of the Great War, with his elder brothers already under arms.

William achieved his ambition on his 18th birthday and joined the Royal Navy at Devonport. He later readily acknowledged that he was lucky to have avoided the horrors and sacrifices of the War, as hostilities ceased whilst he was still in training. He did succumb to the great Spanish flu pandemic and saw at first hand its terrible effects, but he was also able to witness the scenes of great joy that greeted the end of the conflict and to marvel at the sight of the tops of the scuttled German fleet protruding from the waters of Scapa Flow, in 1919.

Life on board ship, especially for a stoker, was undoubtedly hard in those early years. Even so, William took to Navy discipline and routine. It perhaps suited his own determined character to 'get things done' – an important part of the Royal Navy ethos, as I well remember from my own Service career.

Although Navy life meant long periods away from home, for William it opened up a world which, even today, only a minority have the opportunity to see. He recalled with pleasure his time based in the

Mediterranean and South Africa, and the year-long world 'Empire Cruise' when serving on HMS *Hood*. As a result, these 20 inter-war years were amongst the most exciting of his life.

In 1939 everything changed with the onset of the Second World War. No doubt, William, like me, wondered how he would react to his first direct experience of war. Later, when journalists would ask him this question, he would say, 'There was no time to think. You just got on with your job.' A sentiment I share. He saw at first hand the horrors of the Dunkirk evacuation, survived the dangerous icy waters off Russia and the near sinking of his ship during the Sicily Landings campaign. At the conclusion he felt lucky to be alive.

I recall one of the meetings with William at the celebrations marking the 200th anniversary of the Battle of Trafalgar when he had participated in the Drumhead ceremony, at Southsea. As we shared a joke, I was struck by his obvious zest for life and his infectious smile – all from a man already into his second century! I was also struck by how clearly he remembered with pride his time in the Royal Navy.

There is no doubt that the Royal Navy shaped much of William's character and continued to influence his life long after he had left the Service. His sense of duty and determination to enjoy life to the full became his hallmark and the packed church at his funeral in January 2009 illustrated the affection this engendered amongst all those who knew him.

Who could not have been moved by the sight of William and his two fellow World War One veterans, laying wreaths at the Cenotaph on 11 November 2008, to commemorate the 90th anniversary of the Great War Armistice? The last time that William was to do so. As the last man left to have served in the Royal Navy in two world wars, William's passing closes a chapter in our proud maritime history. He was the last embodiment of all that this period stood for, in our history and memory. Born into an unremarkable position in society, he left upon it a remarkable legacy and lived an extraordinary life.

H.R.H. Prince Andrew

All the nice girls love a sailor,
All the nice girls love a tar.
For there's something about a sailor –
(Well, you know what sailors are!)

Bright and breezy, free and easy,
He's the ladies' pride and joy.
Falls in love with Kate and Jane,
Then he's off to sea again.
Ship ahoy, ship ahoy!

(A.J. Mill and B. Scott, 1909)

INTRODUCTION

F leet hero William 'Bill' Stone was a boy from rural Devon who joined the Royal Navy prior to the armistice in the First World War, travelled the globe just before the British Empire's light began to fade and saw action in some of the most significant sea stories of the Second World War.

Afterwards he returned to Devon to run a barber's shop, an altogether more peaceable existence. Later, through years of retirement, he tended his garden, unaware that celebrity was stalking him. For, as the years progressed and the century turned, he became one of a dwindling number of men remaining who'd served in the First World War. This meant that in some of the most momentous anniversaries clocked up recently – including the 90th anniversary of the end of the First World War – William was a guest of honour. His life bridged two wars and encompassed the exceptional episodes and adventures that fell to a British sailor of the era.

Now with the passing of Henry Allingham (113 years) on 18 July; and Harry Patch (111 years) a week later on 25 July, we have lost our final eye-witnesses to the Great War. This makes this account you're about to read even more valuable as a piece of British history.

Just one among many, William played his part diligently and with distinction to help shape our world. It was an ordinary life lived in extraordinary times and consequently he brushed with many of the noteworthy events of the age. Before his death aged 108 he had become an internationally known ambassador for veteran sailors everywhere. His death comes as the Navy looks to embrace new challenges in ships that bear scant resemblance to those that William knew so well in a world that shrinks with every bold technological advance. His was a different kind of boldness. This is his compelling story.

I

A HERO'S FUNERAL

Snowdrops dipped their silky heads as his body was borne shoulder high before them. Above, in a watery blue sky, majestic red kites wheeled and dipped on a keen wind in the winter sunshine, issuing the occasional mournful shriek as the coffin was carried into a country church. In packed pews, veterans from the Armed Services stood tall, their chests clinking with hard-won medals. For Stoker Stone they all gave a final salute.

For 27 years William Stone was a sailor – a quarter of his long life – and thus the Royal Navy defined much of his existence. 'Once a Navy man, always a Navy man,' as the saying goes. But William was much more than the sum of his Naval service. He was a husband and father, a singer of sea shanties, a successful seller of Armistice Day poppies, a celebrated guest at state functions, a barber, a gardener, a joker and a font of knowledge about seamanship. Without seeking to be, he became an icon of the age. Above all, he was a lucky man. He had cheated death on numerous occasions and proved hugely durable in what became a throwaway society. Unfortunately, at the age of 108 and in one of the coldest winters for a decade, he finally succumbed to a chest infection. He was rewarded for all his considerable achievements with a hero's funeral.

His funeral cortege had been given a police escort on its way to the crowded church service. As it moved in stately procession down the High Street in Watlington, Oxfordshire, local people were lining the route, heads bare and bowed. They were keen to show respect to a friend and neighbour of some 20 years' standing. Soon afterwards, standard bearers from The Royal Navy, The Royal Naval Association, The Royal British Legion, HMS *Hood* Association and The Dunkirk Veterans Association slow-marched before the hearse. His coffin, draped in the union flag, went into an ancient town church through a lychgate built to mark the death of Queen Victoria, who had claimed a quarter of the known world as her own. William Stone was already an infant when the Empire was bereaved and the gate's foundation stone was laid.

Inside, the congregation, which had gathered by the hundred, was listening to some of William's favourite music. The event was sombre, the mood respectful. And then the unmistakeable notes of the theme to *Monty Python's Flying Circus* quivered through the church's numerous and upstanding organ pipes. William knew it better as 'The Liberty Bell', a march written by American John Philip Sousa in 1893 and popular throughout the services. Whatever personal associations the notes held, it was impossible to keep a smile from the lips.

'Typical William,' snorted a man in the fourth pew, struggling to suppress a laugh. He had known William well and discovered, to his relief, that the funeral exuded a similar warmth and revelry to the man himself. 'Sousa's March' was followed by 'Tiptoe Through the Tulips', another popular tune from William's era.

Everyone was told beforehand that the funeral would be a celebration rather than a lament. On this occasion, these were not empty platitudes but sincere sentiments, for it was a life well lived. The service was tailored to reflect William and marked not the tragedy of his death but the triumph of his long life. It was imbued with the same infectious optimism that kept William sprightly as a centenarian.

Accompanying the coffin into St Leonard's Church in the arms of a Navy man were William's medals, which were then laid upon it, next to a sumptuous spray of spring flowers. There was room on the coffin lid too for more flowers, delicate posies offered up by his great-granddaughters Sophie, and Annabel – who had recently survived a serious heart condition thanks to ground-breaking surgery in the USA. Their mothers Seena and Susie were both weeks away from producing more great-grandchildren who would have delighted William. That he never saw the new additions to his family or held them in his surprisingly strong arms would have been one of his few regrets.

A 14-strong choir in cranberry cassocks together with a hearty congregation sent the hymns reverberating to the top of the church's vaulted ceiling. William would have approved. Moreover, even a week before his death he would have been able to sing out the hymns confidently and clearly with the best of them, without reference to a song sheet.

Pupils from Watlington Primary School placed snowdrops on the coffin as choir and congregation sang 'I Vow To Thee My Country'. William was a familiar figure at the school, invited in as 'living history' to talk about his experiences.

And incredibly William was already an 'Old Salt' in the Royal Navy when this moving song became popular. It had begun as a poem by diplomat Cecil Spring-Rice (1859–1918), initially penned in 1908 but substantially revised to reflect the losses of the First World War. The tune, known as 'Thaxted', was an adaptation of a section of *The Planets* by composer Gustav Holst. It was first performed in 1925 and became an element of ensuing Armistice memorials. Indeed, William would have known the little-used middle verse:

> I heard my country calling, away across the sea,
> Across the waste of waters she calls and calls to me.
> Her sword is girded at her side, her helmet on her head,
> And round her feet are lying the dying and the dead.
> I hear the noise of battle, the thunder of her guns,
> I haste to thee my mother, a son among thy sons.

Patriotism that was commonplace in William's youth was reflected in the words that even today evoke the carnage of the First World War.

Not a particularly well-educated man, he nonetheless possessed the wisdom of ages before his death. He had decades of experience behind him and was an accomplished people-watcher. Those characteristics blended with the gift of geniality drew people to him. He was as happy in the company of princes as paupers and, in his own small way, William helped to overturn a class system that had been entrenched in Britain for years, simply by paying no heed to it.

Most of the mourners, bodies creaking under the weight of the years, were at least a generation behind William. None of his Royal Navy contemporaries who straddled the two wars are now left alive although three British-born veterans from the First World War survived him. One of them, Claude Choules, served in the Royal Navy in the First World War and the Australian Navy in the Second World War. The numbers of those who participated in the Second World War are in steep decline.

William had many friends drawn from numerous organisations in which he was a stalwart. There was the Dunkirk Veterans Association, Royal British Legion, The Royal Naval Association, Western Front Association and the Freemasons. That's just a sample. He was a familiar face in Watlington as resident and a perennial poppy-seller. His was a life of near-misses and he was happy to mark the sacrifice of fellow servicemen in the knowledge it might well have been him reduced to gothic lettering on a town's war memorial.

The coffin left the church on the shoulders of six stokers – now known as marine engineer mechanics – to the strains of 'Wish Me Luck As You Wave Me Goodbye'. Outside, muffled church bells rang 108 times while British Legion bearers lowered their standards in a nod to William's passing. As a bugler sounded 'The Last Post', reality dawned. When he lived William was older than a vast array of modern inventions we now take for granted: the escalator, vacuum cleaner, teabags, instant coffee, traffic signals, parking meters, Tupperware, credit cards and a host of other objects that have overarched modern life. But now the man who outlived the twentieth century had finally yielded up his stake in life.

Yet the ceremony wasn't over. Bill's daughter Anne, with Revd Angie Paterson, Chair of Watlington Parish Council, planted a shrub in the churchyard on behalf of the community. His long-time church-going companion Lady Mogg unveiled a commemorative plaque. Mourners braced themselves against the bitterly cold weather to observe how one small community that had taken William to its heart marked his passing. Then, to the strains of 'Somewhere Over the Rainbow', played by Watlington Concert Band, people drifted away assisted by sticks, frames or fellow veterans, knowing that life would from here on be a little less sunny for his departure.

2

Edwardian Childhood

At the foot of Devon, among lush green fields bordered with hedgerows humming with bird song, lies the village of Ledstone. Even in the twenty-first century it is tranquil, with hills falling into gentle folds that are smoothed down by sea breezes.

That's where I was born on Sunday, 23 September 1900, when it was still quieter and more serene even than it is today. I was born into a farming life that had stayed much the same for centuries, before the first tractor ploughed Devon's rich, red earth. There were steam engines, certainly, but the plough was horse drawn back then rather than mechanised. Almost all the jobs that needed doing were done by hand, not machine. We depended on the land to live. We wasted nothing.

Two days after I was born a British general election brought Winston Churchill to Parliament for the first time and gave the fledgling Labour Party two seats. Churchill became a lifelong hero of mine. This national news would have meant little to my neighbours, though.

Ledstone was a rural community in the South Hams, and its population was almost solely concerned with rural issues. The price of butter and the hay harvest rated far more highly in terms of importance than occurrences in distant London.

The hamlet consisted of about a dozen houses occupied by farm labourers and there were a couple of farms. There were no shops although there was a thatcher called George Heath. He was kept busy because most properties had a thatched roof back then. If you had no access to a horse or pony then you'd walk everywhere. People walked to the next village, Goveton, about a mile away every day and would think nothing of walking to and from Kingsbridge, the nearest town, just over two miles down the road. There were tracks instead of roads, just wide enough for two horses to pass.

We were a large family, though not unusually so for those days. I was the tenth child of a family that eventually comprised eight girls and six boys born to William Frederick and Emma Celia Stone. There was George, Alice, Jack, Annie, Susie, Elsie, Carrie, Walter, Nellie, myself, Lawrence, Mabel, Florrie and Cecil. Neighbours of ours had 19 children!

Pound House was so called because people used to 'pound' apples there to make cider. That all happened in an area below the living quarters in the house. A horse was harnessed to the arm of a mechanism that turned a large stone, which would crush the apples as the horse walked round and round. The pulp was put in a big press between layers of reeds and squeezed; then the juice was put in barrels. Different farmers used to bring their apples there, returning home with cider, which served as part of farm labourers' wages. Cider was also used as a remedy. For example, cider boiled with a sprig of rosemary was thought to be a cure for colds and coughs. At the time the cider press was in use most farms had a cider apple tree or two. 'Redstreak' was a favourite variety for its flavour.

But when we lived there the cider making had finished up, although the large crushing stone still remained. The area below was used as a stable where we kept Tom, the pony. Standing in the kitchen you could hear Tom hit his head on the floor when he was eating hay from the rack. On Sunday mornings when I was a small child we would hitch up the pony and trap and drive to Kingsbridge post office where we could collect the post between 7 a.m. and 9 a.m.

Next door to the stable there were two pigs. We always had two pigs because father said one pig on its own was 'picky'. With two pigs it was a race between them to see who could eat the quickest and the most. Father used to sell them as meat. Sometimes he would keep about half a pig and salt it in. Mother used to put a peeled potato in the big container of water and add salt until the potato floated. Then it was good enough for salting in the pork. They had to do this because there was no refrigeration.

Also below there was the space for coal, wood and 12 fowls. It was always amusing to us children when the cock would crow at about 5 a.m. Father used to get in a rage, saying he would cut the cockerel's b****** head off soon, although he never did. We always kept a ferret as well, for catching rabbits.

Upstairs there were three bedrooms, a living room, a large back kitchen and a little pantry. It never seemed overcrowded. Although there were lots of us there were often no more than four children at home at any one time. As soon as the girls came of age they went to situations – that means living in service as maids. The boys went to live and work on farms.

Father's mother lived in one of the bedrooms until she died aged at least 80. She was confined to her bed through asthma and old age.

The roof was half thatch and half slate. As there was no gas or electrics, we used to use oil lamps and candles to light up the house. Kingsbridge had gas installed after I was born but we never had it in the country. I can remember us children many times were looking for things on the top shelf that ran around by the roof by candlelight. How we never caught the thatch alight I don't know.

There was one stove in the living room used for all the cooking and heating. It was fuelled by coal which cost half a crown a hundredweight and was stored in the back kitchen. It came on a horse-drawn wagon from Kingsbridge. Mother was a good cook, baking lovely meals and cakes and apple pies.

The lavatory was in the garden. Whatever went into the lavatory went into a big pit. What a stink there was when Father used to put the contents of the pit on the garden as manure. The lavatory was closed in, with a door at the back. An overflow led into a nearby field. My father used to grow a lot of vegetables in our garden, so rich and well-fed was his plot.

Inside the house there were no taps. We children had to fetch all the water in buckets from a 'well' up the road. The water used to run through the bank into a stone trough and was ever so pure. It then overflowed down the road. Every Sunday Father used to bring out the boiler. We put as much water as we could on the stove so Mother could do washing on Monday morning. She used to get up at 5 a.m. on Mondays and the washing would be blowing on the line within an hour or so. There was another well the other side of the hamlet and, in the summer, both tended to run low on water.

My mother went to different homes during the week to do handwashing. She used to work for Grannie Smaridge, a local farmer's wife, and she used to get 15d a day for doing the washing and scrubbing out the kitchen but she'd say: 'I don't want that my dear. What I want is to put my feet under your table, because what I eat up here, 'tis a bit more for them down home.' Sometimes, if a farmer's wife was ill, she would go there and make butter by hand. My poor mother worked so hard. Strong as a lion, she was.

My father worked on farms all around the South Hams area of South Devon. He was skilled and could turn his hand to most jobs that cropped up on a farm. He could operate many agricultural machines like the steam-driven threshing machine or steamroller. He also slaughtered and butchered pigs, a man they used to call the 'Pig-Sticker'. He learned how to do that when he was living on a farm near East Prawle during a severe snow storm. With about 6 ft drifts of snow all around they couldn't leave the house and had to kill the pig for food.

Most people in those days kept a pig or two. My father charged a shilling (five pence in today's money) for killing and cleaning up the pig and an extra sixpence – or two and a half pence – to return the next morning and cut up the carcass, for which he used an ordinary saw. He was left-handed and the local butcher said that he could tell which pigs Father had butchered by the way they had been cut up.

As children, we all helped him with his work on occasions. In those days animals from local farms were not stunned before they were killed, nor were they taken to an abattoir. No, their throats were slit or a sharp stick was put through their jugular veins. My father, known among farmers as 'Sticker Stone', would allow us to work on the rear of the animal whilst he dealt with the head. We would sometimes have an informal biology lesson. Father would explain that the pig's insides were in many ways similar to a human's and would show us things like the animal's appendix. I don't know what he would think of the modern idea of using a pig's heart in a human – it's not something I would want myself.

Once butchered, the meat was salted down. Although all of us boys helped Father when we were young, we thought that it was a dirty job and none of us followed his trade when we grew up.

My father also used to pull 'flat-pole' cabbages planted by Mr Cole, the farmer, in several fields. He would put the cabbages in bunches of 100s and he got 3d per thousand. When we children came home from school we would help.

My father's father, also called William, and mother Sarah once lived at Stanborough Cross, on the Totnes to Kingsbridge Road in South Devon, in a turnpike house owned by the Cubitt family. That was where road users were charged before they could pass. It was more of a track than a road and those passing through would have been wagons or horse-drawn coaches. There was a water supply there as well, which was useful for the horses. My grandmother was often in on her own so she used to put two sailors' collars on the back of a chair facing the door. If tramps came by she used to shout upstairs: 'Come on, you boys!' Seeing the sailors' collars and hearing that, the tramps would soon be off, believing a couple of strapping sailors were about to set upon them. There's nothing remaining of the house today.

For a while my father worked at Fallapit House, in East Allington. When he was there the pig broke its leg so Squire Cubitt ordered it to be killed and buried. Father and the other man he worked with thought it was a pity to bury all this lovely pork. They decided to cut up the best parts and bury the remainder.

At their cottage my mother put the curtains across the windows and shut the door while she was salting the pork. This was very unusual so a neighbour came in and asked: 'Mrs Stone, why ever have you got the door shut and the curtain across the window?'

Of course, she saw all this pork so my mother gave her some and told her not to tell anyone. Well, this neighbour told her husband and her husband told people at the pub and soon everyone knew about it, including the Squire himself.

The Squire gave orders that the two men had to apologise in the drawing room at Fallapit House or they would have to leave their jobs and their homes. The other man agreed to apologise but my father was stubborn, even though it was a serious business to lose your job back then. A relative of his implored him to say sorry but he said he wouldn't. Eventually, on Saturday night he condescended to do so.

But when he went into the room at the appointed hour and saw the other man on his knees in front of the Squire, with all the rest of the staff lined up to watch, he turned around and said: 'I'm not going to bloody well apologise.'

So he shut the door and he left. He and my mother lost their home, which was two doors from the pub.

Squire William Cubitt (1834–91) was the son of one of Britain's most celebrated architects. Thomas Cubitt (1788–1855) takes credit for some of the most familiar aspects of London, including significant sections of Bloomsbury, Belgravia, the creation of Battersea Park and the eastern end of Buckingham Palace. He found royal favour for his work on Osborne House on the Isle of Wight, reputedly Queen Victoria's preferred residence, and was a pioneer of urban sewage systems. He and his brother William formed a building company that figured largely in the creation of squares and fascias around the capital. When Thomas Cubitt died Queen Victoria called his death 'a real national loss. A better, kind hearted or more simple, unassuming man never breathed.'

William Cubitt was his sixth child of ten. Comparatively little is known about him, except that he was a Justice of the Peace in Devon and was once a lieutenant in the Coldstream Guards. He bought Fallapit House from the Fortescue family prior to 1870, kept foxhounds there for a couple of seasons and financed the restoration of St Andrew's Church in East Allington. He was also a noted supporter of the local school although appears to have had no children of his own. Given what we know of the feudal approach at times adopted by Squire Cubitt, it is intriguing to note an inscribed brass plaque commemorating him in St Andrew's Church was paid for by people working on the Fallapit estate and speaks of their 'admiration and respect'.

Curiously, the Cubitt family links to William Stone were echoed in the twenty-first century. In 1883 the family building firm was taken over and became known as Holland, Hannen and Cubitt. And it was this company that built the Cenotaph in Whitehall. Before its familiar, stark outline, William became a celebrated visitor as a longstanding survivor of two world conflicts.

Squire Cubitt's older brother George (1828–1917) ultimately became 1st Lord Ashcombe and he also maintained links with East Allington through support for the church and school. It is George Cubitt's three grandsons, Captain Henry Cubitt (1892–1916), Lt Alick Cubitt (1894–1917) and Lt (William) Hugh Cubitt (1896–1918), that are remembered on the East Allington war memorial plaque. All died on the Western Front, which underscores the Stone family's good fortune in that all three serving sons came home safely.

With the death of the eldest three, the baronetcy went to a fourth son, Roland, whose daughter Rosalind was the mother of Camilla, Duchess of Cornwall. William met Camilla at Buckingham Palace in 2007 when he and fellow veteran Henry Allingham went first to a Ministry of Defence lunch and then an audience with the Queen held at Buckingham Palace during a garden party. A lifelong royalist, he was thrilled to greet the Queen, Prince Philip, Prince Charles and his wife Camilla, the Duke of Kent, the Duke and Duchess of Wessex and Princess Alexandra. With his characteristic cheeky humour William asked both Camilla and Sophie for a kiss. But both were wearing wide-brimmed hats festooned with feathers and laughingly declined, claiming the extended headwear made a kiss an impossibility.

William and Emma had lived at East Allington but, at the time of the 1891 census, they were living at Lower Merrifield, Slapton, with their first four children. Later they came to a rented house in Ledstone. It was a great place to be a child.

We used to play hopscotch, ring-a-ring o' roses and hide and seek. We used to hit a hoop with a stick to make it wheel around. We put chestnuts on string and fought with them. Father used to play the accordion and I often used to dance around the kitchen with my sisters.

And we used to get up to mischief as well. We would go 'scrumping', pinching apples from the orchard next door to our place. We used to break open a locked door leading from our garden. The farmer used to chase us off.

Father used to keep a hogshead of cider with a wooden tap. [A Devonshire hogshead contained 63 gallons.] We used to help ourselves until he realised what was happening. Then he put a cap on the tap which had a key. We tried all sorts of ways to get it off but we never could.

We children had a trolley and we used it to collect wood from the meadows for burning. On Saturday mornings we took the knives and forks outside to clean them using brick dust, which is what we used before Vim was widely available. Although you could buy Vim at the time – which had the advertising slogan 'When things are dim, give 'em Vim' – we didn't have enough spare money for it. Don't forget, cutlery was made of mild steel at the time which used to mark quite easily. Stainless steel wasn't around until I was a teenager. To help out at home we'd pick mushrooms, blackberries, hazelnuts and chestnuts from the woods near our home. On Fridays one of the children would have to go into Kingsbridge to collect the local newspaper for ourselves and some neighbours. We used to go to bed when it got dark and got up when it was light.

At three years old I started school in Goveton, the next village, where I was one of about sixty children. It sounds early but all the local pupils began school life at that age. Our teacher in the infants was Miss Elizabeth Gillard, who saw many of the Stone children through their early education. The oldest pupils there were aged 13. My father had only managed one day of school in East Allington although my father-in-law stayed at school until he was ten.

Life for children like William in Edwardian England was a world away from the one known by youngsters today. The children's toy industry was gaining momentum during William's childhood, although it is unlikely to have had an effect on the Stone brood. At the time upper or middle class children might have played with clockwork toys, puzzles, books, train sets, dolls and dolls houses, toy animals or soldiers, or a rocking horse. Wax dolls were made in Britain while luxury dolls were usually imported from France. In 1901 Frank Hornby patented his new toy called 'Mechanics Made Easy' which was re-launched six years later with the name 'Meccano'. And it wasn't until 1902 that Richard Steiff produced the first jointed soft bear in Germany.

At around the same time an endearing cuddly bear was produced in the USA, mimicking a cartoon that was popular at the time. The cartoon showed Teddy Roosevelt, who was President from 1901 to 1909, refusing to shoot a baby bear that had been captured for him to dispatch following an unsuccessful hunt in Mississippi. Soon both American and German makers of cute cuddly toys were using the name 'Teddy' bears to differentiate them from the fierce-looking creatures that had been made previously.

Children rich and poor delighted in sweets in Edwardian times. They had a choice that included peppermint lumps, sherbet, liquorice allsorts, satin pralines, penny everlasting toffee strips, cinder toffee, aniseed balls and coconut ice. As the popularity of day trips increased, more children than ever were sampling 'penny licks' of ice cream, served on thick glass plates.

Children's clothing tended to be made from thick material including flannel or starched cotton and was worn in layers for warmth. Although moving pictures were frequently attractions in travelling fairs, the first purpose-built cinemas only started appearing after 1908. It's unlikely William's childhood in rural Devon would have featured a trip to the cinema, books or, for that matter, a teddy bear.

Until 1891 – just nine years before William was born – there was nothing standard about schooling in Britain. All the evidence shows that education wasn't high on the agenda in Victorian England. For centuries the churches had run schools of varying standards, focussing largely on learning the Scriptures. They ran alongside 'Ragged Schools', run for poor children and paid for by the rich. Still, schooling was only available to the few. And that's the way many people liked it. Some wealthy folk, who had access to fee-paying schools for their own offspring, were concerned that schooling would reduce the labour supply. They knew that more educated people were less likely to tolerate the shocking conditions that often prevailed in industry at the time.

Meanwhile, hard-up families were also suspicious of education because it often cost money and took children into the classroom when they could have been at work. Although the employment of children aged nine and under was forbidden in 1833 the lower age limit was often not enforced.

In 1870 The School Act *had the country divided into districts, each with an education board. The schools run by the board cost money but the poorest children were paid for by charitable donations. These schools were run alongside church schools but attracted better teachers thanks to enhanced wages. Ten years later school became compulsory for children aged between five and ten. But it wasn't until 1891 that education was finally made free when Parliament overruled belligerent members of the aristocracy who'd felt it was unwise to spend taxpayers' money on schooling. Eight years later the school leaving age was placed at twelve. In 1903* The Employment of Children Act *decreed that no one should leave school before the age of 14 without a standard education. The aim was to improve the levels of reading, writing, maths and general knowledge among the workforce. This sometimes penalised the quick learners who were able to quit full-time education clutching a certificate saying what they'd achieved much earlier than those who were less gifted. The Act also stipulated that no child under the age of fourteen should be employed in any occupation before 6 a.m. or after 8 p.m. or for more than nine and a half hours a day or on a Sunday. These regulations outlawed many of the bad practices linked to child employment but were hard to enforce, particularly in remote mining and farming villages, or large cities with a high proportion of migrant labourers.*

Goveton was a busy place with lots of children. There was a post office, a blacksmith and a hunt kennels in the field adjacent to the school. When you sat in class you could hear the hounds of the South Pool harriers howling. There was a carpenter's shop behind the school and up the lane was an engineer who used to do all the work for local farmers, like sharpening the blades of harvesting machinery. There was no pub but the house where we lived later, during the

1920s, Brook Cottage, once sold cider. The schoolhouse was used as a chapel at weekends. The school could use the chapel organ in the daytime. Squire Hubert Brunskill, who lived at Buckland House, was a keen cricketer and once captained the Devon side. He also enjoyed hunting. If he went through the village the schoolgirls curtsied and the boys doffed their caps.

Before school I had to fetch the milk each morning from local farmers and make deliveries around the village. It was a chore mother made all us children do at one time or another. It was scalded milk and it cost a penny a pint. I used to get it for the neighbours as well and they used to give me a lump of cake for doing so. We had other ways of earning extra money as well. My brother and I would cut weeds in the local farmers' fields for a few pennies. We would send away for Christmas cards and sell them around the district. Also, we would pay local families a half penny for rabbit skins and sell them on for a penny.

We went to St Peter's Church in Buckland Tout Saints. I can remember seeing Squire Brunskill, his family and servants file in and take their allotted pews. I used to be given a penny for the collection. But on one occasion I changed this into two halfpennies. I put one into the collection and used the other to buy Woodbine cigarettes. My misdemeanour was soon discovered and my father soon used his trouser belt to send me the clear message that this sort of behaviour would not be tolerated. I never did it again.

My brother Lawrence, who was eighteen months younger than me, and I joined the Boy Scouts when I was ten. The scouts used to meet once a week at the Market Hall in Kingsbridge. On one occasion we went to Salcombe, camping. It was the only holiday I had when I was a boy. As for my parents, they never had a holiday.

Like thousands of others, William and his brother joined the scout movement within the first few years of its formation. It had originated with Robert Baden-Powell who, during his army career, noticed how men of the ranks benefited from learning survival skills associated with scouting. At the time 'scouting' referred to the tracking and camping that army reconnaissance units undertook. At the Siege of Mafeking (13 October 1899–17 May

1900) during the Boer War he witnessed boys happy at work in typical military scouting activities. Afterwards he wrote Aids to Scouting, *which became a best-seller both inside and outside army circles.*

Although still in the army, Baden-Powell returned to Britain and contacted youth organisations already in existence in Britain, including the Boy's Brigade, suggesting some new ideas. He was by now a national hero and his suggestions carried plenty of clout.

By 1907 the first scout camp was held at Brownsea Island and Baden-Powell experimented with the patrol system which still exists today. This had the boys organising themselves in groups with elected leaders. The same year he wrote another best-seller Scouting for Boys, *containing information he had gleaned from his own experience and culled from other youth groups of the era. Since its publication in book form in 1908 it has become the fourth best-seller of all time after* The Bible, *the* Koran *and Mao Tse-Tung's* Little Red Book. *Although he was from a military background, Baden-Powell's new movement was considered less regimented than the Boy's Brigade and soon overwhelmed its rivals through a popular groundswell.*

Other treats were few and far between. We'd go up to Buckland House sometimes to see the Christmas tree there and we'd go to the Rectory at Charleton for tea parties occasionally. School records show that the 'Wild Beast Show' came to Kingsbridge in 1906 and most of the pupils skipped the classroom to see it. I can't remember now if I went. However, in that same year, I received an 'honourable mention' at school so perhaps I stayed for lessons instead.

We all enjoyed local events, like the 'Kingsbridge Show'. Everybody went after haymaking. There were lots of stalls on the pavements selling things like toffee apples, cinnamon sticks and cherries. There was a roundabout driven by a steam engine and a boxing booth. Once I was so delighted because when I was ten I was riding our pony, who was thirteen hands high, in the Kingsbridge Show and I got first prize. My photo was in the newspaper captioned: 'William Stone: the youngest competitor in the show'.

At Christmas we never knew if we would be eating turkey or goose for dinner until late on Christmas Eve. The butcher's shop in Fore

Street, Kingsbridge, had all the turkeys and geese hanging in the windows and, after 9 p.m., the prices were cut down. Father would wait opposite in the Exeter Inn until he got bottom price.

We used to hang our stockings up and we'd get an orange and apple, some sweets and some chestnuts for roasting. We were pleased with things like that, indeed we were. We always had lovely Christmas puddings. In fact, Mother used to make two so that we could have one when Jack, my older brother who was away in the Navy, came home. There were always silver three-penny pieces in it. Mother and Father would make sure the youngest child got at least one by slipping the coins in when they dished it up.

When William was born it was not only a new century but a time of great social change for both children and adults. Britain turned a page upon the death of Queen Victoria on 22 January 1901. There was national grieving on an unprecedented scale as Victoria, on the throne for 63 years, was considered the 'Mother of the Nation'. Everyone was expected to wear black, no matter what age or background. The national mood was in any event sombre because of the on-going Boer War and a scandal unfolding about the appalling conditions in concentration camps run by the British for refugee Boers. The atmosphere was further blackened when the coronation of King Edward VII (9 November 1841–6 May 1910) had to be postponed, as he was seriously ill.

However, by August 1902 Edward was sufficiently recovered from appendicitis to enjoy his coronation and the war had been won, albeit without the glory that Britons sought during the era.

The next great battle on the home front was against poverty. Child poverty was extensive across Britain. Although his family were poor, William was certainly better off than counterparts in towns or cities where disease was rife and accommodation unsanitary. At least his family had the option of growing food or eating what they killed. And there was probably less evidence in the countryside of the prejudice against the poor that prevailed.

People soon fell into the poverty trap if they were too old or sick to work. Children were poor because of their parents' and their own low wages, the death or illness of the family's main wage earner and the large size of families. Jobs were also getting hard to come by as Britain was being challenged for her 'top-of-the-pile' position in the world by both America and Germany. Evidence of the declining health of the nation came about with the Army's recruitment figures during the Boer War, when between 40 and 60 per cent of applicants were rejected because they were not sufficiently fit.

There was a long-held suspicion in Victorian times that poverty was endemic among those who frittered their money on drink. But by Edwardian times this notion was being challenged by reformers including future Prime Ministers David Lloyd George (17 January 1863–26 March 1945) and Winston Churchill (30 November 1874–24 January 1965), who felt the state of the nation's poor was a national disgrace. The two established political parties – the Liberals and the Conservatives – were also eyeing the rise of the Labour party. By speaking for the disadvantaged in this new age of enlightenment, there was anxiety that Labour would corner some of the vote, still restricted to men over 30 who satisfied various qualifications – amounting to less than a quarter of the population. A number of local councils began slum clearance programmes which improved the lot of the inner city poor.

King Edward VII did his bit by providing dinners for some 456,000 poor and destitute people in London to mark his coronation at a cost of more than £30,000.

When I was about ten or eleven I used to work after school at Bowcombe poultry farm for a man called Mr Edmonds. I had tea when I got there and supper before I left. On Saturdays and Sundays I spent all day there and I got a total of sixpence a week.

I used to drive the pony and trap to different places to collect broody hens. Mr Edmonds' spaniel, Tudor, used to leap on the back just as I was setting off and would sit beside me in the front seat. We must have looked a funny pair. I would put the broody hen in a crate with 13 chicks and drive them to Kingsbridge Station. On one occasion I took two pigs to Totnes pig factory. I took my younger brother Cecil when he was only about four or five. The pigs were squealing, Cecil was crying. There seemed a terrible commotion. We had some relatives nearby so I dumped Cecil there and picked him up on the way back. Two tramps held out their hands wanting a ride. I said: 'Go to hell.'

The census taken in 1911 shows that there were ten of us living in Pound House, Ledstone. In addition to my father and mother there was Elsie, seventeen, who was a domestic servant, Nellie, twelve, myself, Lawrence, eight, Mabel, seven, Florence, aged two and one-year-old Cecil, as well as my grandmother Sarah.

School was very nice because in the juniors Miss Minnie Collins was a good teacher. We were taught to read and write and studied Scripture. By today's standards the school was primitive. There was no drinking water. That had to be fetched from a tap in the village. There weren't enough desks for the infants and it was rather dark as there were no electric lights. The school was heated by an open fire place. A urinal was finally built in the school while I was an infant. In March 1904 the school was shut for four weeks because Miss Collins was ill. On several occasions it was closed on account of Mrs Brunskill who liked to hold dances and jumble sales there. Many times children stayed away from school to help at home or on the farm. Sometimes the whole school was closed for blackberry picking. At the end of what turned out to be my final term I remember the teacher, Miss Collins, saying, 'I shall not need you again next term, Billy' and that was that.

3

FARM BOY

Having finished my schooling I needed to find myself a job. My father was able to point me in the direction of a farmer, George Giles, who had mentioned that he needed a boy to help out. I went along to the farm, Sherford Down, at Sherford near Kingsbridge, and said: 'Father says you wants a boy.'

'And what wage do you want?' asked the farmer. 'Well, my father says half a crown a week,' said I. 'Ooh, pretty much isn't it?' he said. Of course, it wasn't a lot at all as my father knew the going rate. 'When can you start?' asked the farmer. 'Now,' I replied. And I did.

So, aged thirteen, I left my family home to live in there although it was only two or three miles away. I shared a bedroom with two others, the head horseman Bert Tucker, who was several years older than me, and the second horseman Dick Tucker. They were cousins and both came from Sherford. I had a little bed in the corner. They shared a bigger bed. Some years later Bert joined the Royal Marines and was lost along with Lord Kitchener when HMS *Hampshire* was sunk. The battlecruiser, en route to Russia, is thought to have run into a mine off the Scottish coast on 5 June 1916 and there were only 11 survivors from a crew of 655. By then everyone knew Lord Kitchener's face.

As Secretary of State of War he was the recruiting 'sergeant' for the Empire, appearing to point out of posters which carried slogans like 'Your Country Needs You'. Once, Kitchener had been a hero after military campaigns in the Sudan and South Africa. But at the time of his death he was less popular. There were plenty of theories about the ship's loss at the time. It was thought to have been sabotaged by a Boer or by Irish republicans. The slow pace of the rescue was thought by some to be a sign that Parliament was pleased to be rid of him. However, his death was supposed by most to be a disaster for the war effort.

I had often done odd jobs on the farm during my boyhood days – helping to clip hedges and jobs like that in the evenings or at the weekend. It earned you a few pence that you could look forward to spending, particularly when the fair visited Kingsbridge.

Now I had all kinds of jobs on the farm. In those days most farms didn't specialise in one form of livestock like they do now. The farm that I worked on kept cattle, pigs and hens as well as growing fodder crops.

At 5.55 a.m. the farmer would ring the bell from his bedroom, and five minutes later ring it again for us to get up.

In the summer I would go and fetch the cows from the field, bring them into the house [shed] and give them feed. Being a local man born and bred, the farmer would only keep South Devon cattle. The Tuckers would get their horses in as well.

A whistle was blown at 7 a.m. when it was breakfast time. On the menu was bacon and mash. Only on Sunday did we get an egg. To begin with, I couldn't eat all my breakfast as it was fat bacon. The dog used to sit with his head between my legs. I would look around at everybody and give my bacon to the dog when no one was watching. He wolfed it down. But after a short while I would offer my plate up for more. I'd got used to eating fat bacon as I was hungry.

Of course back then, all milking was done by hand. I remember the first time I had a go at milking, I happened to choose a cow which had just had her first calf. Like me, she was new to the game of milking and didn't take kindly to it. As soon as I started she kicked violently and over went the bucket. For a while after that I was designated a novice and the farmer made a point of following me around. He always managed to get more milk out of the cow than I did. It was important that all the milk was drawn out of each animal as if this was not done they would dry up sooner. Most days we would each milk 12 to 14 cows and eventually I mastered the technique. I also got the hang of choosing the cows that were less likely to make a fuss about being milked.

The farmer would keep a supply of full fat milk for use by his family and sell some to the villagers. Some was put through a hand-operated separator, which removed the cream from the milk. It was my job to turn the separator handle. The cream that it created was used to make butter and the remaining thin milk given to the pigs and cattle. The farmer's wife would make the butter by hand (sometimes my mother would help) and on market day take it, together with eggs from the hens, to sell at Kingsbridge.

The bull was kept in the field as well. When I went to get him he roared like mad. I couldn't stretch my arms around his neck, he was so huge. But I used to have to get him to his own house. There I'd put a handful of cake [feed] into his straw. He liked that.

I cleared the manure from the sheds and the other men cleared the stables. All the manure was put into a large pit behind the stables and later in the year taken by horse and cart and spread over the fields. The farmer grew acres of mangolds, a sort of root vegetable, which were used as fodder for the cattle. When the mangolds were ready to harvest we would pull them up, cut off the tops and store them by a hedge, covered in straw and hedge parings to protect them from the winter frost.

There were odd jobs, like cutting down weeds and hedges. I fetched the cows back in again at 4 p.m. for the evening milk and turned the separator again. It was the same routine all over again; twice a day, seven days a week.

In the wintertime the cows would lay in. Breakfast was later and I used to go out about 7 a.m. and feed them and give them more straw to lay on. I helped at calving many times, using a rope around the front legs of the calf to 'pull it off' its mother. You could get called to help with calving any time of day or night. It was my job to make sure newborn calves were feeding. You had to put your finger in their mouths to get them to start sucking, then take them to their mothers. And I had to feed the young pigs and the calves when they were just weaned. I took the cows out into the field again then I had to come back and clean out the houses, putting new straw in. To help prevent foot rot I would empty lots of lime into the gateways.

Along with my 'official' duties at the farm went my other role of rat catcher. Mr Giles, the farmer, would give me a penny for each rat I caught and I remember that at one point I was doing so well that he thought I was bringing the same rat to him twice! 'I've paid you for this one before, haven't I Bill?' he would say. After that, just to make sure he was getting his pennyworth he made a point of cutting off the tail of each rat as I claimed my reward so that he knew that a second claim could not be made.

The housekeeper was Alice Giles, the farmer's sister. She used to wash my feet sometimes. It was her way of helping look after me, I suppose.

On Sunday mornings I would change into my other clothes after breakfast and I would attend the church service at Sherford. In the afternoon I used to go home to Ledstone to change my vest and pants for clean ones. When I got back to the farm I used to put overalls over these, my best clothes, to carry on work. Then, in the evening, we used to go to church in Stokenham. It was about three miles away and I would walk there. Afterwards we lads used to go into the pub, have half a pint of beer and have a sing-a-long. You weren't allowed in a pub until you were 18 but the landlord was always pleased to get you to have a glass of beer. I couldn't stay too late, though. I had to be home at Sherford by 10 p.m. or I would be locked out.

Farmer Giles got married while I was there. His bride was called Mabel Evans and she was a nurse. Her mother was a schoolteacher from Salcombe. Miss Giles had to give up the reins and she didn't like it very well.

On one occasion Mr Giles said: 'I know what a harvest moon is, but what is a honeymoon?' And she said: 'I'll tell you what it is. You get married and then you go away and talk silly. Then you come home and you talk sensible again.'

She spoke sharply because Miss Giles was irritated by her brother's 'lovey-dovey' behaviour. Mr Giles used to say 'yes darling' to his wife all the time and I think it was terrible to Miss Giles. I believe Miss Giles went to live with another sister after her brother's marriage.

In Victorian times one of Britain's best loved patriotic songs was amended. Instead of 'Rule, Britannia! Britannia, rule the waves', the exhortation was changed to '. . . Britannia rules the waves . . .' In simple terms, she did.

Overseas, Britain under the rule of Queen Victoria amassed a number of lucrative foreign territories to inflate its prestige and world standing. Key to the maintenance of the colonies was the British Navy.

Britain was also dominant in terms of world trade. Such was this small island's astonishing success, some Britons believed they were exercising a God-given right to rule. Others were more canny, realising that a new dawn would bring a different world order, one that would see Britain challenged for its place at the head of the table.

Germany was a clear favourite for the title of 'Young Pretender'. It was created as recently as 1871 when politician Otto von Bismarck (1815–98) unified its previously disparate elements in central Europe, embracing Polish, Danish and French minorities. Germany's monarch, Kaiser Wilhelm II – grandson of Queen Victoria – was keen to emulate the imperial spread of the British Empire.

France had long viewed Germany with deep-rooted suspicion, distrusting the self confidence and power associated with unification. If there was a race for colonies in Africa and the Pacific, the French certainly had no intention of being second or worse. While the French defeat at Waterloo in 1815 was largely a distant memory in the streets of Paris, it remained a potent symbol for the British. But a generally held suspicion of the French was superseded by concern about the aspirations of Russia that were encroaching on the British Empire. The focus for a possible clash of interests was Afghanistan, which became a buffer state between India and the Russian empire.

Although the USA was still stinging after the civil war, it was spreading fledgling wings and discovering a taste for international influence. Following the Spanish-American War of 1898 the US found itself heading an empire of its own, including Cuba and the Philippines.

While every international player of note was both keen to expand to new fields of fortune and to defend its own a shakedown of national and foreign interests was inevitable. As the twentieth century unfolded, its stage was being set for a shakedown of epic proportions.

A year after I started work the First World War (1914–18) began. My elder brothers had joined the Royal Navy and soon I was eager to follow suit. In 1915 I went to Kingsbridge to enquire about entry and passed all the necessary tests. You could join the Navy as a lad between the ages of 15 and 16½, training on shore until you became a Boy, First Class when you could go into cruisers or bigger ships. It certainly sounded a lot more entertaining than working on a farm day in, day out. However, when I took the forms home for my father to sign he refused to do so, saying that he already had two sons in the Navy and that I was too young anyway, so the papers were sent back. If I had joined up I perhaps wouldn't have lived such a long life. That was in the first half of the war and I could have perished at Jutland, for example, which took place when I was 16.

One of the youngest ever recipients of the Victoria Cross was John Travers Cornwell, who was only a matter of months older than William when he died at the Battle of Jutland in 1916. Born in Leyton, East London, John – better known as Jack – left his job as a Brooke Bond tea van assistant to join the Navy in 1915 and trained at Devonport. After that he was posted to HMS Chester *as a Boy, First Class.*

When the Battle of Jutland got under way at the end of May 1916 he was acting as a sight setter on one of HMS Chester's *forward 6 in. guns. As the pounding duel continued, the ship took several direct hits. Even though members of his gun crew were lying dead or dying around him and he himself was mortally injured, Jack stayed at his post calmly awaiting orders. He was apparently oblivious to the shards of metal piercing his chest. He died on 2 June in Grimsby Hospital.*

Later, Captain Robert Lawson, from HMS Chester, *wrote to his mother Lily:*

I know you would wish to hear of the splendid fortitude and courage shown by your son during the action of 31 May. His devotion to duty was an example for all of us. The wounds which resulted in his death within a short time were received in the first few minutes of the action. He remained steady at his most exposed post at the gun, waiting for orders.

His gun would not bear on the enemy; all but two of the ten crew were killed or wounded, and he was the only one who was in such an exposed position. But he felt he might be needed, and, indeed, he might have been; so he stayed there, standing and waiting, under heavy fire, with just his own brave heart and God's help to support him.

I cannot express to you my admiration of the son you have lost from this World. No other comfort would I attempt to give to the mother of so brave a lad, but to assure her of what he was, and what he did, and what an example he gave. I hope to place in the boys' mess a plate with his name on and the date and the words, 'Faithful unto Death'. I hope some day you may be able to come and see it there. I have not failed to bring his name prominently before my Admiral.

As news of Jack's bravery spread a memorial fund set up in his name exceeded £21,800. Perhaps curiously, it was used in part to provide portraits of Jack for schools around the country. His body was exhumed from a pauper's grave and given a more fitting monument. Within months the grave also contained the body of his father, a serving soldier who had died from bronchitis. Soon afterwards Jack's mother was presented with the VC by King George V.

Cornwell's name became a byword for bravery as Sir Edward Carson's comments reveal. 'I ask people who grumble if they ever heard the story of John Travers Cornwell . . . I feel that this boy, who died at the post of duty, sends this message through me as First Lord of the Admiralty for the moment to the people of the Empire: "Obey your orders, cling to your post, don't grumble, stick it out."'

Around the same time, aged about 15, I left the farm and got another job. For a few months I worked for Mr Cole at Ledstone, sleeping at home but eating on the farm. Then I started work for a haulage company at Kingsbridge driving a horse and cart for Mr Whiting delivering flour, amongst other things. I also used to deliver coke from the gas works to the quay where the boats were moored and tip it into the holds. On one occasion – not when I was driving – the horse and cart both fell in with the coke. They had to get a crane to haul them out. I don't think the horse was hurt very much. I would take loads of cracked stone to nearby beaches like Thurlestone, deposit it and load up with sand from the sea front and bring it back. It was hard work but I got about 25s a week.

Then I went to work for the council. In the summer I would water the streets with a horse-drawn water cart to dampen down the dust. There was no tarmac on the road in those days so when the wind was blowing we had to water the street or it became unbearable for road users.

Later, I was employed by the council as a second 'hand' driving a steamroller. We used to work on the local roads laying chippings and rolling them in to make a metalled surface. Later still I moved up to a 12-ton engine. Again, this was steam powered and similar to a traction engine that one might see at fairs these days. Operating such a vehicle was a two-man job. One man would be responsible for driving it which involved keeping the boiler going and dealing with steam pressure and the like. The other man was responsible for steering. We would rotate these jobs so that we kept our hand in at both duties. The steamroller and its trailer jack-knifed on the way into Kingsbridge on one occasion, and blocked the road for hours. Once there was a girl servant in a house nearby waving to me and I nearly went into the hedge while I was driving.

I travelled with the steamroller to Strete, Slapton and Stoke Fleming, sleeping in a council caravan. I hitched it to the back of the engine and parked it near to where the job was, in a gateway or farm entrance. It was a lovely little caravan with two bunks, oil lamps, a little stove and seats around it. I took food like bacon and eggs, pork, rabbit and a loaf of bread with me. I got milk from local farms. The farmers would always come and have a yarn with me. Sometimes my sister Annie visited me as she was living and working out that way. It meant the engine driver could go to his home in East Allington, leaving me to fire up the engine in the mornings.

When I was staying at Slapton another council worker wanted to play a joke by frightening me. He opened the door of the caravan and made a spooky noise. I had no idea what it was but I said: 'If you don't b***** off I shall pick up a saucepan and smack you over the bloomin' head.'

'Don't do that Bill,' he cried and that's when I realised it was someone I knew playing a trick. But I never felt scared or alone when I was in the caravan. I really enjoyed my time there.

Then I got offered another job to drive a steam engine. The council's surveyor asked me why I wanted to leave. It was very difficult to find young workers at the time because the war was on and most men had joined up. He asked me if I wanted more money but I turned him down because I wanted to operate the engine. It was a stationary engine in a copse. We pulled the wood to the engine using a winch with chains around the engine drum and then we cut it up into planks with a circular saw, driven by the engine. The tops of the trees went as pit props. We would take the wood to Kingsbridge station and leave the engine there for the night. By this time I was earning good money. Father worked with me, cutting up wood for the government. This was my last local job before I joined the Navy and oddly it had an influence on my duties during my first weeks of service.

The family had a great Naval tradition. My father had three brothers who had 'done their full time' during the previous century – one had been a Master at Arms. My mother also had a brother who had done his full time. Three of my brothers and I all joined the Royal Navy. My father never saw military service himself as he had fallen off a horse when he was younger and had broken his arm. The arm had not set correctly and was always a bit crooked. I remember that he also had a pit in his forehead which had been caused during the same accident – as he had fallen from the horse, he had hit his head on a plough shear.

My eldest brother, George, broke with the family's Naval tradition and joined the Royal Horse Artillery. The last time I ever saw him was in about 1908 when he cycled down to South Devon all the way from London. What happened to him after that I never knew, though I gather he died in India. I think my father was hurt that he didn't get in touch but he always said: 'If he doesn't write letters home, we don't have to answer them.' Years later another of my brothers, Jack, who was also in the Royal Navy, was in India and tried to find him, but George had apparently died some time before.

Jack served in the Royal Navy for 22 years, rising to the rank of Petty Officer. I remember that at one time he was on the destroyer HMS *Isis* and I was on a party from HMS *Hood* that was responsible for refuelling her.

Walter, who was about three or four years older than me, also served his full time in the Navy.

Lawrence, who was 18 months younger than me, followed me into the Navy. In fact he did more than that – he followed me to my first ship, HMS *Tiger*. Lawrie finished his Naval career also holding the rank of a Petty Officer, having served about 24 years.

My youngest brother, Cecil, followed George by joining the Army and was in the REME (Royal Electrical and Mechanical Engineers). Of course, Lawrence and Cecil both served in the Second World War only, having been too young for service in the First World War.

In the eighteenth and nineteenth centuries, Britain had dominated the world, not least because her navy was acknowledged as the most powerful and the best. Thus, joining the Royal Navy had a certain kudos. Its sailors had no doubt they were helping to make Britain great. Furthermore, Britain had superior internal communications, was a major tariff-free market and did not have to maintain a large standing army, thanks to the Navy's flexible and long reach.

Ultimately Great Britain defeated France, her main opponent at the time, by a combination of sea and military power applied on a global scale in theatres of operation in Europe, North Africa, India and North America. Backing British efforts were superior external maritime communications and industrial and financial muscle.

For nearly a century afterwards, British global dominance, hailed as 'Pax Britannica', was rooted in her battle fleets and merchant navies. But by the beginning of the twentieth century maritime strategies were changing in the wake of a new world order. New centres of industrial and naval power – the United States, Germany and Japan – were elevated to the 'Great Powers', joining the established nations of Britain, France, Russia, Italy and Austria–Hungary. By 1914 Imperial Germany possessed a navy second in size only to Britain's. Based just across the North Sea, it posed a direct threat to metropolitan Britain and the heart of British global power.

At the same time, the importance of sea power was eroded by the new nineteenth-century technologies of the railway, telegraph, combustion engine and radio. These enhanced the internal communications and strategic viability of the Continental Powers, particularly the United States and Russia. Evolving twentieth-century developments of the aeroplane, submarine, mechanised armies and logistics, electronics, and missile technology further consolidated the global influence of these vast self-sufficient centres of industrial and military power which were invulnerable to typical and traditional naval strategies.

New technologies in propulsion, communications and weaponry also influenced the way war was conducted at sea. Diesel-engined submarines, an impressive new weapon system, appeared early in the twentieth century, while coal-fired engines were increasingly replaced by oil-fired turbines in surface warships. Weight for weight, oil gives out more heat than coal and occupies less space. So turbines were smaller, more powerful, and needed less manpower. The days of shovelling coal into the furnace were being dispatched to history. As the overall performance of warships was increased, so armaments, armour and internal protection on ships were improved. Refuelling at sea – the domain of stokers like William – increased the effectiveness of naval forces across the globe.

With its new role there came an image change for sailors and stokers. Previously, stokers were seen as rough, fierce men likely to settle any argument with their fists. In the twentieth century, engine room recruits had to show some dexterity and aptitude with the array of machinery now lining the bowels of a modern ship. Also, fewer stokers were now needed for the same job. Those that managed their tasks well could now expect to progress to officer class, an unthinkable notion just a few short years before. The King's Navy, a book published in 1925 by Frank C. Bowen, amply illustrated the point:

All would-be recruits have to come up to a high standard of conduct, intelligence and physical fitness, as is clearly shown by the figures for a recent year in which only 7,000 were accepted from 42,000 candidates. Apart from the definitely skilled ratings, the rank and file of seamen, Royal Marines and stokers are in their everyday duties constantly handling mechanisms of the greatest complexity and delicacy, and handling them with skill and assurance.

Knowing the qualities of their men, it was not surprising that naval officers were disgusted with the tone of the report made by a committee of businessmen which in 1923 inquired into the pay of the fighting services. So far as the Navy was concerned, the committee seemed almost to think that it was still manned by the sweeping of jails and the press-gang, or at any rate, that the bluejacket was on a par with the lowest unskilled labourer.

4

CALL OF THE SEA

As my 18th birthday approached, I again started to think about joining the Royal Navy. Then, two weeks before my birthday, some papers arrived in the post informing me that I should report to Exeter to undergo a medical in preparation for joining the Army. My father brought them to me at work. 'Not likely,' I said. 'I'm a Navy man.'

I asked my father to take over work on my engine and I went straight home to get changed. I caught the next train to Plymouth to join the Navy. That way I escaped conscription into the Army. I had my lunch whilst I was there, the Navy office gave me half a crown for my return fare and sent me home. I agreed to sign on for five years and seven in the reserve and I joined as an ordinary seaman.

When I got home my two brothers, who were stokers, told me I had joined 'the wrong regiment'. They felt I should have joined the engineering branch like they did. Anyway, I didn't hear anything for a week. But then just before I was 18 they called me up and I went to Plymouth to join full time. I can remember vividly leaving home to catch the 7.25 a.m. train from Kingsbridge. My heart was in my mouth. I met an uncle of mine who was a postman. 'Buck up, Bill,' he said. 'You will go a long way in the Navy.'

'Yes,' I said. 'They might send me to China.' And at the time China didn't sound like a great place to be.

My Navy records start on my 18th birthday. I was doing my training in the naval barracks when the First World War was on.

After I joined up I was sent to St Budeaux, near Devonport Barracks, where we were all billeted in tents at the time – about four to six men in each tent. We had to march twice a day between there and the Naval barracks where we did our training. My first dinner there was bully beef, boiled potatoes and marrowfat peas.

Whilst I was undergoing my initial training at Plymouth the country was struck by a Spanish flu epidemic. Thousands died during the outbreak and I was quite ill myself for a while. I had collapsed over my dinner as I was eating it and when I woke up I was in the Naval barracks. We were put into the gymnasium because the sick bay was full. I was there for about ten days and I don't remember much about it. Certainly, it was far worse than any flu I've had before or since. Part of our treatment involved being fumigated. We were marched into a room about 50 at a time. The room was then filled with a mixture of steam and disinfectant fluid that combined to look like a thick fog. Our clothes were given a similar treatment and we were advised to gargle regularly. When I had recovered I was sent home for about ten days' leave.

Tens of thousands of men died with the flu. It killed more men than all the battles of the First World War. Just about every Royal Naval ship and barracks was affected. And those men who escaped the virus had reason to complain too. They were taken out for lengthy route marches every day in the belief that fresh air and exercise would ward off infection.

William was one of an estimated billion sufferers worldwide. Spanish flu – so called because neutral Spain broadcast its effects when censorship stopped publicity about it in other countries involved in the First World War – claimed an estimated 50 million victims. The war's death toll stood at about 16 million.

The influenza pandemic defied expectation because it picked off young, healthy humans ahead of infants and the elderly. Within twenty four hours of showing symptoms about one in five victims was dead.

Those symptoms included bleeding from the nose, ears or lungs and a bluish tinge to the face. Victims generally died either from blood loss or pneumonia. Sometimes Spanish flu was mistaken for dengue fever, typhoid or cholera, other prevalent diseases of the era.

The first wave of the disease, which emanated from America, was relatively mild and occurred early in 1918. Its second wave between September and November 1918 – when William was struck down – caused the most serious loss of life. It wasn't in abeyance until June 1920. Troop movements and transport improvements hastened the progress of the disease around the globe.

Eventually, I returned to good health and finished off my training. After basic training I changed from ordinary seaman to stoker. Just two months after I joined up the war finished before I even got to sea. The gates of the barracks were flung open and we had free entry to every venue around the city. There was dancing and singing in the streets and everybody went mad.

In Plymouth soldiers and sailors paraded in the main thoroughfare alongside wounded men still in their hospital clothes. People rushed forward to shake the hands of the injured men. There were flags everywhere, hanging from poles, from trams or house windows. Although the vast majority were union flags there was the odd stars and stripes and there were some French and Belgian emblems also. Soon there was bunting across the city as well as placards. One read simply: 'Thank God'.

It was terrifically noisy with sirens and hooters blasting, people blowing paper trumpets and then the toll of church bells.

Everyone gathered outside the offices of the *Western Morning News* to wait for official confirmation of the armistice to be posted in the window. When it appeared there were cheery celebrations. As these were going on two wagon loads of German POWs came by. They looked just as pleased about the end of the war as the British soldiers guarding them.

There were lots of sailors on the streets as the patrol vessels in the Channel returned to Plymouth when it seemed certain peace was at hand. Typically, soldiers and sailors were swapping hats and dancing with every woman in sight.

On 12 November 1918 the Western Morning News – *costing 2d – gave an insight into celebrations held in Plymouth:*

There was in some respects boisterous rejoicing but there was a happy absence of the wild and unrestrained behaviour which, from its state of origin, has received the name 'Mafficking'.

This was perhaps in large measure owing to the restrictions on the opening of public houses and the sale of liquor, restrictions which in Plymouth were wisely and patriotically extended by the licensed victuallers themselves many of whom at the mayor's request closed at the early hour of 7.30 p.m.

Hence, while there was plenty of noise and jubilation there was very little to which reasonable objection could be taken. To most people, indeed, the declaration that hostilities had ceased came with a sense of relief too deep for light manifestations of joy and for too many homes the occasion was saddened by the thought of dear ones through whose sacrifice the glorious victory of right over wrong, of liberty and justice over slavery and tyranny, had been brought about. Never surely were the thanksgiving services so widely held more fervent and sincere. On the whole the entire nation and not least the people of the West Country have received the news in the manner which does them credit from the personal and patriotic point of view.

The word 'Mafficking' was coined after the jubilation which spread through London in May 1900 following the relief of the besieged town of Mafeking during the Boer War resulted in noisy and unfettered demonstrations of joy. Such public frolicking was generally thought bad form by a hierarchy that was keen to see society held at bay.

As my brothers and I had survived the war, we were what was known as a blessed family. Around Britain there were some blessed villages to which all the fighting men dispatched to the battlefields had returned safely. Even then I thought someone 'up there' was looking after us in the Stone family.

Back to training. The flu had disrupted it but I knew there were certain things we had to learn and we did them day in, day out to prove we could. Firstly, we had to learn how to march. Apparently the marching pace of the Royal Navy is the longest of the three services. When we paraded, a loud drumbeat kept us in step and the joke among the officers was: 'Seamen will march off in columns of four, stokers will follow in a bloody great heap.'

Clearly, not a great deal was expected of or delivered by those destined for the engine room branch. Some of the men just could not get the hang of marching, to the fury of the commanding officers. It wasn't too much of a problem for me, knowing that there was the threat of a rodeo if training didn't go according to the officers' plans. A rodeo meant trotting endlessly around the parade ground with a hammock held at arm's length above the head.

We had to learn the art of *dhobeying* which, in one of the Indian languages, meant washing clothes. That entailed stripping off and scrubbing all our clothes and kit until they were spotless. The challenge was to wash the uniform collar so that the blue of the collar did not taint the white stripes. But perhaps the most difficult item to tackle was the boiler suit, which seemed to take forever to finish. Last to be done was the hammock and bedcover. Everything was hung on racks and taken by trolley off to a hot room near the boiler house.

On *dhobeying* days there seemed an extraordinary amount of kit. Basically, as far as laundry went, the Navy went by the motto: 'One on and one in the wash.' So, in addition to our black boots, we had two pairs of thick, blue woollen socks, two sets of underpants and vests, two white shirts, two serge uniforms, two caps, a black and a white one, two blue sailors collars, two large black silk squares and two boiler suits. There was also a webbing belt with a pouch pocket which we wore beneath our uniform because we always carried our money with us; a woollen navy-blue jersey, and a black oilskin coat. We were better off than sailors of the generation before us who had to make most of their kit in an era when officers were obsessed with kit order. Learning to keep kit scrupulously clean was good practice for life in the engine room where everything was kept spotless. We were also issued with a 'hussif' – or 'housewife' – which was a container with needles, wool, a piece of beeswax, buttons and a block of wooden printers' type, used to mark items with our initials.

The kit had to be laid out in a set manner, each item exactly folded or rolled to Naval requirements. It was one of many regimented aspects of Navy life. Once a fortnight on a Friday we paraded in the drill shed to receive our pay. Paymaster officers sat behind a line of tables that corresponded to the first letters of surnames. There was nothing casual about it. Using our right hands to grab the left side of the cap's brim, we took off our caps and came to attention. After calling out our pay number, we held the cap upside-down in front of the paymaster. A Chief Petty Officer called out the amount due and the paymaster would empty the contents of a prepared envelope into the cap. Then you used your left hand to cover the money as you did a sharp right turn. Money in pocket usually meant a trip to the naval stores to buy cigarette or pipe tobacco and bars of Pusser's Soap. This yellow soap costing a few pennies was used for *dhobeying* and personal washing.

According to Frank C. Bowen in The King's Navy, *attention to detail as far as uniform was concerned was being relaxed during William's early years in the Navy when a generation previously inspections had gone to extraordinary lengths.*

The word 'bag' in the Navy means a man's kit, the greater part of which he keeps in a cylindrical canvas bag, which gives its name to the whole. 'Mustering' it consists of laying out every item which the Regulations prescribe, each in its exact pre-ordained place, each folded or arranged in one particular manner, each showing the name of its owner. The inspecting officer, in a comparatively perfunctory inspection, will see that the bag is complete and clean, entering the numbers of each kind of garment in the appropriate columns of a printed form or book and seeing that shortages noted at previous inspections have been made good.

But a really searching inspection, such as was common in the days of uniform mania, ran an uncompromising tape measure over nearly every item. Trousers, for instance, must be 11 in. across the foot and ten across the knee, and the pocket on the breast of a jumper not only measure exactly six inches by three but also be placed in an exact spot in relation to the shoulder. A fraction of an inch too much or too little meant that the trousers or jumper had to be altered and the whole bag mustered again in some subsequent dinner hours. In ships where things were carried to extremes, even the needles and buttons and skeins of thread and cotton in a man's 'housewife' were counted.

We got a hammock, a set of hammock ropes and clews and two metal rings, plus two bedcovers and a wool blanket. All of this had to be marked with our names and kept in a kit bag.

Of course, we had to learn how to sling a hammock and also how to lash it when it was not being used. A properly lashed hammock could double as a life support in the sea. This was done on orders from the Petty Officer to 'lash up and stow'. The edges of the hammock were brought together and the long hammock lashing bind was turned seven times evenly around it. The tighter it was lashed, the more effective it would be in open sea. Anyone who didn't secure their hammock properly was liable to a charge of having a 'slack hammock'.

And I mustn't forget the PE kit, which was shorts, singlet and plimsolls, all in white. We used to call the physical training instructors 'Muscle Bosuns'. If you were in PE kit you had to carry out all orders and movements at the double.

When William joined the barracks at Devonport it was known as HMS Vivid. *Although the dockyard itself dated from the seventeenth century the barracks were not built until the last half of the nineteenth century on what had been fields and market gardens. The limestone buildings clad in Portland Stone cost £250,000 and consisted of two accommodation blocks for 5,000 men, a drill shed and a Commodore's house. Replacing rundown and unsanitary hulks, or beached ships, it was a vast improvement for sailors but was considered by some in authority to be an outrageous waste of money. It was occupied for the first time in June 1889.*

Construction work during the 1890s that linked Devonport and Keyham docks called for tons of concrete and the contractor, Sir John Jackson, sought to supply the necessary raw materials by dredging off the coast of the South

Hams villages of Hallsands. Some 160 villagers, dependent on fishing for their livelihoods, protested, suspecting the dredging would irreparably damage the beach. However, an inquiry found in favour of Jackson until in 1902 the beach at Hallsands fell away and the sea wall was damaged by fierce autumn storms. In 1903 Jackson's licence permitting the dredging was revoked. However, the shoreline struggled to recover its defences and in January 1917 swathes of the village were swept away or undermined in a winter gale. The village's pub and 37 houses now lie beneath the sea and only the chapel survives.

The barracks clock tower was added in 1896 and two years later the site was further extended with an officer's wardroom and further rooms for another 1,000 men. Gunnery training took place there from 1907. In 1934 it was re-named HMS Drake. *Like the rest of Plymouth, Devonport was a target for German bombers during the Second World War and was hit during a heavy raid on the night of 21 April 1941. Sailors stationed at the barracks helped to clear the rubble at Devonport and throughout the city. After 1961 Devonport barracks was used solely for accommodation and accounting.*

I then received my first draft. I was to proceed to Rosyth by rail to join my first ship the Battlecruiser HMS *Tiger*. One of Admiral David Beatty's 'Splendid Cats' of the 1st Battle Cruiser Squadron, *Tiger* was a famous ship, which had seen action during the First World War at Dogger Bank and then Jutland.

However, another duty awaited me before I joined ship. There was a national rail strike during September 1919 and my papers showed me as an engine driver. (The notes should have read steam engine driver.) On the basis of this faulty intelligence I was sent to Newport in South Wales to help out with essential work on the railway during the strike. The government was worried about food supplies and had quickly cut sugar and meat rations while the strike was on.

The end of the First World War did not bring about domestic harmony. Prices had risen two and a half times during the conflict. Recently demobbed soldiers and sailors were discovering there was little by way of opportunity or reward for them in 'Civvy Street'.

Britain was in debt. One sure fire way to resolve this problem was to export more. But that would have meant slashing spending – especially in defence – and that would have been chronically unpopular with an already hard-pressed population. And all the while Britain was a major importer, particularly with food.

Before the war had ended the police force went on strike. There was a host of other industrial disputes, including the railway strike that William witnessed first-hand in Wales. Liverpool and Glasgow suffered widespread civil disturbances.

But Britain was not alone in suffering waves of unrest. In the USA an estimated four million workers took part in 3,600 strikes in the months after peace broke out. In Germany, Hungary and the Baltic States there were full-blown revolutions. Governments everywhere were alarmed by what they perceived to be the threat of Bolshevism. Russia had fallen to the Bolsheviks before the end of the First World War. Allied forces had taken up arms against the revolutionaries in Russia but had failed to dent its victory. (Stan Smith, a year older than William and a fellow sailor, was among 28 Royal Navy volunteers imprisoned in the notorious 'Black Hole of Baku' after they were sent to stop the Bolshevik revolution spreading to Georgia. Kept in two cells with earth floors, they all witnessed terrible atrocities carried out on the civilians by their captors before they were finally released after two years.)

Speaking at the Paris Peace Conference in 1919, US President Woodrow Wilson declared: 'We are running a race with Bolshevism and the world is on fire.'

In fact, for most working people in Britain the Russian revolution of 1917 highlighted the potential of 'people power' rather than sparked a desire in the war's victorious forces for a sharp political left turn. They knew that the days of virtual serfdom for working people were at an end. Although there were comparatively few Marxists among Britain's cities and shires there was widespread recognition that things had to change in post-war Britain. Governance by the privileged class was under scrutiny and found wanting. The question of land distribution was key and here there were lessons to be readily learned following the conflict. Sharp-eyed observers realised the attractions of Australia and New Zealand where land was cheap and plentiful would do much to lure a discontented British population. In HMS Tiger's *ship magazine of 1918 there is a view that is far from revolutionary but reveals that most people knew the page on Britain's social history had to turn. It is possibly the best representation we have today of a sailor's view of events at the time:*

> If the British Empire is to be retained for British people, drastic changes in its land policy are essential. No longer must the land be allowed to be owned by a few large owners but by thousands of small ones. Each of the overseas Dominions have, with commendable effort, been engaged since the outbreak of the war in preparing plans in the direction of assisting their forces to settle on the land but such has not been the case in the United Kingdom where it is even more urgent. For if the lands of the Mother Country are not going to be used as the cradle and nursery of the future British race, the dangerously empty spaces of the Dominions will be populated with people from enemy countries. Moreover it has long been an acknowledged fact that the cities and industrial centres of the Empire have, for a long time past, been congested with people on a scale altogether out of proportion to the population of the country districts. And if this longer continues the backbone and sinew of the British Isles will drift away to foreign countries and Great Britain will become a resort of multi-millionaires and the cheap labour of the continent . . . to weaken the heart of the Empire at the close of a war which has drained Great Britain of her best would be a suicidal policy and there is no need to do so.

When I got to Newport I was able to clear up the fact that my driving had been in traction engines rather than in railway engines. However, when the authorities found out that I was joining the Royal Navy as a stoker, they decided that I should practise my new trade by working as a fireman or prospective engine driver for two to three weeks. In fact, I'd occasionally had a go in a steam engine in the sidings of South Devon during my youth so I did have an idea of how to drive a train. However, during the strike, my own engine driving was restricted to shunting around the station and goods yards. One engine I drove was called *Baden Powell*. But some of the Engine Room Artificers from the Navy got to do longer runs on the main line.

In my first few days there I slept in the sheds but after a while I went to temporary accommodation in Newport.

Of course, we sailors were not very popular with the strikers. We were called 'Black Scabs' to begin with by the locals. Our reply was that being in the Navy we went where we were pushed. We were subject to 'King's Rules and Admiralty Instructions', which was a governing principle of the Navy. Eventually most of them accepted that we were not volunteer strike breakers. Like sailors everywhere, we tried to dispel problems by organising football matches. At any rate, the strike only lasted a few days into October.

You got 42 days' leave a year in the peacetime Navy on home duties. That was usually 14 at Easter, 14 at Whitsun and 14 at Christmas. When I came home on leave I used to go hunting, for all sorts of animals. We used to hunt badgers, going into the woods and putting dogs in the badger sett. One of the dogs had his jaw bitten away by the badger. We had a ferret and Father and I used to catch rabbits. We'd put nets up over the rabbit hole, put the ferret in the warren and out came the rabbit, into the net. It was entirely legal. A farmer would sell the rights to hunt rabbits on his land to a rabbit trapper. I remember one who had about two hundred gin traps which he would load up on to a donkey. As he walked around the fields he would throw the traps to the ground, then go back and set them. It wasn't only rabbits that got caught in them, though, and they are not legal now.

Farmer Cole was drinking with Father and I during one leave when he said: 'Come on Bill. What about breaking in my horse tomorrow?' Immediately Father said: 'You can't go riding a horse on Sunday.' But I did!

I had no saddle so I went into a field bareback with someone leading the horse. When he couldn't hold it any longer he let it go and the horse galloped across the field to a heap of husk left over from threshing. He tipped right over and I was thrown off. But I got back on straight away and rode him into the farm. It was the end of his high spirits. My persistence broke him.

My mother was mad about whist and, if I was home, I'd sometimes go with her to play. She couldn't believe that I'd ever win the top prize but once I did. I don't know if I was lucky exactly. It was 300 cwt of coal, not exactly the ideal prize for a stoker who got sick of the sight of it at work. Still, I daresay it came in handy at home. She would drive us to the pubs holding the whist drives in the pony and trap, which had big candles encased in lamps either side like headlights.

We used to go to dances in the town hall in Kingsbridge, or in East Allington and Slapton. I often used to go to the Salcombe Regatta.

At home we had a gramophone and we used to play records one after another. I still know all those songs by heart and I often sing them. You had to turn the handle to make the turntable go round. I used to put the horn out of the bedroom window so everyone on the other side of the village knew one of the Stone boys was home on leave. And they could tell if it was me that was home – I always used to play band music – or Lawrie, who preferred songs. The music we both enjoyed was played by music hall stars like Harry Lauder, who wrote 'Keep Right On To The End Of The Road', and Billy Williams, who sang 'When Father Papered The Parlour'. We used to buy our records in Kingsbridge.

On Sunday evenings we read our prayer books and sang hymns together. Often Mr Cole used to join us.

It was about this time when one of the local farmers offered to sell me a cottage in Goveton for £50. Of course I wasn't married then so I wasn't interested.

5

HMS TIGER

When the rail strike finished I took a train north to join *Tiger* at Rosyth. On that journey, I remember sleeping in the luggage racks in the compartments.

The first thing that I had to get used to on joining *Tiger* was the routine of shipboard life. We stokers slept in hammocks on the mess deck and each morning the Chief Stoker – who is the Navy's equivalent to a sergeant major – would come around to make sure that everyone got up on time.

On the first morning that I was aboard, the Chief, a man called Darby Kelly, came around at 5.15 a.m. and I somehow managed to get up. The next morning it was about 5.30 a.m. when he came around shouting: 'Out of those bloody hammocks!' Everybody seemed to be out of their hammocks except me. He came right up to me and shouted: 'What the bloody hell's wrong with you? Out of that bloody hammock at once and run down the passage singing "Should Auld Acquaintance Be Forgot."' I fell out of my hammock – much to the amusement of all my messmates who all knew 'Chief' of old. They tell me 'Chief Stokers never die . . .' I suppose he had to be pretty hard as there were about 400 stokers on HMS *Tiger*.

I was issued with the *Stoker's Manual* and got some advice from its pages. In the introduction I was instructed about my career path:

Although on joining a stoker knows little, he will at first generally be working under a petty officer or higher rating and he should obey orders cheerfully, do his best, be observant, ask questions and try to get on. Within a year or even less time if he shows himself to be particularly smart he will be examined by an Engineer officer for the rating of Stoker I, a rating which carries with it increased responsibility and pay.

As a First Class Stoker he may be placed in charge of a dynamo engine, refrigeration plant or some similar watch-keeping duty, and after two or three years if he shows zeal, intelligence and ability to take charge of men he will be rated an acting leading stoker, and at the end of the commission he will be sent to the mechanical training establishment at his home port for courses.

Depending upon the ability shown in these courses and subsequently a stoker can become a Chief Stoker or a 'Mechanician', the latter rating leading to Warrant rank.

I'd no idea at the time that I would be a textbook case by following this path exactly. Career advancement wasn't uppermost in my mind at the time. But I kept the manual for my entire life so there must have been some words of wisdom in it.

Having managed to get up, the day's routine would start with breakfast before setting to work. Then, at 11.30 a.m., came the call 'Cooks to the Galley'. Two men from each mess would be assigned as 'Cooks of the Day' and it was their job to prepare the food for all the men in their mess. This might involve jobs such as peeling potatoes, preparing vegetables and cutting up the half a pound per man meat allowance to make a pie. Having put on the crust you would take the pie and other food back to the galley to be cooked. Inevitably it was all accompanied by extensive cleaning of mess tables and chairs. There was no fresh milk and we drank tinned with our tea. I quite liked it. There were plenty of cooks aboard. It was their job to cook the food in the galley rather than make it. Great improvements had recently been made to the galleys. Even at the turn of the century breakfast on board ship was cocoa and a ship's biscuit and supper was bread and tea. By the time I was on *Tiger* there were recognised meals produced by trained cooks in well-equipped galleys.

There was always plenty of cleaning to do. Often sailors were down on their hands and knees 'holy stoning' the deck with sandstone. It was never a popular job but the officers didn't let anyone slack. Stokers worked hard as well. I worked as a stoker in the Engine Room department where there were 39 Babcock and Wilcox boilers fuelled by coal. I well remember the duty of coaling ship when all hands including the officers would join in as we took on thousands of tons of coal. Even the Marine Bandsmen had overalls on. We'd be nearly all day and all night coaling. Of course, being the most experienced, we stokers were responsible for trimming the coal in the bunkers, working down below. It was hell at times.

Each boiler had four furnaces. The coal-burning boilers would get covered in clinker, which we stokers had to clear out. Having let the fire in the boiler to be cleaned burn down, we would then pull out the clinker and ash. You'd have to put a hose on the ashes, which made everything fly up into the air then it went out the side of the ship through ejectors. Taking live coal from the other furnace you'd start the fire anew.

When I came off watch I would remove my thick flannel trousers and vest. And by the time I went on watch again my trousers would still be standing up on their own, thanks to the perspiration and the coal dust they had absorbed. You always had to wear a cap because drips from the pipe of boiling water would drop on your head. It was hot and you got thirsty so I used to keep a piece of coal about the size of the end of my finger in my mouth to stop it drying out, like the miners did in pits. It was grim and tough. In addition to keeping the engines turning, one of the most important jobs performed by the stokers was the production of drinking water by a boiler.

When we weren't on watch there wasn't much to do. We did our *dhobeying*, wrote letters or read. Gambling on board ship was strictly forbidden – although sometimes it happened. If anyone wanted to gamble – and the dice game 'Crown and Anchor' was popular – it entailed posting a lookout for punishments could be severe. Sometimes the ship's policemen, or 'Crushers', were on patrol.

More likely though men played *Ludo*, known in the Navy as

'Uckers'. The board was a large piece of painted canvas and the dice was a block of wood acquired from the chippy. It was rolled out of a bucket. Observers used to shout: 'Gilly, gilly for a six'. If two pieces of the same colour landed on it square it was called a 'blob'. Veterans from the China station sometimes played Mah-Jong and there were hands of whist, bridge and cribbage going on. Only on special occasions when ships' companies met did we play bingo, which we knew as 'Tombola'. The last house of the night was always a doubler; the price of the ticket and consequently the value of the prize was doubled to make it a really worthwhile win. Rather than shout bingo, most men would yell: 'Here you are!'

There wasn't much privacy aboard a ship like that. We kept everything that was precious to us in 'ditty boxes', small wooden boxes about 12 in. by 9 in. and about 5 in. deep. They had a lid, a lock and a tray inside to store letters, photos and other small personal treasures.

At about the time I joined HMS *Tiger* the ship's magazine was published containing a dictionary of lower deck phraseology. I no doubt found this helpful in my early days in the Navy. Here's a selection:

Bake: Failure or the worst has happened.

Batchy, Wet or *Potty*: An insult applied to one who is *non compos mentis*.

Buzz or *Wheeze*: Rumour.

Dodger: Caretaker.

Elephant's part: A scornful term applied to one who habitually prefers to watch others working [rather than do it themselves].

Flap: To work with zeal.

Fowl, crow, pigeon, bird or *pheasant*: All these ornithological expressions are applied to an individual who is habitually lazy and troublesome. The relevance of the term lies in their ability to sleep in any position (even standing up) and at any time they desire.

Gens: General leave.

Gobby: Signifies coastguard. Also, a seaman attached to the quarter deck for ordinary duties.

Goffer: Any effervescent drink.

Ledstone village, where Bill Stone grew up.

Pound House, where Bill was born on 23 September 1900.

Bill's birth certificate.

The Stones' local church – St Peter's – at Buckland-Tout-Saints, near Kingsbridge.

Bill aged ten, winning first prize at the Kingsbridge Show, photographed by a national newspaper.

Bill's parents, William (Senior) and Emma Stone, in the village of Ledstone.

A confident-looking Bill Stone at 16 years of age, wondering what life held for him.

Harvest time in Ledstone was typical of agricultural life in Devon in the early 1920s.

The Spanish flu pandemic struck the post-Great War world very hard. It would kill over 50 million people across the globe. (© Getty Images)

Bill would witness the many German navy shipwrecks poking above the waterline at Scapa Flow. (© Getty Images)

The Empire Cruise 1923–24: HMS *Hood* slowly makes her way – with Bill onboard – through the engineering miracle that was the Panama Canal.

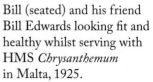

Bill (seated) and his friend Bill Edwards looking fit and healthy whilst serving with HMS *Chrysanthemum* in Malta, 1925.

On the rifle range with his unit from HMS *Chrysanthemum* on Malta
(Bill is far left, back row), 1925.

Back home from Malta, Bill is at the wheel of his beloved car, minus ladies underwear!

On his new posting, *P40*, with his crew. Bill is third row from the front, and first on the left, holding the rail.

The aircraft carrier HMS *Eagle*. Now a Leading Stoker, Bill stands for a picture with Argentine tourists as the ship sails along the South American coast in 1930.

Above all others, Bill (sitting, far right) enjoyed his posting to Simonstown in South Africa, where he served on HMS *Carlisle*.

Now a Chief Stoker, Bill (on the right) and a friend take a stroll at an exhibition in Johannesburg, South Africa, in 1936.

A married man: Bill and Lily celebrate their wedding on 27 May 1938.

Gold-dust or *Pay-Bob*: The ship's paymaster.

Harry Freeman: Signifies immunity from payment i.e. 'Harry Freeman's tram ride' means travelling without obligation to pay.

Jaunty: The most senior ship's policeman.

Jimmy Bungs: A cooper.

Leather-neck, Bullock or *Turkey*: A marine.

Mudhook: The anchor.

Nutty or *Bonso*: The nickname for someone with a large head.

Pusser: Ship's purser or steward.

Putty: Ship's painter.

Red lead: Tinned tomatoes.

Rocky: People who are serving for the duration of hostilities.

Round the buoy: A second helping.

Sand king: A boatswain.

Stokers tended to keep their own company, rather than mixing with ordinary seamen. There was always an unspoken rivalry between the engine room and the upper decks. They say that oil and water don't mix. I know the nickname for stokers among seamen was 'Bilge Rats', which doesn't sound very affectionate. But we were tough guys in the engine room. Some of my shipmates had been at the Battle of Jutland in 1916, but they never spoke about it.

Shortly after I joined HMS *Tiger* under Captain William Boyle, we were at Scapa Flow where the German High Sea Fleet had been interred at the end of the First World War under the terms of the Armistice to await a decision on its ultimate fate. It was there on 21 June 1919 that Rear Admiral Reuter gave the secret signal for the entire fleet to be scuttled. About 70 ships went to the bottom. The action took the British by surprise and they were furious, because the ships were worth millions of pounds. During my early days in *Tiger* you could still see the funnels and masts of some of the ships, which had gone down in shallow water. It seemed a remote and haunted place at times.

To my mind the scuttling of these ships was probably the best thing that could have happened in the circumstances. I think that, had the Germans not taken the initiative, there would have been a lot of political arguments between Great Britain, the United States and France about how the High Seas Fleet was to be divided up between the victors of the First World War.

Following the scuttling of the High Seas Fleet, *Tiger* spent a while in the docks at Rosyth having some of her coalbunkers converted to be powered by oil. Then she was 50 per cent coal, 50 per cent oil and would normally start a trip on coal before switching to oil.

Our next cruise took us to Gibraltar and around some of the Spanish ports where the Mediterranean ships were painted a lighter shade of grey. I remember visiting Vigo, where I seemed to land up a lot of the time, as well as Malta. In Gibraltar the main street was lined with shops that looked like Ali Baba's caves. The name of the game was to haggle, to beat the vendor down to his best price. That's what the old hands had advised us to do and so we did. At times it looked as if the sellers were about to lie down and die, our demands were so outrageous to their ears. They were good actors and usually everyone enjoyed the long, drawn out transactions. I remember buying 4711 Eau-de-Cologne for Mother, which was all the rage at the time, and a black Jacobs pipe for Father. There were at least two large beer halls, the Trocadero and the Continental. One of them hosted a ladies' orchestra, which was very popular among the British sailors. Then there was Malta, where British ships lined the docks and British sailors filled the bars.

In 1920 came my first contact with the mighty HMS *Hood*. *Tiger*, together with nine of the Navy's newest destroyers, accompanied *Hood* on her first overseas cruise, which was around Denmark, Norway and Sweden during May and June of that year. There were two reasons for going. Firstly, *Hood* had a high profile diplomatic job to do. While we were in Scandinavia King Gustav V of Sweden, King Christian of Denmark and King Haakon of Norway were entertained aboard the *Hood*. Secondly, it was to warn the Russian Bolsheviks that we were close at hand if they tried anything in the Baltic states, which were at the time independent.

When we anchored at Nynashamn, a group of us sailors went ashore and caught the train to Stockholm. We should have caught the midnight train but got back in time to see it leaving the station.

I think we'd had a little too much liquor. We eventually reported back to ship '12 hours adrift' and were put in the Commander's Report. My excuse was that I couldn't find the station, to which the Commander replied: 'Next time don't leave the station.' We were stopped four days' pay.

In 1921, we went on the usual spring cruise to the Mediterranean. On this occasion, we were not allowed to be in contact with the men from the ships of the Mediterranean Fleet as they were suffering from another epidemic of flu.

There were, however, still regattas and races between the visiting ships of the Battle Cruiser Squadron. In these *Tiger* did not fare so well. The reason for this was that, when *Hood* was first commissioned, many of the men had been taken from the *Tiger*'s sister ship HMS *Lion*. These men were the finest oarsmen in the fleet and *Tiger*'s crew stood little chance when pitched against them in the cutter races. I used to take part in the cutter races myself. A cutter was a boat, which was 'pulled' [rowed with oars] by eight men.

Sport was always rated highly in the Royal Navy. In Victorian times the PT instructors would keep their biceps in trim by swinging hefty clubs. By the time I got on to ships PT instructors were known as 'Club Swingers' – and they didn't let anyone 'swing the lead'. I used to practise with the ship's boxing team. I had to give up boxing though, as my nose would always bleed and there would be blood all over the place.

I also remember another incident whilst we were at Gibraltar. I was out for a run trying to keep myself fit when I passed by a brothel. The girl on the door spotted me as a sailor and greeted me with shouts of 'Over here, Jack,' but I kept running. I don't think all the British sailors passed by, though.

In these early days we would regularly call in at Malta, which I remember as being a great place to be. There could be a dozen big ships in the Grand Harbour in those days – HMS *Tiger*, *Ramillies* and all the others. Smaller ships berthed at Marsamusciett Harbour or Sliema Creek while submarines pulled into Manoel Island.

By the jetty there were two clubs run for the Royal Navy, the 'White Ensign' and the 'Vernon'. Tombola was a favourite game here among the sailors. There were various sports grounds as well as the towns of Valletta and Sliema.

The streets would be packed with sailors. Most were drawn to *Strada Stretta*, otherwise known as the 'Gut'. It was a narrow alleyway full of bars, restaurants, dance halls and cabarets, all of which were well run and very cheap. I tended not to go ashore myself until later on in the month – just before payday was a good time. That way the place would be a bit less busy as a lot of the sailors would have run out of money. Every door seemed to be either a pub or a café. Spirits were always high among servicemen in Malta.

The whole Maltese economy seemed to be based on the British Fleet in those days. Without it I can't imagine how local people would have scratched a living. The locals would come on board to clear away after meals and do the washing up. They took away any leftover food – known as 'gash' – and sold it in the towns and villages on a 'penny a dip' basis. That used to make me laugh as the larger your hand the more you got for your penny. We would often give them a loaf to take away as well. There were also locals running ferries to and from the jetties. Others came on board to take away the washing, which they would return the next day. You could even have someone come on board and measure you for a suit.

After I had been in *Tiger* a while I started to look around for a spare time occupation aboard ship from which I might be able to earn a little extra cash to supplement my Naval pay. In due course I decided that I would have a go at tobacco rolling. Back then, tobacco arrived on board in the form of loose leaves. Of course, most men smoked in those days and it was common for someone to buy 1 lb of tobacco at a time to last them the month. A pound of tobacco cost about 18d back then. Having bought the whole loose leaves, men would bring them to me to prepare. The first stage of the preparation process involved cutting out the black stems of the leaves – from which snuff could be made. Having done that, you then had to dampen the leaves and roll them tightly into an elliptical shape, which was fat in the middle and tapered to two pointed ends. Canvas was wrapped around followed by spun yarn – wound tightly all around. The leaves could be stored in this form and remain fresh. I worked at a rate of 6d per pound. The men would cut tobacco off to use for roll-ups, as they needed. When cigarettes were made up and stored in tins they were known as ticklers.

At this time most men and an increasing number of women in Britain were smokers. A leap in tobacco usage has often been linked to conflict and the numbers of smokers worldwide increased during the First World War. There were smokers in Britain after Sir Walter Raleigh (1554–1618) brought tobacco back from the New World and introduced Queen Elizabeth I to the habit. However, it was after the Crimean War (1853–56) that smoking became more widespread in British society. It was Scottish Crimean veteran Robert Peacock Gloag who opened the first cigarette factory in England in 1856. Temperance groups, formed to stem the evils of alcohol, also condemned the use of tobacco but it remained freely available. In 1888 five 'Wild Woodbine' cost a penny while a loaf of best bread was selling for sixpence.

In 1907 the British Medical Association heard from GP Doctor Herbert Tidswell about the perils of smoking. Tidswell suggested every girl and boy in Britain should be encouraged to sign a pledge that would prevent them taking up the habit. Further, he highlighted the risks of cancer of the tongue and lip. Tidswell's gloomy forecasts were echoed in 1912 by Dr I. Adler who believed smoking was linked to lung cancer. However, both men were opposed by other doctors who argued that no clear case had been presented against moderate use of tobacco.

Scientists in Paris in 1923 claimed that smoking was beneficial as the chemicals in cigarettes fought bacterial infections. Four years later at an International Tobacco Exhibition held in London a doctor claimed categorically that there was 'no risk of cancer from tobacco'.

Even as late as 1933 there was doubt in the public's mind about the dangers of tobacco, exploited by cigarette manufacturers. A Chesterfields advertisement began with the words: 'Just as pure as the water you drink . . . and practically untouched by human hands.'

Cigarettes were used as a metaphor for sex on the silver screen when Hollywood was tied down by The Hays Code in 1930 that aimed to restrict the content of films. Anything that could be deemed even slightly risqué was ruled out – and that's where cigarettes came in. Stars of both sexes developed the art of smoking suggestively. Thus, most of the celebrities of the era were seen smoking freely by people who flocked to cinemas to see the latest releases. Tobacco was part of servicemen's rations in both the First and Second World Wars.

After the war, however, Britain and America were suffering extraordinarily high levels of lung cancer. Studies by Sir Richard Doll and Sir Austin Bradford in 1949 and 1951 finally made a statistically irresistible link between smoking and lung cancer. Cigarette companies responded by putting filter tips on smokes in the 1950s.

Sir Richard Doll continued to highlight the deadly nature of smoking. 'It wasn't until the media themselves changed their minds – journalists and TV presenters were often smokers – that the public began to be convinced. By this time doctors had nearly all given up smoking. Media coverage about the doubts continued until the early 1970s with the media giving disproportionate weight to the tobacco industry,' he said. Still, prior to the 1970s most people smoked without being fully aware of the dangers.

I left *Tiger* in 1921 and returned, as one always did, to barracks at my homeport of Devonport, known to sailors everywhere as 'Guz', to await my next draft. During the day we used to march into the dockyards to clean up the ships that were refitting. I also used to prepare vegetables in the Chief Petty Officers' mess. Then we used to march back again.

I continued to earn extra cash by rolling tobacco. I also made rabbit nets to sell at 6d each because, don't forget, Naval pay was comparatively low at the time, perhaps £1 a week. While I was in the barracks I met an old Chief who was leaving the Navy on a pension. He had been the barber in his ship and wanted to sell his clippers now that he was leaving. I thought that this might be a good way to earn a little more money whilst aboard my next ship so I said I would buy them from him. I paid £1 for which I got a full set of clippers (No. 1, No. 2, No. 3), a comb and scissors. Although I had no experience of hairdressing my father used to cut our hair when we were boys so I had seen how it was done. I had also watched closely when I went to the barber's shop myself. I didn't realise at the time that not only would this purchase earn me extra cash to supplement my Navy pay, but it would be the start of a whole new career for me – one that would even outlast my days in the Royal Navy.

Many men on board ships looked for ways to supplement their income. Often, a pair of leading stokers would start a *dhobeying* firm, another sailor might take up tailoring or boot mending while someone else practised the art of tattooing. It brought in extra income and it often improved life for men at sea.

Eventually, there came news of my draft to HMS *Hood*. Usually, when one was drafted a number of men stationed in barracks went together, but my draft to *Hood* was unusual in so much as I was the only one who joined her at that time.

6

HMS *HOOD* AND THE EMPIRE CRUISE, 1923–24

In January 1923 I joined *Hood* at my homeport of Devonport. She was the grandest ship in the Atlantic Fleet and it was a prestigious posting. Although it only took about a week to get to know your own department it took much longer than that to learn where everything was on this mighty ship. When I first went on board everyone was at divisions and I wanted to go to the lavatory, so I had to find it myself. That proved quite a challenge. A lot of people used to say to me: 'Oh, so-and-so serves on the *Hood*. Do you know him?' And I would have to explain that there were 1,400 men on the ship and you couldn't possibly get to know them all.

Once aboard, I decided to lose no time in putting my barbering skills to the test. *Hood* had a cabin fitted out as a barber's shop with space enough for two barbers. Unfortunately, when I joined, both positions were already taken. Rather than wait for a vacancy, which might not happen for some time, I decided to set up 'in business' on 'the flats' (the small open areas between the decks).

Not long afterwards, some of the crew had made it known that they were not happy with one of the barbers occupying the barber's shop, who couldn't cut butter. One of the Commanders asked the Master on Duty if there was anyone else who was able to cut hair. He replied there was a young stoker who might be interested. I was offered the job and I was delighted to take it. This was the official start of my hairdressing career, which would yield many happy memories as well as earning me as much money as I got from my Navy pay packet.

I used to cut hair in my spare time and, of course, I wasn't excused duty to do so. If my turn at engine room watch keeping was in the early evening when the barber's shop was at its busiest I would ask a fellow stoker to take it on my behalf. I would slip him a bottle of beer in return for the favour. Beer was hard to come by for the ordinary seaman. Although it was distributed to officers it was never given to other ranks, who had to make do with rum tots. (And sometimes we suspected the rum had been watered down.) Other stokers were very pleased to get a bottle of beer. And while they were doing my watch I was saying: 'Next please.'

The barber's shop in *Hood* was on the port side of the upper deck – one deck down. I remember that it was a lovely room with a 6 ft wide mirror, a water geyser and all the equipment that a budding barber needed. There was plenty of room so I used to sleep there because it was so crowded on the mess decks. I used to call it my cabin. The other thing that struck me about the room was its rather odd shape. One of the walls was curved, formed as it was by the massive vertical steel cylinder or 'barbette' running down through the ship, on top of which sat 'B' turret.

I shared the barber's shop in *Hood* with a Marine Bandsman. We each charged 4d a time and paid 30s to the Sports Club fund at the end of the month. The balance of the money was shared between us so it was a good way of topping up Navy pay. It also meant that you were not ashore spending your money all the time. Instead, you were in the ship, earning it. I soon discovered that there was no shortage of customers, most of whom became regulars.

When the officers had their hair cut they would often say to me, 'How much do I owe you?' I would reply, 'Well, you can give me a bottle of beer if you like, sir.' It was useful for currying favours and I also liked a beer as a change from the daily issue of rum that we had in the Navy back then. The ratings would often pay me in kind with their tot of rum. After working in the barber's shop I used to have a tot of rum – or 'Nelson's Blood' as it was called – and then go up on deck for a walk. I'm sure it is the rum that has kept me going so long. We celebrated crew birthdays with rum. The birthday boy was traditionally offered 'sippers', a sip of everyone else's rum ration.

There was a chief aboard who always insisted that I cut his hair. One day, after I had been on duty, I noticed he'd had a haircut. When I said that it was me who always cut his hair, he told me I had. Not only did I cut his hair I also shaved him with a 'cut throat' razor. I told him I couldn't remember a thing about it. Then he said, 'I thought you were pissed when you did it and now I know you were!'

Another good thing about being the barber was that you were often the first to hear what was going on. I remember that whilst we were at Gibraltar in *Hood* during the spring cruise of 1923 I was cutting a commander's hair when he summoned the Engine Room Commander. Being in the engine room myself I thought it might be worthwhile finding out what he had to say, so I made the cut last a bit longer than usual. When the Engine Room Commander arrived I heard them talking about the ship going through the Panama Canal and how much clearance there might be. 'It's going to be tight. There will be about 6 in. spare each side, I reckon,' was the Engine Room Commander's view. That was the first time I heard mention of the Empire Cruise, which HMS *Hood* was to lead in November 1923.

Unfortunately, a while later I found out that the Marine Bandsman with whom I shared the shop was 'playing dirty' with me. We each charged 4d for a cut, 2d for a boys' cut and 2d for a shave, with all the money supposed to go into a kitty to be shared out at the end of the week. Being the new boy I had accepted this arrangement in good faith. However, I started to think that my share seemed pretty low for the number of cuts that I was doing and eventually realised what was happening. The bandsman was often being given a sixpence by his adult customers, which he would put in his top pocket. He would then give them 2d change out of the shared kitty, which I was filling with my own takings. This meant that of the 4d that I put in only 2d remained there for the payout at the end of the week. When that arrived, and the money was halved between us, I was ending up with only a penny a cut. One night when he went out I took the opportunity to check the top pocket of his jacket. I found several sixpence pieces which confirmed my suspicions. When he came back I confronted him and said that, because the profits were so low, one or other of us had to go. I didn't tell him that I had found the evidence of his deceit in his top pocket – his conscience would tell him that. It didn't come to either of us having to leave in the end but the takings were a lot higher from then on, although I never really trusted him again afterwards.

Money was a touchy subject on the lower decks. At the end of the war stokers and able seamen found they were not only paid substantially less than their counterparts in the American navy but also fared far worse than munitions workers at home. With mutinous rumblings in the air, the high command decided to review pay and conditions. In 1919 a new pay structure was introduced into the Navy that meant able seamen received four shillings a day, up from one shilling eight pence, while a petty officer now got seven shillings rather than three. The Daily Telegraph *welcomed the news by claiming: 'An old scandal, which lay heavily on the nation, has at last been removed.'*

But these golden days were not to last. Sailors were splashing their cash a little too freely, as the head of the Naval Personnel Committee remarked. 'Undoubtedly the lower deck are very well off. Some of the higher ratings keep motor bicycles and can afford to take the more expensive seats at local entertainments and their meals at places which officers patronise. In some cases they are able to buy their houses . . .'

Clearly, in the eyes of the braided ones, it had all gone too far. By 1925 Naval pay rates had been cut. New recruits would be earning even less than the discontented crews of 1919. This pay cut occurred even though a treaty signed in 1922 limited the size of the British fleet and meant the Royal Navy could not spend money on modern large ships even if it wanted to. Luckily for William, existing personnel stuck to the raised rates. The net result was that men working side by side doing the same job were paid differently, depending on when they joined up. Later, when the government looked to axe pay rates during the 1931 economic crisis, those like William who had served since 1919 were bought into line with the 1925 wage rates. Once again, luck was on his side. He and the rest affected by this unpopular move were largely sheltered from its effect by an existing agreement on protected allowances. In 1934 half of the 10 per cent pay cut imposed in 1931 was restored. Four years later – happily coinciding with his wedding – marriage allowances in the Navy were substantially improved.

When I first joined *Hood* the Admiral flying his flag from her was 'Titchy' Cowan. Walter Henry Cowan was a terrible chap who never missed a chance of telling off any of the officers or ratings. I remember that he would often report the boat crew boys for not pulling properly. On one such occasion, he had a group of boys sentenced to five days in the cells. Boys could not be given time in the cells so he had the whole group rated to Ordinary Seamen so that they could be jailed. I heard that this was subsequently overruled and that they were rated to boys again but it is a good example of what a hard man he was and how he would always find a way of exercising his will on the men under his command. At divisions on the first Sunday of the month Cowan would stand on a spit-kid on the quarter deck, and the whole ship's company would march past and salute him.

But when he needed to address the crew he had to stand on a box if anyone were to see him, for he was a very short man. In command with him was Captain Geoffrey Mackworth who was likewise severe and sometimes cruel. Cowan's on board mascot was a goat that he had won in a rifle competition. The goat was known to eat cigarette ends, ledgers and assorted ship's equipment.

In 2001 I received a letter from Elisabeth Gilbertson of Oxford whose father, Reverend Arthur Gilbertson, was chaplain on HMS *Hood* under Cowan. She told me her father once received an instruction from Cowan which read: 'I hope you will not have the litany in my flagship; but if you insist, will you please omit the petition where we ask to be delivered from battle, murder and sudden death. Hang it! I've never been trained for anything else!' That goes to prove what a rather sarcastic and unfeeling man Cowan was to his men.

When I wasn't in the barber's shop I was generally employed on one of the picquet boats taking liberty men ashore and fetching them again. In the picquet boat you would be on your own in the small Engine

Room with just a Chief Petty Officer in overall charge so there was a lot of responsibility and you had to do everything yourself. We used to have regular unofficial races with our boat pitted against the other picquet boats. When you got back to *Hood* the brass funnel that each picquet boat had would be covered in salt from the spray and you would have to clean it so that it shone before your duty finished.

I also did watch keeping on dynamos and in the engine room. And I spent days on end cleaning brass and copper pipes. We also polished the steel floor plates until they were like mirrors.

In May 1923, Rear Admiral Cowan left *Hood* and was replaced by Rear Admiral Sir Frederick Field. He was a popular man who was both diplomat and entertainer – he was a member of the 'Magic Circle' – and ideal for the task ahead. Towards the end of the summer the rumours of our world cruise were confirmed. Rear Admiral Field was to be promoted to Vice Admiral to lead what was to be unofficially known as the 'Empire Cruise'. The voyage would be a complete circumnavigation, calling in at various outposts of the British Empire in order to 'show the Flag' and encourage the nations of the Empire to combine their naval resources. *Hood's* captain was to be John Im Thurm.

Everyone aboard the *Hood* considered themselves lucky to be on such an adventure. Luckier than most was Bandmaster Henry Lodge who had raffled his motorcycle to raise some ready cash. Gambling was prohibited in the Navy and Lodge could have been court-martialled. Instead when Captain Im Thurm discovered the misdemeanour he cautioned Lodge who then joined the crew for the voyage as planned. Im Thurm's generosity on this occasion boosted his popularity among the men.

Also aboard was author Scott O'Connor whose contemporary account gives us an astonishing insight into life and attitudes at the time. According to the flag-waving author of *The Empire Cruise*:

> The First World War had become a thing of the past; the vast and terrific energies it had created had died down to exhaustion; a period of reaction had set in.

The empire, strained to the foundations of its being, lay breathing deeply, its pulse low, its hand shaken by the mighty contest from which it had emerged victorious. Five years of hardship, of unemployment, of a grinding and bitter taxation – in England the heaviest in the world – even of disillusionment had followed. And then, just at that time, there had begun slowly to appear upon our horizons a dawning of new light. It seemed as if the gloom and depression of those years might presently pass away. There were symptoms of a revival of trade, of a decline in the cost of living; there was the feeling that if the empire was to continue to exist and prosper it must draw together in peace as in war. And in this country at least it was clear that we meant to face our obligations without shrinking or evasion. We alone of the great nations engaged in the war had begun to pay our debts and it was plain to all men that our word, long honoured, would continue to be our bond. We might with an open countenance enter upon our destiny and face the world.

One man who wasn't aboard, however, was nineteen-year-old crewman James Horton who died in a drowning accident two days before HMS Hood *sailed.*

Horton was visiting his family in Dudley prior to his planned departure when he happened upon a group of boys left floundering in freezing water after playing on thin ice. They were among 30 choristers who went to Allport's Pool after Sunday school and spent 45 minutes larking about before the ice covering the pool cracked. Although he used a pole to reach the struggling boys and spread his weight across the ice Horton fell in and drowned, along with two fifteen-year-old boys.

At Horton's funeral – which took place as HMS Hood *eased its way into warm African waters – women and children were crushed by mounted police attempting to control some 20,000 mourners. Police lined the church wall at Kingswinford to prevent people from scaling it. A report from the* Dudley Herald *observed that many people were contributing to collections in hats and a bucket but no one knew who the money was for.*

Horton's coffin, covered by a union flag, was taken to the church on a gun carriage drawn by six black horses and a Naval party fired above his grave. Among the floral tributes there was one from HMS Hood.

Officially it was the 'World Cruise of the Special Service Squadron'. To sailors and stokers it was the 'World Booze Cruise'. Few of us could believe our luck, looking at the itinerary that had been drawn up in some of the most exciting and exotic locations in the world. HMS *Hood* was the flagship and we sailed in the company of the Battlecruiser HMS *Repulse* and the 1st Light Cruiser Squadron comprising HMS *Delhi*, *Dauntless*, *Danae* and *Dragon*. And we started in the company of HMS *Dunedin*, on its way to joining New Zealand's navy.

We left Devonport on 29 November 1923 by which time the press had labelled the venture the 'Empire Cruise', which is how it is known today. We didn't get a big send off – it was a very low-key affair with just family members at the quayside. We would not return home for another 11 months.

In the early days of the cruise we passed within sight of the Canary Islands with dolphins and porpoises playing at the bow and flying fish in the wake at the stern. We continued on down the west coast of Africa to reach our first port of call – Sierra Leone. I remember to this day how very hot it was there. The steel and iron of the ship almost glowed with heat. Dugout canoes paddled by local people drew alongside, with locals diving for coins tossed in by sailors. There was a film crew aboard and as soon as we landed they went ashore to photograph the locals and such sights as there were. Unfortunately, one of the seamen who went with them soon returned to the ship suffering from sunstroke and my services as ship's barber were required to shave his hair off so that ice bags could be applied to his head. When he recovered he was not at all happy about what I had done to his hair!

While we were there we were presented with one of the first gifts that *Hood* gathered on the trip, an elephant's tusk mounted in silver from the city council.

Sierra Leone's first settlers were a group known as the 'Black Poor from London' – comprising slaves whose freedom was guaranteed by Britain in return for fighting in the American War of Independence and assorted others who had washed up in London, frequently via service in the

Royal Navy. The notion to transport them to a new colony was far from straightforward. Many black men had settled in London, married or co-habited with white women, had no knowledge of Africa and were fearful of being enslaved once they got there.

In 1787 the first group to arrive were nearly eradicated by disease and disputes with local people. However, another group of mainly black Nova Scotians came to Sierra Leone and its symbolically named settlement Freetown with Thomas Peters, a charismatic freed slave from North Carolina, and John Clarkson, brother of the slave trade abolitionist Thomas Clarkson. This time the settlement was more enduring. By 1827 the first university in Africa, Fourah Bay College, was established. The descendents of the settlers were called Creole and spoke with a distinctive tongue that betrayed an African, American and British background. Their way of life was likewise a blend of traditions.

However, indigenous people still had difficulties with the influx and were particularly offended by the British tax system which encompassed the very huts they lived in. In 1898 there was a revolt that cost hundreds of lives on both sides, finally suppressed by the ruling British.

Observing the imposition of white, Western ways on the people of Sierra Leone, O'Connor reflects the prevailing belief that colonialism was beneficial to both Britain and the lands she occupied. However, he has enough empathy to comment: 'Poor Africa, she has suffered almost as much at the hands of her benefactors as at those of her deadly enemies.'

He is, however, in no doubt that the colony was benefiting enormously from British influence:

> If the hand of England were removed from this Colony it would be a disaster for its people; the slow progress it has made in the course of hundred and thirty years of its history would cease and a spurious independence would be achieved at the cost of financial embarrassment and a lethargic and self-interested officialdom – as in Liberia.

At the time Liberia was struggling to define itself economically. For a century it had been the destination for freed or free-born slaves from the United States who dreamt of a new life in the continent from which their ancestors had been forcibly removed as slaves. It became Africa's first independent republic in 1847. Indeed, Liberia is similar to the Latin word for freedom and Monrovia, its main city, was named for James Monroe, who was President of the USA from 1817 to 1825. However, the incomers who largely colonised the coast found difficulties living with the indigenous people of the interior. A naive political approach permitted countries like Great Britain to evade import and export taxes. At the time of the Empire Cruise the government of Liberia had only managed to secure large-scale outside investment from one company, Firestone Tire & Rubber. Thus the peaceful certainties brought about by Imperial control made Sierra Leone seem a better option to O'Connor.

Something else that stands out in my memories of the early days of the cruise is the fascination we all had that, along with all our other equipment, we had brought along a Rolls Royce car complete with driver. This was needed for various ceremonial occasions but it must also have been an excellent way of showing off the best of British motorcars throughout the Empire. It often cut an incongruous sight when it was hoisted off the ship, though.

Leaving Sierra Leone, we continued to make our way down the west coast of Africa until we reached the equator – known to all seamen as 'the line'. For centuries there's been a tradition that all sailors who haven't yet crossed the equator, no matter what their rank, are inducted by those who have. Anyone who has crossed the line is known as a 'shellback'.

Once it was a notoriously brutal ceremony. Men were towed in the water behind the ship and some were even killed in the high-spirited celebrations. Even in my time it was boisterous. The ship's routine came to a halt for a night and a morning as 'King Neptune' – a role usually taken by the most experienced shellback aboard – held court. He was accompanied by an incarnation of the Greek sea goddess Amphitrite and 'Davy Jones', who has always been more of a satanic figure. Then there was a squad of 'bears', shellbacks clad in seaweed who assisted King Neptune.

It started with the Vice Admiral getting a mock award known as 'The Order of the Bath'. Then it was officers first to undergo the ceremony – and that included the *Hood*'s captain John Im Thurm. I was nervous before it started because at the time I couldn't swim and I knew we were all in line for a ducking.

Indeed, most of the ship's company had not been south of the equator before so we lined up anxiously in our bathing suits to be initiated. On hand there was a 'barber' who looked more like a butcher wielding a huge wooden razor with red stains on his apron. Each of us was lathered up on a stool while being beaten with inflated football bladders and then thrown down a slide into a huge canvas bath, which had been erected on the quarter deck. The bears were there to meet us and ducked us as many times as they thought necessary. No one was spared this ordeal as King Neptune treated officers and men alike. By lunchtime no fewer than 950 men had matured into shellbacks. After the ceremony we received our certificates to record this occasion, then King Neptune decreed that we could continue on our way. Neptune was in fact Chief Petty Officer Alfred Punshon. Sadly, when we got to Australia he was rushed to hospital following a heart attack and that's where he died just a few months after this ceremony. There was a similar initiation ceremony for those going above the Arctic Circle for the first time, when sailors get the 'Blue Nose Certificate'.

At sea we carried out all sorts of exercises. On the way to South Africa *Hood*'s efficiency against gas bombs was put to the test. Although gas shells had never been used at sea, we all knew the devastating effect they'd had on the Western Front during the First World War. We also knew they could now be dropped by plane.

But when natural ventilation was cut off to protect the crew from the effects of gas it became unbearably hot and one officer even collapsed with heatstroke. Fortunately, gas was never used during the Second World War on land or at sea.

At least we were steaming a little faster now and that helped keep us cooler. The weather remained fine with hardly a ripple on the water and the nights were lovely. Each morning all seamen and engine room ratings off watch would fall in on the quarter deck and would have a church service, the Captain usually officiating. The Royal Marine Band played the hymns and I always enjoyed singing out in the open sea.

Our next port of call was South Africa where we arrived on 22 December. We got a warm welcome although the Afrikaans newspapers apparently hadn't mentioned our visit. Clearly there was still some antipathy towards Great Britain following the Boer War, which had ended some 20 years previously. We spent Christmas in Table Bay. We were greeted by great storms and winds known locally as the 'south-easter', which made it very difficult to get boats ashore. Our entire visit to South Africa was dogged by fog, rain and swell. It meant that thousands of people who had hoped to tour *Hood* were disappointed. We had to miss out a planned trip to Port Elizabeth entirely. On Christmas Eve there was a march of 900 seamen and 300 marines through Cape Town. In addition we visited East London and Durban and had bad weather at all of these places, but were given wonderful receptions by the people. All sorts of events were organised, including athletics, boxing, football and hockey matches. Anyone in a British sailor's uniform was let in free of charge to pubs and clubs and plied with drink.

On leaving South Africa we rounded the Cape and made our way up the east coast of Africa until we reached Zanzibar. It was an exotic place peopled by Arabs, Hindus, Persians and Parsis as well as Africans. What I remember most about there is the youngsters who used to come up to you and say something like, 'You very good man, master,' to which came my reply, 'What the hell do you want?' All they wanted though was to swap some of the local fruit for some of the food that we had on board ship. They came bearing great bunches of bananas and other fruits. The air in Zanzibar was filled with the scent of cloves which grew everywhere.

But it was hot day and night. There was no air conditioning in the ship, of course, so a lot of men slept on the deck when they could. If they didn't their hammocks would be wringing wet with sweat. The heat caused sweat rash, an itchy condition that affected most of us. Everywhere the atmosphere was stuffy. It was hard to keep your eyes open when you woke up in the morning. A canvas bath on deck was filled with sea water so those who were off watch could cool down. We were all overcome with a kind of lethargy that accompanies extreme, still heat.

There were two reasons for placing Zanzibar on the itinerary. The Sultan of the day, Sayyad Khalifa ben Harud, proved his loyalty to the Empire during the First World War by providing 5,000 soldiers for the East African campaign and £70,000 in funds. Secondly, the British ship HMS Pegasus was sunk by the German cruiser SMS Königsberg in 1914, in full view of locals, with the loss of 38 lives. This episode was a major source of embarrassment for the British, supposedly the most eminent navy in the world. The cruise was a timely reminder to those in Zanzibar at least that the Royal Navy was back on top of its game.

Having crossed the Indian Ocean, we came to Trincomalee, Ceylon [Sri Lanka]. I had some leave and took a trip up into the hills to have a look at the coffee plantations. I also visited Kandy, the capital of Ceylon, with a group of officers and men. It's an ancient city full of temples, one of which allegedly holds one of the Buddha's teeth. Right next to the ornate 'Temple of the Tooth' there's a Christian church. Some of the officers joined a shooting party and one of them bagged an elephant. Sadly, Stoker Petty Officer George Wood, from HMS *Repulse*, was killed when a bus overturned during this trip. His funeral and burial were later held in Kandy.

The next stop was Port Swettenham in Malaya. Hard to believe that rubber plants came to the Malay peninsula only in my life time, from Kew Gardens where the seed had been cultivated. Now the coffee plantations and natural forest were giving way to rubber, which was much more profitable, and the countryside was covered in it. As rubber became more abundant the demand for labour grew. Consequently there'd been an influx of Indian and Chinese workers. The wealth rubber has brought has turned nearby Kuala Lumpur from a rural settlement into a swish city. In Kuala Lumpur we left the body of Able Seaman Walter F. Benger who had died from malaria.

It was a relatively short hop to Singapore. Also in port were HMS *Hawkins*, *Carlisle*, *Bluebell* and *Petersfield*, which at the time were part of the China fleet. Apparently venereal disease was rampant in Singapore. We were all given a lecture about it before anybody went ashore from *Hood*.

There was the usual round of ceremonial and sporting activity. I know the Special Services Squadron was victorious in the boxing against the China fleet. I suppose it must be the weather that sticks in one's mind most though as I clearly recall it raining very hard whilst we were there. I went shopping and bought a tea set for £5. I still have the tea set today. Compared to other parts of the Empire we had visited, there were a lot of English women in evidence.

By Singapore the sick bay was bulging. According to O' Connor: 'The level of vitality lowered; men fumbled over work and accidents became more frequent.'

Our passage through the Indonesian Islands took us south through the Pacific and towards Australia. First we passed the volcano Krakatoa, issuing a faint spiral of smoke. Only 40 years before, it had exploded with the loudest explosion known to man, one which was heard hundreds of miles away causing deadly tsunamis and a worldwide change in weather patterns. We had to cancel a planned stop at Christmas Island because of heavy seas so it was onwards to Freemantle in Western Australia where we moored alongside the wharf. We were overwhelmed by the thousands of visitors who had come to welcome us.

Everyone wanted to present the ship with a memento and often this took the form of a live animal. In Australia we were given a wallaby called Joey who travelled with us all the way home. He was a great favourite among the crew and became something of a celebrity. His favourite treat was a pinch of tobacco. He also used to box with members of the crew. (In addition to Joey we gathered a ring-tailed opossum, a flying squirrel, two beavers, two pink cockatoos, assorted parrots and a kiwi.) Meanwhile, everything on shore in Australia was free to those in a British sailor's uniform.

When we arrived at Adelaide, I again had a period of leave and met up with a man named John Cole who had been born at Ledstone – my own home village back in Devon. I had known John during my childhood days and had last seen him in 1908. He'd been expecting a telegram but there was no trace of it in Ledstone. He asked my brother and I to go to East Allington to see if it had arrived there, but it hadn't. He was now a butcher in Adelaide and was really interested to hear how things were at home. I had written to him when the cruise was finally confirmed and arranged to meet him. His house, I remember, was covered with a vine laden with grapes. I also met up with another man named Bert Heath who had also been in the village during those early years of the twentieth century and who was now enjoying life in Australia as a sheepshearer. He used to cut wool with hand-held shears and I suppose he must have been pretty good at it. Visiting friends in Australia was a strange experience. Their homes had the same furniture as ours, similar pictures on the wall and we ate and enjoyed the same food. But the landscape and, of course, the weather was so alien.

On 17 March – St Patrick's Day – we arrived in Melbourne. It was a magnificent welcome, even by the high standards already set on the tour.

During his trip ashore the Vice Admiral said, 'Words fail me to describe the extraordinary enthusiasm with which we were received in every part of Melbourne through which we drove. All the streets were beautifully decorated in honour of the Squadron's visit and enormous and enthusiastic crowds were gathered whenever we stopped to pay calls. Warm as our welcome has been in all the places previously visited it was altogether surpassed by the reception accorded to us by the citizens of Melbourne which can only be described as amazing.'

Ships' crew as well as the officers acted as ambassadors for Britain when they took shore leave. Their excellent behaviour did not go unnoticed. The Sun News Pictorial *in Melbourne said:*

> [British sailors] leave behind them a feeling of comradeship and take with them much more than formal expressions of goodwill. Their conduct has won the unstinted admiration of all classes.

The Commissioner of Police added: 'The British sailor ashore behaves like a gentleman. Melbourne has something to learn from him.'
Remarked O'Connor:

> British sailors, besides having a special way with ladies, are naturally kind and hospitable and little inclined to discriminate

between people who come on board, whether white, black, brown, or yellow, great or small; so that visitors, besides being delighted at the honour of coming on board a ship-of-war, come full of smiles and heart-flutterings. There are none so forlorn or humble that some seaman, or marine, or boy, will not be found to take them in hand and show them over and explain in plain or technical language the mysteries of our ships. Some of this information doubtless goes over the heads of their guest; much of it is of the common language of humanity. Every man on the ship thus becomes a sort of envoy from the Homeland and unconsciously 'does his bit' in that respect.

Of course, the highlights of our time in Australia came with the open days. The public were allowed free entry to the ship and the freedom to roam wherever they liked. Officers and men remained aboard to act as guides. I recall that some of the younger chaps were very quick to pick out the nicely spoken and best dressed amongst our visitors in order to make sure that they got a healthy tip at the end of their guided tour.

I acted as a guide in the *Hood*'s engine room and it was packed to capacity down there. On one occasion I showed two ladies around and spent some time explaining to them the circulation and condensing system. Only later did I discover that both were married to engineer officers so I had only explained to them what they undoubtedly already heard about on a regular basis from their husbands!

We found out that people had come from miles around, often staying with strangers in Melbourne who had thrown open their doors for the occasion. Sailors couldn't help but notice the number of limbless ex-servicemen in evidence, symbolic of Australia's sacrifice during the First World War.

Some musical wit on board came up with a song that entertained the public. It was accompanied by a young lieutenant on his ukulele.

Oh, oh, oh, the S.S.S.
There never was a squadron like the S.S.S.
North, South, East and West

We'll show the world we're better than their best.
All Australia visited the *Hood*
But they couldn't sink her, nobody could.
There never was a squadron like the S.S.S.

Next port of call was Hobart in Tasmania. Hobart was a lovely place but I will always remember it most of all for a small 'diplomatic incident' that happened whilst we were there. The Admiral had gone ashore and had given a speech in which he had said that the Navy today was mainly men drawn from prisons and borstals whereas in earlier times they had come from good homes. Of course, he had meant to say this the other way around, but soon the local papers were full of 'the Admiral's gaffe'. I gather that he had to make an apology. After that, whenever we went ashore at Hobart we had conversations with the locals along the lines of 'How long have you been in the Navy then?' 'Oh, just over five years.' 'And how long have you still got to do?' 'Oh, another seven.'

To which came the reply 'My goodness, whatever did you do – it must have been something quite serious!' It was all good-humoured leg pulling.

About the same time the *Hood* jokes started. (We were getting used to being called 'Cook's Tours'.) One joke that stands out in my mind is this one. 'Why is the Empire Cruise like a Ford car?' Answer: 'Because the *Hood* is the best part of it!'

It was back to Australia and New South Wales after Hobart. The sea was so heavy that a Japanese steamer *Honolulu Maru* began listing badly after her cargo shifted. *Dauntless* and *Dragon* peeled off to provide assistance while we anchored in Twofold Bay. Next day, 5 April, we went into Jervis Bay, a fantastic vista deserted except for the Royal Naval Australian College.

Our visit to Sydney coincided with the Royal Agricultural Show, just about the most important event in the city's calendar. The whole place had a festival feel to it. No fewer than 156,000 people visited *Hood* and *Repulse* while we were in port. On 11 April the city and harbour were lit up by the Special Services Squadron searchlights and those of the anchored Australian fleet. Meanwhile a Venetian carnival took place on the water. Of course, the place looks completely different today. There was no bridge when we were there – that wasn't built until 1932 – and it was another half century before the Opera House was finished.

Before we left we paid homage to HMAS *Australia*, scuttled off Sydney Heads on 12 April. Although only in commission for nine years, she was scrapped so that Britain could fulfil its ship quota agreed at the Treaty of Washington two years previously. It was a big sacrifice for Australia to make in the circumstances.

When we left Australia we were leaving behind more than 140 men from the squadron who had decided to desert. There were only six million people living in the whole of Australia. There was plenty of room there and the climate was warm. No wonder some men with no ties at home decided to jump ship. Of course, they would have been in trouble if they had been caught.

However, we took with us HMAS *Adelaide*, which was to accompany the squadron for the rest of the tour.

The politics behind the Empire Cruise were evident in Australia. Britain was conscious of Australia's contribution to the Allied victory in the First World War but yearned to see a more committed defence strategy. For its part, Australia was mindful of its debt to England but unwilling to pledge itself to a shipbuilding programme.

At a ceremonial lunch in Melbourne, the Premier of Victoria said, 'We have had the protection of the British navy in our infancy and in our youth and we pay tribute and homage to those who have provided that protection. We honour the traditions of a country to which we are attached by the strongest ties of gratitude and kinship and we stand for those traditions and ideals. Britain still retains the leadership of the world.

'I take no narrow view. I know well that other nations have contributed to the cause of humanity and civilisation. I appreciate the qualities of other nations. When I went to America I was struck with the wealth and initiative of the Americans. But when I reached Britain I felt that there was something different there. Why was it, I asked myself, that these little isles had been able to lead? In the main because our ideals were spiritual, because we had sought to do things justly and to do that which was right; even though we had sometimes failed.'

For his part the Prime Minister said, 'While with the passing years we have evolved our own nation and are Australian in all our thoughts and sentiments and our people have a patriotic love of their own country which transcends all other affections; we are yet at the same time an overwhelmingly British community. Our forefathers came from Britain and 98 per cent of our people are of pure British descent. We share its glorious traditions; in our veins there runs the same blood. We are, in fact, the most British nation in the world.'

The editorial of the Melbourne Sun *said:*

To say that Australia was cradled in the strong arms of the British Navy is more than a figure of speech. It was the command of the seas that made a British Australia possible. It is due to British sea power that Australia is the only continent that has never had to suffer an invasion.

O'Connor explains the Australian position:

In all these speeches it was apparent that all men were agreed upon their loyalty but that some took one view of action and some another. The Labour Party, pursuing its ideals of a world peace, its detestation of war, places its hope in the League of Nations and in a general disarmament. The rest of Australia is no less peace loving, no less inspired by a revulsion from war as a means of settling differences between honest and civilized. But it points to the fact that the world is still armed and that the League of Nations has no power to endorse its will. It asks, where is the policeman acting for justice and right who will enforce the law? The Self-Governing Dominions in conference laid down as their cardinal principle the maintenance of the peace of the world; they affirmed that this could best be accomplished by the preservation of the integrity of the Empire; and next by the promotion of good and better relations between the English-speaking peoples. They desired to promote the prestige and authority of the League of Nations. In other words, a strong Empire could be used to promote the cause of peace, even if it resorted to strong-arm tactics.

Onwards to New Zealand where we arrived at Wellington on 24 April 1924 – the day before ANZAC Day, when the sacrifices made by the Australian and New Zealand Army Corps are remembered. More than 75,000 Australians and New Zealanders died after Australia's Liberal Prime Minister Joseph Cook observed in 1914, 'If the old country is at war so are we.'

The city was paralysed by a rail strike. On ANZAC Day officers from the ship joined memorial events. 'I beg of you,' the Rear Admiral told veterans, 'to regard this day not as one of mourning but rather of thanksgiving that we are of the same flesh and blood as the heroes we now honour and also as a day of earnest resolve to emulate their great example.'

Once again thousands of people flocked to the ship. It was here that the main capstan on the foredeck was rigged up as a merry-go-round. A leading hand stood in the middle to make sure all the children who took a ride on it were safe.

A few days later hundreds of us were involved in a ceremonial march through the city, watched by thousands of people. The Governor-General, Prime Minister and other members of government took the salute. My Uncle George was looking out for me and he came to march alongside me.

After the march we met up. As a lad I had spent the odd weekend in Plymouth with Uncle George who was a stonemason by trade. His son had emigrated to New Zealand in about 1920 and he followed shortly afterwards. They came back with me on board *Hood* and, the following day, I went to ask the Commander if I could have some leave to spend time with them. The Commander was not very happy with such short notice and told me that I should have applied weeks ago. But I did manage to get seven days' leave and spent it at their home. They took me all over the city. I also got to meet all my relatives over there: Uncle George and Aunt Polly and many cousins, one of whom, Ida, had married an army tailor named John Adams who had also gone out to New Zealand from England.

That meant I missed the usual hospitality that occurred in ports visited by the Empire Cruise, including balls and sports competitions. But I didn't mind not being aboard for a bit. In New Zealand and all the other ports we visited the throngs of trippers made it difficult to move about the ship easily. Happy though we were to host everyone we still had our jobs to do and it took much longer to go about our business. And it was all getting a bit 'old hat' now.

While in New Zealand the ship was visited by Admiral John Jellicoe. We all knew Jellicoe well as the Commander-in-Chief of the Grand Fleet at Jutland during the War and, afterwards, as a First Sea Lord. At the time of our visit he was the Governor-General of New Zealand although his term of office was coming to an end. When we left Admiral Jellicoe travelled with us in *Hood* on to Auckland and that felt like a great honour. After we arrived Lady Jellicoe and their daughter Lucy were guests at an official dinner held on *Hood*. It was the only time that women attended an event like this on the ship during the cruise.

At Auckland, the crowds were so huge and riotous that the ship's fire brigade ended up pointing hoses towards shore in case they got out of order. People didn't seem to mind, though. I was again allowed leave and took a trip by train up to the hot springs at Rotorua, a system of mud baths and geysers on Maori-owned land. Rear Admiral Sir Hubert Brand, who was in command of the Light Cruiser Squadron, came with the party. We discovered that the Maoris kiss by rubbing noses. The Maoris also told us that they used to have wars, 'but we let the British do that for us now'. We all laughed at that one. They also told us that Captain Cook's pig had fallen into the hot springs and that they had rescued everything bar the grunt. They asked that the next warship built in Great Britain be named for the Ohinemutu tribe. I don't think the request was ever granted.

I remember from that trip that Admiral Brand was a really pleasant man. Sadly, while we were on the cruise, he received the news that his wife had died back home in England. His bereavement made the entire squadron gloomy as he was a popular man. Still, he remained at his post. It wasn't as if he could hop on a plane to get home in time for the funeral.

Leaving New Zealand behind, we sailed to Fiji, heading back into a warmer climate again. The strongly-built Fijians danced and entertained us with fire walking. The pits they used were scorching.

But it was hard to forget that just two generations ago they were known as cannibals who called human flesh 'long pig'.

I was once again suffering with prickly heat. The sick bay issued lime juice and barley water as a remedy.

Then on to Honolulu, crossing the date line en route so two days in succession bore the date 27 May. We crossed the equator for the fourth time. As we passed close to Samoa the days and nights were delightful. The stars of the southern sky that we had grown used to gave way to those that shine on the northern hemisphere.

I remember Honolulu for two things. Firstly, the very modern docks at Pearl Harbor and secondly the fact that we couldn't get drinks because of Prohibition. The Vice Admiral had forbidden the consumption of drink aboard ship so as not to cause offence to our American hosts. It probably stopped locals coming on board and drinking us dry.

Prohibition meant the manufacture, transportation, import, export and sale of alcoholic drinks was either restricted or entirely illegal. It was a law brought in throughout America in 1920 reflecting a belief that families, women and children were at risk from alcohol abuse.

Although drinking in bars was now against the law, legislation did little to change the drinking habits of the nation. Alcohol was still widely available at 'Speakeasies', covert drinking bars that sprang up everywhere to beat the ban. Many people brewed their own alcohol or smuggled it in, especially from Canada via the Great Lakes. Private homes were often well supplied with bootleg liquor too, for private parties. Wine production was largely halted, although it could be supplied for religious purposes i.e. Holy Communion. Meanwhile whiskey could be obtained on prescription and this fact substantially enlarged patient lists. Ships that were three miles from the American coast were exempt.

If the ban on drinks was bad news for ordinary Americans, it was an excellent turn of events for gangsters like Al Capone. Mobsters took over the supply of alcohol, reaping enormous cash dividends. This brought mayhem to the streets in some quarters.

Incredibly it wasn't until 1933 that the 18th Amendment, which introduced Prohibition, was reversed. Even then some states continued with Prohibition. By 1966 all Prohibition legislation was finally repealed.

It was the first time during the whole cruise that we had dropped anchor in foreign waters. All our other destinations had been within the boundaries of the Empire but Hawaii belonged to the USA. Flights of aircraft came to greet us when we arrived on 6 June. People flocked to the docks to hear *Hood*'s concert party performing on the fo'c'sle. Much to our shame, *Hood*'s men were beaten at cricket by a team of baseball players.

During our stay more than 47,000 people visited the ships and one of them stayed. Tom Frazier, a 15-year-old boy scout, was due to represent Hawaii at the International Assembly of Scouts in Copenhagen but had missed his steamer connection for America. When he heard about young Frazier's dilemma, the Vice Admiral suggested he came aboard, slept in the boys' mess deck and hitched a ride as far as America where he could resume his planned journey.

On our departure the *Honolulu Times* said:

> The excellent behaviour of the British sailors ashore has been widely remarked. They gave a fine example of discipline and good conducts. They fraternized informally and freely with American sailors, soldiers and civilians. The British squadron is circling the globe on a mission of friendship as well as of Naval development. In this port it succeeded 100 per cent. As an advertisement of the British Navy it certainly made good, from its genial and able Commanding Officer to the newest Midshipman and the youngest sailor.

The Squadron continued its journey across the Pacific and came eventually to Canada, calling first at Victoria and then at Vancouver. Whilst there we were told that a contingent of crewmen was to travel by train through the Canadian Rockies to rejoin the ship at Halifax on the east coast of Canada. My name was initially amongst those scheduled to take this passage but I said to the Chief that I didn't want to miss the Panama Canal. My request to skip the Rockies tour was granted and so it was that I ended up staying on the ship. When I look back now I wonder whether I made the right decision, as I would have loved to see the ravines of the Rockies. Then again,

I would not have wanted to miss the unique opportunity of being on the largest warship in the world as she passed through the Panama Canal.

As we made our way down the West Coast of the United States we parted company with the light cruisers. They were peeling off towards South America, visiting several different countries and rounding Cape Horn, where everyone knew they would face rough weather. Now it was *Hood* and *Repulse* in the company of *Adelaide* heading for the Canal.

First we stopped off at San Francisco and once again alcohol was off the menu. But sailors who went ashore soon learned that locals there too had found many and various routes around the law that banned drink.

Then we dropped down to Latin America and the passage of the Panama Canal which was, to me, the highlight of the entire cruise. The Rockies was a natural spectacle but this was an amazing feat of engineering that was still considered new. I was most fortunate in that the week that we made our passage through the canal I was scheduled for a motor boat course which was to take place on the ship's boat deck, so I was in an ideal position to see all that was going on.

The most spectacular part of all was when *Hood* passed through the canal's locks. As the Engine Room Commander had suspected at Gibraltar more than 12 months before, the clearance on either side was minimal, no more than 30 in. in total. There wasn't much room fore and aft, either. There were four small engines known as 'mules' which ran on rails and were lashed to *Hood* with wires. The mules were there to ensure that *Hood* was kept straight and away from the sides of the lock as she eased her way through. As the lock filled it was incredible to think that water alone could lift *Hood*'s 45,000 tons with such ease.

At the time the canal toll was 50 cents a ton. The bill for the *Hood* amounted to $22,399.50. Behind *Hood* came *Repulse* and *Adelaide*.

Apart from the narrow locks, other sections of the canal were quite wide – like a broad river. I remember that we spent a day moored at Panama City and, whilst we were there, there was another torrential rainstorm.

The opening of the Panama Canal in 1914 was a culmination of more than 30 years of arduous efforts by both the French and the Americans to create a shortcut for shipping across Latin America. Before the canal opened ships making the transcontinental journey would have to journey around the tip of South America, almost always a rough and treacherous passage. After the 48-mile (77 km) canal was constructed, ships of all shapes and sizes could cut from the Atlantic to the Pacific in as little as ten hours. However, the project was not without cost. In terms of dollars, the cost to America alone exceeded $350 million. Worse, the death toll among workers from its nineteenth-century inception to the canal opening was in the order of 27,500. It also involved the creation of Panama following a coup contrived by the US in 1903 after Columbia became intransigent in negotiations. When William travelled through the canal the five-mile canal zone that surrounded it belonged to America. Now the land is owned by Panama, a country bisected by what remains a phenomenal piece of modern engineering.

Having completed our passage of the Panama Canal we headed north, calling in at Jamaica, Halifax, Quebec and Newfoundland before heading home across the North Atlantic. We felt the last of the hot weather in Jamaica during a ceremonial march. After that the temperature dipped and thick fog delayed our arrival at Halifax. Our visit coincided with a city carnival marking the 175th anniversary of its founding. But most of us had lost our desire to drink in the atmosphere of foreign parts. We were tired and we wanted to go home. On 21 September the squadron sailed from Topsail Bay, Newfoundland, after a 15-day stay.

Field faced some tough questioning in Canada. On the right there was consternation that Canada had no ship suitable to accompany the squadron on its prestigious tour. On the left, peace rather than armaments was driving the agenda. So when Field responded to press questioning with the notion that Canada should maintain ships to protect its lengthy seaboard it caused a storm of protest, mostly centred on accusations of unwarranted interference. Insisting he had been misquoted, Field won apologies from several newspapers, which helped to soothe the row.

We returned to Plymouth on 28 September 1924. This wonderful cruise had taken us 11 months and a distance of over 38,000 miles, crossing the equator many times. It was the first occasion such a voyage had been undertaken by the modern Navy. (My family recently surprised me by obtaining from the Imperial War Museum a video copy of the official film made during the cruise – of course it is 'silent' and in black and white.)

By the end of the World Cruise 1,936,717 people had come aboard the ships of the Special Services Squadron. Of those, 1,803,885 were British subjects, of whom 1,423,157 were Australians and New Zealanders. They saw the face of the modern British navy. But O'Connor discovered the Navy had changed considerably in living memory. One stoker on the cruise told him:

> Life in the Navy was very different when I first went to sea. In those days it was 18,000 miles from Devonport to Esquimalt. There was no milk on board and you drank your tea without it. There was no fresh meat either and no refrigerators. There was beef in casks: black it was and tough to look at and I have seen a man pull stringy bits off it and lace his boots with them. Afterwards, boiled mutton was introduced in tins – 'Fanny Adams' – it was quite good stuff to eat and we liked it. Things have changed, maybe not all for the better. Seamanship now, there's not so much of it about as there was.

I found that my barbering had made me a considerable amount – £100, which was certainly a great deal in 1924.

On returning from the Empire Cruise I was due to leave *Hood* but I really wanted to stay in the ship. I came up before the Commander, who asked me: 'Why do you want to stay?' I had not planned my reply particularly effectively and just said something about having invested time and money in setting up the barbering in *Hood*. This did not impress the Commander, who pointed out that I had done over six years in the Atlantic Fleet and that I was now due for foreign service.

Not long afterwards I found out that even if I had managed to convince the Commander of my value to *Hood* it would have made little difference as the ship was transferred from Devonport to Portsmouth so I would have left her anyway.

By the time I left *Hood* I think I must have done every job in the ship that I was eligible to do as a stoker. There were a number of jobs right down deep in the ship – looking after the dynamos and so forth – that meant that you had to be in a room all on your own. I found the main difficulty in those jobs was to keep myself awake, as there was no one else with whom to exchange a few words. I often think of what it must have been like for those chaps down there when the ship was lost.

On leaving *Hood* I returned to barracks at Devonport. Whilst I was in barracks I was placed on standby to be drafted to HMS *Emperor of India* at one point. However, that all came to nothing and I was told that my new ship was to be HMS *Chrysanthemum*, which I was to join at Malta.

As Bruce Taylor observes in The Battlecruiser *HMS* Hood:

> Large-scale cruises continued to be made, notably those of *Renown* to Australia in 1927 and *Eagle* to South America in 1931 but nothing would ever approach that of the Special Services Squadron . . . For a fleeting moment the World Cruise united technology, treasure, organisation and opportunity in a spectacle never to be repeated, the high point of British sea power between the wars. For the 4,600 men who took part, the two million who visited the ships and the millions more who witnessed their passing, the Empire Cruise left memories and experiences only now fading into oblivion.

Excerpts from HMS *Hood*'s log:

8 December 1923 (at Sierra Leone)

14.00 His Excellency the Governor of Sierra Leone visited Vice Admiral Sir Frederick Field.
Fired salute of 19 guns
20.00 oiler cast off – received 2,053 tons of oil fuel

9 December 1923

09.00 Landed Presbyterian and Weslyan Church parties

10 December 1923

11.00 Carried out gunnery programme
Took aboard 3,940 lbs fresh meat and 8,000 lbs fresh vegetables

12 December 1923

10.00 Took aboard 4,000 lbs fresh meat and 8,286 lbs fresh vegetables

26 December 1923 (at Cape Town)

09.30 worked main derrick
Discharged one rating to RNH Simonstown
10.00 carried out gunnery programme
Took aboard 1,000 lbs fresh meat
14.00 ship open to visitors
20.00 Squadron Ball

31 December 1923 (at Cape Town)

06.30 cleaning ship
Worked main derrick
Took aboard: 10,300 lbs fresh meat; 13,000 lbs vegetables
13.00 Ship open to visitors
14.00 Make and mend clothes

1 January 1924 (Cape Town)

10.00 Carried out gunnery programme

Took aboard: 10,320 lbs fresh meat; 13,000 lbs fresh vegetables.

13.00 ship open to visitors

14 January 1924 (Zanzibar)

06.30 Cleaning Ship

07.00 USS *Concord* sailed

Landed small arms companies, Royal Marines and field guns for ceremonial March Past.

08.30 Worked main derrick

10.00 Landing parties returned

Noon: Temperature 82 degrees

Took on board 5,000 lbs fresh meat, 9,000 lbs vegetables.

28 January 1924 (at Trincomalee)

06.00 Cleaning ship

07.00 Discharged two ratings to Columbo Hospital

09.30 Cleaning side and preparing for painting ship

Took aboard: fresh meat 5,000 lbs; vegetables 8,500 lbs

13.00 Ship open to visitors

14.00 hands painting ship

6 February 1924 (Port Swettenham)

05.30 Sent funeral and firing party to Kuala Lumpur for internment of A.B. Walter Benger

Cleaning ship

08.00 Landed 200 men for Kuala Lumpur excursion

Ship open to visitors

Noon Temperature 80 degrees

12.30 Fired 17 gun salute for Sultan of Perak

Fired 17 gun salute for Sultan of Pahang

Fired 17 gun salute for Sultan of Negri Sembilan

14.00 Ship open to visitors

15.00 Hands make and mend clothes

16.00 Quarters

15 February 1924 (at Singapore)

06.30 Cleaning ship

07.30 Landed small arms company, Royal Marines, Field and Machine Gun sections for ceremonial route march

10.00 Landing parties returned

Noon temperature 77 degrees

Took aboard 7,000 lbs fresh meat, 12,600 lbs vegetables

13.00 Discharged M. Babstock Wordoff to General Hospital

Ship open to visitors

14.00 Make and mend clothes

21.00 Burned searchlights

7

AN ODYSSEY AND SOME
UNEXPECTED GUESTS

For most of my time with the sloop HMS *Chrysanthemum* I was based in the Mediterranean. And there were worse places to be than Malta, the home of the British navy in the Med, between 1925 and 1927.

I remember that *Chrysanthemum* was the subject of some mess deck gossip and leg pulling at the time. About a month before I joined her she had been taking part in one of her usual duties, towing targets so larger ships – battleships and the like – could practise firing. The canvas targets, which were quite large, were towed about 50 yards behind *Chrysanthemum*. The idea for the other ships was not to hit the target but to get close to it. On one occasion, however, things had not gone to plan as the *Emperor of India* – the ship that I had almost joined – put a 6 in. shell through *Chrysanthemum*'s stern. There was no explosive in the shell so it went right through the ship and out the other side. There wasn't much damage, just two holes where it had entered and left. By the time I joined the *Chrysanthemum* the metal plate holed by the shell had been replaced and was mounted on the quarter deck as a sort of 'battle honour'. The thing I have always found hard to understand is that after this incident *Emperor of India* was awarded a cup for best gunnery!

Once when I was on *Chrysanthemum* the engines suddenly stuttered and leapt forward. Instantly the captain asked me what had happened. I said I thought something had gone wrong with the target attached to the ship. Sure enough, when he looked, it was no longer there.

One of the regular duties of *Chrysanthemum* was to put to sea at about 9 p.m. on Sunday night. The Fleet usually put out for exercise on Monday morning and it was our job to provide advance warning about the weather conditions. We were usually accompanied by the boat that took the mail to Syracuse.

I must say it was hard work for us stokers when we were steaming and towing two battle class targets. The boilers, fuelled by coal, each had four doors. And one of the fires had to be drawn out every so often. It was quite a hot job, I can tell you. It was so hot in the summer when we were at sea towing targets that we had to wear flannel gloves as the iron ladders got so hot we could not touch them with our bare hands. Although it was hard work we more than made up for it by playing hard when we were ashore in harbour. And I never minded hard work. It didn't kill us.

I had some good times in *Chrysanthemum* where I continued with my barbering. I was often sent for by other small ships to act as a travelling barber. I remember one day I ended up a bit drunk as the sailors were all paying me in kind with their tots of rum.

On another occasion when at Moudhros on the Greek island of Limnos, I was again slightly inebriated when I came across a local man who was trying to push a donkey into the sea – presumably to wash it. I decided to lend him a hand but ended up pushing him into the sea as well as the donkey. At that point I decided to dive in myself. Up until then I had not been able to swim but afterwards I never again had any fears of going into the water. The next day, when they piped 'Hands to bathe on the starboard side', I jumped over and swam. The Officer of the Watch said, 'Look at that damn rating – he couldn't swim yesterday. He can swim like a fish now.' In fact, a couple of months later I found myself goalkeeper in the water polo team.

We had a few smashing trips around the coast of Italy and I recall anchoring at Naples from where I went to the ruins of Pompeii with some messmates. We also visited Capri where I swam in the Blue Grotto and I still remember the wonderful clear blue water.

I really enjoyed my two and a half years based in Malta. I had good pals, there was plenty to do, lots of sport, the weather was often fine and we saw sights that we could never have dreamed of seeing if we weren't in the Royal Navy. As it was a major Naval base, there was plenty of entertainment – clubs, restaurants and bars. We would visit the Naval Club and I saw my first 'talkie' at the cinema there.

The ships would hold regattas, which I particularly enjoyed. A Royal Naval regatta consisted of a number of rowing races using different ships' boats. Ships would enter teams to compete in each race and at the end of the competition the scores would be tallied up and whichever ship scored the most won. The winning ship was known as the 'Cock of the Fleet' and was given a model of a cockerel as a trophy. And there was plenty of swimming, with most ships fielding at least two water polo teams. All this when there was a general strike and major economic depression at home in Britain.

I attended evening classes in English and Arithmetic as part of the preparation for promotion examinations and was promoted to Acting Leading Stoker just prior to leaving Malta.

About this time I met up with two of my brothers, Jack and Walter, whose ships were returning to England. Jack had spent two and a half years on the West Indies station and was returning home on HMS *Cairo*. Walter was a leading stoker who had been based at Malta. He was with HMS *Emperor of India*.

I also joined the 'Royal Antediluvian Order of Buffaloes', and later in 1932, the Freemasons. Both were alike in that they were associations rooted in brotherhood and charitable acts. The main advantage for sailors like me was that they had places all over the world where you could meet fellow members.

However, the main event that stands out in my mind from my two years in *Chrysanthemum* came in 1927 when we buried Sir Walter Norris Congreve, the ex-Governor of Malta, at sea. After retirement he had lived at Gozo, the small island just off Malta, and had expressed a wish that, when his time came, he should be buried at sea. It fell to *Chrysanthemum* to perform that duty. Several prominent people from Malta attended the ceremony. It was a solemn moment as Sir Walter's coffin slid beneath the waves. Some time afterwards we were detailed to take his widow to Marseilles as she was returning to England. It was a very rough trip and we landed her instead at Hyères. She occupied the Captain's cabin and was thrown out of the bunk once or twice during the journey.

General Sir Walter Norris Congreve (1862–1927) was Governor of Malta from 1924 until shortly before his death. Among the decorations he had received during a long military career was the Victoria Cross, awarded for his valour in the Battle of Colenso during the Boer War. He and three others had dashed through an exposed strip of land being swept with gunfire to retrieve his unit's artillery which had been forced into a gully. Soon afterwards and despite an injury he helped to bring in a wounded man under attack by the Boers. He was still serving in the First World War, during which he lost a hand. His son Major William La Touche Congreve was given a posthumous VC for his bravery at the Battle of the Somme in 1916. They are one of only three father and son pairings to win VCs. Before his death Sir Walter was also known as 'Squib', 'WNC' or, to his men, 'Old Concrete'. The sea passage where Congreve was buried, between Malta and Filfla, is now unofficially known as 'Congreve Channel'.

On leaving *Chrysanthemum* at the end of 1927, I was drafted to HMS *P40* which was a submarine chaser. *P40* was a very small but fast ship. She had been converted from a patrol boat of 750 tons with a single 4 in. gun with a set of three torpedo tubes and depth charges.

She had been built in 1914 and used for patrolling the coast for submarines and German E-boats. During conversion, in the early 1920s, the torpedo tubes were removed as were other parts. She was fitted with an underwater dome to the bottom of the ship which contained the echo sounding gear.

I remember her as the only ship I served in from which I could dive from the upper deck. I was only in *P40* for about nine months while I waited for a place on a course for Leading Stokers. For this I had to return to base. This time it was Portland.

When I was based at Portland the train journey home to the South Hams involved changing four or five times so I bought a little car

– a Swift 8.9 horsepower – for £175 and, after one lesson, I drove it. I would frequently give fellow shipmates a lift and also picked up other people en route. Most important of all, I used to drive a warrant officer to get our pay every fortnight from the Naval depot.

At the time I was the only person in our village to own a car. They were still a rare sight on country roads and it was a pleasure to drive. The road tax cost £9 a year and insurance was £20 a year, although it was not compulsory. The petrol tank was under the bonnet and fuel was gravity-fed to the carburettor. There were no front wheel brakes, no windscreen wipers and no pressure gauges. The dynamo was called an auto charge. That's because it 'oughta' charge but it bloody well didn't, so I carried a spare battery in the car as well as a two-gallon can of petrol. I think petrol was about 2/6 a gallon at the time.

I used to take three chiefs into town at night time. They would give me half a crown each for my trouble. They drank pints of beer and I would drink a glass. Thank goodness there were no breathalysers in those days. Once I drove our Captain, a Lieutenant Commander, and his wife to Torquay on a Friday and picked them up again on the following Monday. Another time, I picked up a tramp – or a 'gentleman of the road' as we used to say. When we got to his destination I asked him if he would like a drink, as we were stopped outside a pub. He said, 'I can't give you one back.' I told him I didn't want him to and I bought him a pint while I had a small beer then I went on my way.

And I had no trouble getting young ladies to come out with me when I was home for weekend leave, thanks to the car. I used to fly two flags in the windscreen which were actually ladies' knickers that I'd bought in Malta. One pair was red, signifying port and the other green, starboard. Everyone used to have a good laugh and give a cheer when they saw the underwear. My mother and brothers and sisters all thought it was a big treat to go out in the car.

Swift cars were made in Coventry by a company that was better known for making bicycles and sewing machines. Although it was an early innovator in the age of the motorcar and produced some popular models, the company closed in 1931 during a catastrophic economic downturn.

At last I was notified that I had a place on the course, which was to be held in old ships moored adjacent to the barracks at Devonport and would last three months. During this course I learned my trade, which was boilermaker/bricklayer. It might seem odd to say that whilst in the Navy I was trained as a bricklayer but the boilers on ships were all lined with firebricks, which had to be replaced from time to time. We were shown how to crawl inside the boiler attached to a rope in case anything untoward happened. Once inside the boiler you had to chip out what remained of the damaged bricks and replace them with new ones. In February 1929 I completed a three-month course in bricklaying.

Later in 1929, I was drafted to the aircraft carrier HMS *Eagle*, again based in Malta. Before I left Devonport I sold the car to a man in Kingsbridge for £75. The Wall Street Crash, which happened the same year, seemed very distant to us in the Royal Navy.

Almost immediately, *Eagle* went in for a refit. My own part in this work involved stripping the brickwork out of number one boiler, laying new bricks and lining them with fire clay. My Engineer Commander must have been pleased enough with my contribution as he remarked to me, 'Stoker Stone, you will be able to build your own house when you leave the Navy.'

Soon afterwards I received a call that was to test my bricklaying skills as well as my ingenuity. The captain of the ship had said that he wanted the tiles of the bathroom floor in his sea cabin replaced as the glazing had worn off. The shipwrights had been asked if they could do it and had said 'no' as they were all tradesmen and considered it a tiler's job. My Engineering Officer asked me if I might be able to do it as I had bricklaying skills that he thought I might be able to transfer to tiling. I said that I would have a go. The preparation was hard work as, when I had lifted the old tiles, I found an inch or so of special cement that needed to be removed. Then came the real problem – how was I going to cut the tiles? However, luck was on my side as, whilst I was ashore at Malta, I happened to meet a local man who knew how to cut tiles and, for a bottle of beer, he gave me a bit of instruction. Following this, I managed to lay the tiles well enough but was then faced with the problem of the grouting.

The cement was brown and would not have looked very attractive as grout but I came up with the idea of mixing the cement with some of the white powder that we used throughout the ship to clean the brightwork. As I had hoped, this combination made a nice white grout. Finally, after I had finished the grouting, I covered the whole area with sawdust for a while which absorbed any excess moisture. One of the shipwrights got to see what I had done and asked me, 'Stoker Stone, where did you get that bloody grout?' 'That's a secret,' I replied. When the captain saw it he was really pleased. So pleased in fact that he asked if I could do his main cabin as well. I did that as well but was not quite so pleased with the result – the tiles seemed a lot more difficult to lay perfectly straight in that room.

Later, whilst I was in *Eagle*, came one of my 'claims to fame' – I got to cut the hair of Major Ramon Franco – a famous aviator and General Franco's brother. In 1929 his Dornier flying boat ditched in the ocean after engine failure and had been lost for days. *Eagle* pilots found him and the ship picked him up together with his three-man crew. They'd been drifting without food or water for six days when they were finally found. And they were lucky. Our pilots were on the point of giving up the search when they spotted the lost crew. Franco's aviation achievements had made him a celebrity as he'd already flown from Spain to Argentina. He was one of the pioneers of the Spanish air force. He was once again trying to forge a route between Spain and South America when his plane was downed.

Afterwards King Alfonso XIII awarded *Eagle*'s captain and senior officers the Spanish Order of Merit and presented the ship with a magnificent silver eagle, which was lost with the ship when *Eagle* was torpedoed in 1942.

My role in all this was a bit more humble – and so were my rewards. Having hoisted plane, pilot and crew aboard, the men, who were in a dreadful state, were given the facilities to smarten up. The Commander then sent for me to cut our guest's hair. I remember that well because instead of paying me with one bottle of beer, as was the custom for the officers, Major Franco said, 'Have two.'

There was too much work on board *Eagle* for just one barber. I worked alongside a Corporal Bandsman on *Eagle* who was a lovely fellow.

On *Eagle* the routine was different, which I liked. There was plenty of room for divisions and such like. One day the ratings were on the flight deck, marching divisions, and I shouted, 'Division halt.' I knew I'd be up on a charge instantly but everyone was laughing. For a moment it felt like it would be worth it. Soon afterwards the captain asked me, 'Why did you do it?' I said, 'I don't know, Sir. I did it as a joke.' He was hiding a laugh when he said, 'Well, you've had your fun, now I'll have mine. Seven days' pay stopped.'

When aircraft were landing the engine room and boiler room crews were notified by the bridge. We were not allowed to adjust the sprayers, as there was a danger of making smoke, which would make things more difficult for the pilots. On the bows of *Eagle* there was a steam pipe by which the captain was able to tell whether he had got the ship lined up correctly in relation to the wind.

One of the cruises on *Eagle* stands out in my mind. We went across to South America and spent a few days anchored off Rio de Janeiro. A few of us took the opportunity of a day's leave to make the ascent of Sugar Loaf, which overlooks the city and bay. We were about two thirds of the way up when I remarked to one of the Chiefs how small the ship looked from the height we were at. 'Yes,' replied the Engineer Commander, 'and she'll look a lot smaller tomorrow when we've gone.'

One day we had an unexpected visitor when one of our own planes returned from Rio with a passenger on board. He turned out to be the Prince of Wales (later the Duke of Windsor). He had been forbidden by his father, King George V, to fly onto a ship but he had taken the chance. He was well entertained and, in fact, attended a dance held in the hangar by the ship's officers and to which various local dignitaries also came.

We headed down the coast of South America to Argentina. During that trip we had the usual ship 'open days' when the public were allowed aboard. Another sailor and I got chatting to a couple of local girls who said that they would return the favour of our guided tour of the *Eagle* by showing us around Buenos Aires and the surrounding district. So when we came ashore they were waiting with an open-top car and took us for a drive. We could hardly believe our luck.

Suddenly they stopped and said, 'Buenos Aires means good air and you sailors are smoking those beastly cigarettes.' We wanted to impress so of course we immediately threw the lighted fags away. We went to their house – they were lovely people – and they drove us back to our ship about 8 p.m. that evening. They said, 'You will write to us, won't you?' We said we would but needed their address and got them to write it on my Players cigarette packet. Of course, the next day I smoked the cigarettes and, without thinking, threw the packet away. I was sorry because they were really nice girls. I still have a photo of us on the flight deck.

We returned to Devonport in 1931 and I left HMS *Eagle* as Acting Stoker Petty Officer. In July that year I was confirmed as a Stoker Petty Officer and a month later, following a few weeks in barracks at Devonport, I joined the sloop HMS *Harebell*, a sister ship to HMS *Chrysanthemum* also fuelled by coal. Our main duties were fishery protection. Although we were based at Portland, we visited, among other places, Reykjavik in Iceland, Buckie in Scotland and Fleetwood in Lancashire. So it wasn't the most glamorous of postings. I left the ship at the end of 1933 and returned to Devonport, having received a good conduct medal. When the officer presented me with it he said: 'It shouldn't be called the "Good Conduct" medal but "Fifteen Years of Undiscovered Crime".'

During my time on *Harebell*, fellow shipmates invited me to become a Freemason and I joined the United Service Lodge at Portland in 1932. I did not know at the time what a long association this would be but in 2008 I was honoured to be presented with a certificate in recognition of 75 years' service to Freemasonry.

In January 1934, I was drafted to a destroyer – HMS *Thanet* – which was part of the Reserve Fleet. Our duties were mainly to go to Belfast once a month to refuel other ships in the Fleet. Sometimes I would make this journey in HMS *Tenedos*. This was an uneventful draft, although I do remember very rough crossings.

William spent much of his service in the Mediterranean. It was one of several foreign Navy bases where British sailors could be sent, including the West Indies, Singapore, Trincomalee and South Africa. Another foreign station where many British soldiers saw action was in China. It was the thought of joining the China fleet that filled William with dread at the start of his Naval career. The UK cultivated influence in China in the nineteenth century to protect British opium traders. Subsequently, the British founded a base at Hong Kong, known as HMS Tamar, *and had concessions including Hankow and Wei Hai Wei as well as centres of influence like Shanghai. There were various spats which involved Royal Naval personnel throughout the early twentieth century. These resulted in the Navy operating a fleet of small gunboats on the primary Chinese rivers, known as the 'Insect Class', reflecting their names. Anti-foreign sentiment among the Chinese was largely forgotten though in the animosity against the Japanese during the 1930s following the Japanese invasion of Manchuria in 1931. When hostilities broke out between the two countries in 1937 following the battle of Marco Polo Bridge the Royal Navy helped to evacuate British nationals from major cities including Shanghai.*

8

FROM AFRICA WITH LOVE

Then I swapped the grey days of Scotland for the sunshine of South Africa. Going back to 1934 I was drafted to HMS *Carlisle*, to serve on the South Africa station at Simonstown.

The two and a half years I spent there were some of the best and happiest times of my life. The weather was good and my shipmates and I made many friends with the local people who had emigrated there from England. They often took us to places of interest and would regularly entertain us at their homes. On one occasion we visited a gold mine in Johannesburg – the deepest in the world.

It was the age of apartheid, although widespread discrimination against black people wasn't called that at the time. Evidence of it was everywhere. While we used to visit the shark-netted beach regularly no black people were allowed on the sands. You weren't encouraged to question it. Everyone was warned about talking to black or coloured people, either by other sailors or people we met. The police, who had a vicious reputation, were always on the lookout for anyone who consorted with black people and they took instant reprisals. If I had 'broken the code', it would have ended in a beating.

Both British and Afrikaners in South Africa were keen exponents of segregation at the time William was in Simonstown. In the uneasy ceasefire between the rival authorities following the Boer War, it was the black and coloured populations that faced brutal crackdowns. After 1905 the British denied blacks the vote and made them use passes for travel. Black and coloured people were kept off the streets at night by a curfew. Police were swift to enforce the racist laws that kept the minority white population in charge. Following the Second World War Apartheid laws were introduced by the Afrikaans National Party, which had a strong government majority among whites. It offered white rulers a stranglehold on the economic and social system. It was reinforced in the 1960s, in the face of growing resentment among a downtrodden black population. Apartheid was finally overthrown in 1994 – almost 60 years after William's visit.

However, the people we met there were very hospitable. My friend Ted and I became friendly with the Matthews and Newman families and they couldn't do enough for us. We ate with them regularly and they ferried us up and down the country. A trip I particularly remember was one organised for a group from our ship to visit Kruger National Park. We were taken by car, stayed two nights, and saw all kinds of wild animals at close quarters, including leopards, baboons and all kinds of deer. On one occasion there was a lion lying down just a few yards from us.

I recall going to the races with my shipmates, and backing the winner. At Durban a group of us had the opportunity of a free flight in a troop carrier plane. Before we took off the South African pilot warned us it was a death trap. But he was just trying to scare us and we told him we would chance it. This was the first time I had been airborne and thoroughly enjoyed it. We made some lovely friends at both the Freemasons and Royal Antediluvian Order of Buffaloes (RAOBs), whose members couldn't do enough for us.

While out there I had the unusual distinction for a Stoker Petty Officer of being Captain of a gun crew. The station had four howitzer guns, which were used in displays that we gave. Three of the guns were crewed by the seamen and one by stokers. The latter was formerly captained by a Seaman Petty Officer but he was court-martialled after a misfire. The Chief was asked if he could suggest a replacement and he suggested me. We trained hard on the football ground in Simonstown.

I well remember when the gun crews went on tour to give displays. We travelled from Cape Town to Johannesburg, and went to Durban and East London as well. We doubled around the exhibition fields, six stokers towing the guns with ropes. Later, dressed in old style sailors' uniforms, we would all sing sea shanties. It was a welcome change from duty on board.

Whilst I was on the South Africa station the Commander in Chief was Vice Admiral Evans – 'Evans of the *Broke*' (1881–1957). I used to go up to his house to cut his hair and remember him as another senior officer who appeared to me to be a very pleasant man. Better known to us as Teddy Evans, he was one of the most famous men in the country during the early 1920s following his exploits before and during the First World War. Before the First World War he had been second in command of Scott's penultimate Antarctic Expedition and he would give us lectures on his experiences there. Sometimes they used to get frozen feet and, he told us, the best remedy was to pee on them. In 1913 he brought the survivors of Scott's disastrous mission to Antarctica home again. Three years later Evans made his name during his command of HMS *Broke* during a famous destroyer engagement in the English Channel. With one other destroyer, they intercepted and sank three German destroyers in the channel. He rammed one to send it to the bottom and there was hand-to-hand fighting on the deck of the *Broke* before the German ship sank. He was one of the great adventurers of the century and it was a privilege to meet him. We used to have long chats while I was cutting his hair. In 1945 he was created 1st Baron Mountevans of Chelsea.

Another of my duties was to drive the Admiral's Barge, ferrying him from shore to ship.

During 1936 it fell to HMS *Carlisle* to make the trip into the mid-Atlantic to supply the smallest island in the British Empire. Tristan da Cunha is a volcanic island covering just 80 square miles that lies some 1,750 miles off South Africa. Its capital has the delightful name of Edinburgh of the Seven Seas.

The thing that stands out most from this trip is the fact that we took with us a live bull. Apparently, it was necessary to introduce some variety into the island's bloodstock – hence the bull. The animal was hoisted aboard and accommodated in a wooden pen, which had been specially made between *Carlisle*'s two funnels. An able seaman was assigned to feed and generally look after it. Of course this led to the usual seamen's banter and leg pulling which this sailor had to fend off. 'I see we've really got some bullshit on board this time,' is one comment that stands out. I can't remember if our 'bull handler' offered a reply. There were other animals too – chickens certainly, plus the more conventional supplies.

When we arrived at the island we had a few days free whilst the stores were offloaded. The islanders had no money – they just bartered. I remember that the fishing there was exceptionally easy – I'd never seen the fo'c'sle covered with fish before – and that the fish were enormous. We were allowed to gut the fish and store them in the ship's refrigerator.

Also, the seaweed was so dense that when the anchor was weighed two shipwrights were needed to cut the clinging tendrils off with an adze.

During our frequent exercises at sea, we would regularly visit ports along the east coast from Simonstown – Port Elizabeth, East London, Dunbar and Lourenco Marques.

We were there for three months before we saw a drop of rain. Whilst at Simonstown, we were often called out to help extinguish fires on the slopes of Table Mountain.

In early 1937 we left Simonstown waved off by a huge crowd of people, including the friends who had been so good to us. They came bearing fruits of all kinds, which made the return journey so much more palatable. I can freely say what a marvellous time I spent with all those wonderful people during our stay in South Africa. And I live on those beautiful memories.

Just as William was leaving Simonstown one of its most celebrated residents was born. Just Nuisance was a Great Dane born on 1 April 1937 in Cape Town and sold to Benjamin Chaney, who ran the United Services Institute favoured by sailors stationed in Simonstown. The dog developed a curious attachment to British sailors who he apparently recognised by their bell bottom trousers. To men in different uniforms he paid no attention. Just Nuisance got his name from lying at the top of the gangplank of HMS Neptune, Carlisle's replacement, making it difficult for sailors to pass him. However, he rewarded their kindness by ensuring they returned home safely from bars across the district – taking the train if he had to round up outlying stragglers. It was his free use of the train that got him into trouble with South African authorities that wished to see him pay a fare. At that point the Royal Navy stepped in and enlisted the dog, as British servicemen travelled free of charge there. Shortly before the outbreak of the Second World War Just Nuisance became part of the Royal Navy, with his trade listed as 'bone crusher' and his religious denomination 'scrounger'. A popular figure among sailors, he nonetheless caused difficulties when he killed the canine mascots of other visiting ships including HMS Shropshire and HMS Redoubt. Just Nuisance was finally discharged on New Year's Day 1944 and died four months later. He was buried with full military honours.

On arrival at Plymouth, we were greeted by another crowd including my sister Mabel and her husband Tom Rundle.

Around this time I began seeing Lily Hoskin again. Lily was to be my wife but it could all have turned out very differently because of bachelor ways that I found hard to shake off. I had known Lily since I was a young man as she lived not far from us and was friendly with my sisters. Lily's father was the local churchwarden and I often used to go around to their house and cut the church grass and spend some time with Lily in the evenings. Lily's mother was Scottish. One evening she must have thought that I was staying later than she would have liked because she put on a gramophone record which began 'Good night, Good night . . .'

On one occasion, not long before I joined HMS *Carlisle* in 1934, I had arranged to go with Lily to Plymouth but I didn't turn up. She wrote to me and said that I would have to decide whether I wanted her or my drinking mates. I didn't answer the letter, probably because I was still enjoying the single life too much, and soon afterwards found myself drafted to HMS *Carlisle* and heading off to the South Africa station.

For the whole time that I was there we lost contact with one another. Lily moved to London and worked in Bryanston Square for two ladies, the Pulteney sisters. One, Dr Isabel Pulteney, was a doctor and Christian who campaigned against birth control. At the end of her life she established a bursary for medical missionaries under the umbrella of the United Society for the Propagation of the Gospel, a fund which was wound up in 2002. She died in 1961 aged 94. Her brother was Lt General Sir William Pulteney (1861–1941) who, following an undistinguished military career, held the office of Black Rod in the House of Lords for 21 years prior to his death.

In 1937 I returned to Devon from South Africa and met up with Lily, who by that time had also returned to Devon as her father had been taken ill. Now I felt differently. I was growing older and the single life, for all its thrills and spills, no longer held the same appeal. For the first time I felt ready for some commitment to something other than the Royal Navy and I'm delighted to say that Lily was still single. I think she had realised that I was going to be late in settling down and, thank goodness, she hadn't met anyone else in the meantime. We resumed a relationship that had begun years before but this time it was serious and I knew it. I wasn't prepared to lose her again for the sake of a night out with the lads.

Following leave, I returned to barracks at Devonport and was subsequently rated to Chief Stoker. I'd got fed up with being a Petty Officer and I wanted to make my own decisions. I failed the exam the first time but then passed it easily the second time I sat it. My brothers couldn't do it, I don't know why. A Chief Stoker is responsible for the smooth running of the boiler room and has to ensure that all the stokers who report to him are doing their jobs. The captain knows what you are up to down below, because of the colour of the smoke coming out of the stack. The Chief is responsible for the colour of the smoke. You can't have it black. That means the fuel isn't burning properly and it gives away a ship's position to the enemy. Then you had to use the fan and the hose. Later on, we got oil and brought it on board through a special hose. We had to check the levels as it was being pumped on board. On *Hood* there were special gauges for that.

In September 1937, I was drafted to the Minesweeper HMS *Salamander*, stationed at Portland, Dorset. She was the ship in which I would see my early wartime service at Dunkirk.

On 27 May 1938, I married Lily Hoskin at St Peter's Church, Buckland Tout Saints, near Kingsbridge. We moved to furnished rooms in Devonport that cost 17s a week and had a delayed honeymoon at her sister Mary's home in Cardigan, Wales.

By this time *Salamander* had sailed to Devonport for refitting and I was stationed in the barracks. But when the ship returned to Portland we rented a flat there where we lived for some months. I was often out minesweeping but was able to return to our home when the ship docked.

Lily became pregnant, but a week before our baby was born the ship left for Sheerness and never returned to Portland. I remember that time well – the air was filled with barrage balloons as defence against air attacks. No one was sure what lay ahead.

Our daughter Anne was born at Portland on 28 August 1939 – just a week before war was declared. Not until the baby was three weeks old and the war had been going on a fortnight was I able to get special permission for long-weekend leave. Eventually Lily and Anne left Portland and returned to stay with Lily's parents, who had now retired to Wrangaton, near Plymouth.

Early in the war I lost one of my nephews, Leslie Edgecombe, who was Nellie's son. Just a fortnight after the outbreak of war he was lucky to be alive following the loss of the aircraft carrier HMS *Courageous* which was sunk in an attack off the Irish coast by the German submarine *U–29* on 17 September 1939. *Courageous* was the first British warship lost in the Second World War.

Later he had told me that, as he was trying to get out, he had heard one of the Petty Officers shouting, 'Follow me.' Although he could not see the Petty Officer, he had followed the sound of his voice and managed to get out and had been rescued. Although my nephew was saved many of my friends were lost with the *Courageous*. The death toll was about 500.

However, my nephew was not so lucky a few months later when, on 8 June 1940, *Courageous*'s sister ship HMS *Glorious* was lost off

Norway following a battle with the German Battlecruisers *Scharnhorst* and *Gneisenau*. *Glorious* was in the region to help in the evacuation of Norway. Leslie was one of 1,200 sailors, marines and RAF personnel lost when *Glorious* and two destroyers accompanying her were sunk. Three days after *Glorious* went down three officers and thirty-five men were picked up by a Norwegian trawler, almost crazy with thirst. The losses of both *Glorious* and *Courageous* were early, critical blows to Britain in the war.

9

DARK DAYS – OPERATION 'DYNAMO', 1940

I *nternational tensions had been building before war broke out and* *servicemen everywhere knew it. HMS* Salamander *– as part of the* *Home Fleet – was put on a war footing during the 1938 crisis, which* *blew up when Hitler invaded Czechoslovakia.*

After a refit at Devonport at the start of 1939 she was on standby to *search for the sunken submarine HMS* Thetis *in Liverpool Bay in June.* *News of the submarine's loss felt like a hammer blow as Britain moved* *inexorably towards war. Ultimately* Salamander *was also involved in* *the salvage operation.*

As pressures escalated worldwide towards conflict, domestic news was *dominated by the tragedy of the* Thetis. *This 270 ft-long submarine was* *taking part in a diving trial in Liverpool Bay on 1 June when disaster* *struck. As attempts were made to adjust its ballast the new craft suddenly took* *on water and plunged to the seabed. There were 103 people aboard, including* *Naval officers and men, representatives from builder Cammell Laird and* *Vickers Armstrong, two catering staff and a River Mersey pilot.*

Men on the tug which had stood by as Thetis *initially struggled to* *submerge soon realised something was badly wrong. But they had no idea* *their vessel had silently drifted four miles from the point where it had* *parted company with the stricken submarine. Rescue boats all headed to* *the wrong area and were then hampered by impending darkness.*

Aboard the submarine there was about 18 hours worth of oxygen available as well as deep sea escape apparatus. Lieutenant Commander Guy Bolus, in charge of Thetis, *was even able to ascend one end of the submarine so it stuck out of the water. It was finally spotted by a search plane the day after the disaster and rescue craft sped to the scene.*

However, the escape hatch was still 20 ft below the surface of the water. While four men managed to make it to freedom, another four drowned in the attempt. By then those still aboard the Thetis *were too weak to even try. They were being slowly suffocated by carbon monoxide gas. An open hatch, possibly linked to the final escape, meant the submarine slowly filled with water. The extraordinary weight snapped the lines that had been established with rescue ships and the craft headed for the seabed once more. This time, everybody aboard was already dead, killed not by drowning but through poisonous gas.*

The event dominated headlines. There were several memorial services and a public fund which almost instantly raised £115,000 for relatives. Due to poor weather, the craft wasn't raised until 2 September. Most of its occupants were buried in a mass grave at Holyhead.

From August *Salamander* was transferred to the 6th Minesweeping Flotilla which, following the outbreak of war, went to the east coast. In those early months of the war *Salamander* was stationed at Grimsby and we were responsible for coastal minesweeping operations around the north-east. I managed to rent rooms in Cleethorpes and Lily and Anne travelled all the way up from Devon by train so that we could be together.

On one occasion the ship had a close call. I was one deck down at the time but I gather that a mine got caught around one of the sweeps as it was being winched back in. Fortunately, someone spotted it and gave the alarm. Winch operators managed to free the mine from the sweep but in doing so, or shortly afterwards, it detonated and blasted the side of the ship. Although there was no damage that threatened the ship itself, one of the plates, which separated the oil tanks, was ruptured and we had to go into docks to have that repaired. It could have been so much worse if the mine had exploded aboard the ship.

That was the problem with being on a minesweeper. At any minute you could have hit a mine and that would have meant an explosion, death and destruction. But you just carried on as if nothing happened. You didn't take any notice of it. Even though the main events in France – where the BEF had been sent to bolster our allies as they sat behind their 'impregnable' Maginot Line – were a concern to all of us, it certainly didn't feel like a 'Bore War' to those of us at sea.

In May 1940 *Salamander* was sailing off the coast of Holland until the Dutch surrender was official. Winston Churchill became Prime Minister at this time. He was a popular choice among sailors as he had twice been First Lord of the Admiralty and was thought to have a special affinity with the Royal Navy. When he had originally been taken back into the war-time government as First Sea Lord, the message signalled around the Service was 'Winston's Back!'

Then, as Germany rapidly advanced through Belgium and France with their *Blitzkrieg* tactics, we were ordered by the Admiralty to the south coast to help with the Dunkirk evacuations that had been urgently organised as the BEF and remnants of the defeated French army sought to escape encirclement. We did three trips to Dunkirk in all, rescuing about 300 or 400 men per trip. Each time we went the experience was worse than before – it was a living nightmare. *Salamander* also took other men to different ships for transport. Although I had been in the Navy for 22 years it was my first taste of active service – the sights and sounds of relentless German bombings, and barrages, the fear of our ship being struck a mortal blow, and the ever-present sight of death are ones I would never forget.

Dunkirk was the most terrible experience of my life. It was awful and got worse as it went on. I witnessed scenes that you wouldn't think possible outside of a Hollywood film nowadays; it was a baptism of war for me, and the thousands of others on those beaches, and in the ships attempting to save them. Hundreds of people were literally killed before my eyes. Scores of terrified men were shot by low-flying German aircraft or bombed as they swam out to boats and possible rescue. Others perished when their ships were blown out of the water by the Luftwaffe or, later, by shore batteries. Some of the survivors and many of the dead were without their clothes. Perhaps they stripped before they swam for the ships that waited to take them to safety or maybe their clothes were ripped from their bodies by explosions. I don't know. But the bodies of the clothed and the naked were covered in oil, which coated large sections of the sea as the swell and tides either took them out, or brought them back into shore. There were oil tanks burning on land, ships sinking at sea and thousands of soldiers lined up on the beaches for hours on end. The dark nights were alive with the sight of tracer bullets and the sounds of gunfire. It must have been hell on the beaches for those men.

All the while was the ever-present fear of capture, as no one knew just when Germans were going to appear on the beach. The rearguard units couldn't hold out forever, we all knew that. We all sensed that, one way or another, our time was frantically short and we had to do the best job we could without reflecting on what we were seeing unfold before our eyes.

We left for Dunkirk from the Humber on the evening of 26 May in the company of HMS *Sutton* and *Fitzroy*. For a long while we were anchored in the Downs at Goodwin Sands and eventually on 28 May we rendezvoused with HMS *Halcyon* and our sister ship *Skipjack* before making our way to France. When we approached the coast there was a ripple of apprehension around the ship. At this point we could only guess what was going on before us by the distant sights, sounds and smells of war. Even from where we were the air was thick with the stench of acrid smoke.

At this stage the rescue was divided into three sections: La Panne, Malo and Bray [see Map 2]. We were directed to La Panne on the western fringe of Belgium and anchored there at about 9.30 p.m. Using motorboats and whalers we took about 150 men aboard during the night. The men were silhouetted by flashes of shell fire and they had to deal with heavy surf. Our attempts to liberate them under the veil of darkness were thus only partially successful.

On the morning of Wednesday, 29 May we were ordered by HMS *Calcutta* to offload those men on to her as she could get no closer to the beach [*Calcutta* shipped a total of 1,750 men to England in two trips].

We went back to La Panne and continued bringing men aboard. In their eyes you could see they'd been traumatised by their experiences retreating through France with Germans on their tails and the uncertainty that prevailed on the beach. We watched them all marching down from the town to the sands at La Panne, from as far back as the eye could see. Enterprising sappers had built a pier of lorries lashed with decking to help them further into the water at high tide. We got troops aboard by using the ship's boats and small pulling boats. They got up the sides of *Salamander* using scramble nets and I was among those helping to haul them over the rail onto the quarter deck. There was some high-level bombing but nothing too much until 4 p.m. when it got a bit too close for comfort.

Nearby, HMS *Greyhound* disappeared in several mountainous fountains of water but fortunately it turned out to be two near misses rather than a direct hit. It was a relief to see the familiar outlines of a British destroyer still upright in the water a cable away. [A cable is the length of a ship's cable, about 600 ft.]

At about 5.30 p.m. there was a second bombing attack. By now we were frantically preparing for departure and heading for the area known as 'Dunkirk Roads'. Steering a zig-zag course to evade the bombers we finally left the dangerous coastline. As we looked back we could see Dunkirk and neighbouring beaches were being heavily bombed. It looked like hell and we were all relieved to be heading in the other direction!

Travelling with HMS *Sutton*, we arrived at Dover shortly before midnight in thick weather. It was a relief to be in the safety of a homeport, even as a Navy man. Goodness knows how the men we delivered there were feeling. They must have been elated to have survived, after the ordeal they had been through. We, of course, were destined to return to Dunkirk, this time knowing full well all the perils involved.

The next day, 30 May, we finally disembarked the troops we had aboard and set off for the French coast after loading up with ammunition and stores – grimly each man aboard stuck to his task as we left the safety of port.

That evening we took aboard almost 400 men, this time from Bray Dunes, once again using the cover of darkness. Leaving our motorboat with HMS *Icarus* we returned to Dover, offloaded and during the evening of 31 May turned again towards Dunkirk. I think all of us were very scared by now – there is only so much good luck one can enjoy, after all. But nobody said so. There was no question of ducking out of it. Little did we know the worst was yet to come . . .

We were travelling once more with *Halcyon* and *Skipjack* aiming to meet up with the remainder of the minesweepers. By the early hours of 1 June we were anchored off Bray beach. Now the beach was under shrapnel fire from inland enemy batteries, a sure sign the Germans were closer than ever. Volunteers manned a whaler which went to shore in darkness broken by the flames of the oil storage set alight at Dunkirk. The whaler returned about half an hour later with one man aboard and a message from General Montgomery saying that everyone was moving westward to Dunkirk as it was by now almost impossible to move off Bray beach. At dawn we sailed for Dunkirk astern of *Keith* and *Skipjack*.

By now the first grey light was breaking. And I could see troops coming down to the beach, wading out to the ships – literally thousands of them – it was almost biblical! There was also a continual stream of small craft heading for us and by 6 a.m. about 450 men were aboard.

Some men swam, risking the treacherous waters for a chance of a safe return. Other groups of men had managed to find boats and rowed out to the ship.

But everything that I had so far seen paled against what occurred that terrible morning, when every ship queuing on the coast came under attack from formations of 30 or 40 enemy aircraft. It was like a panorama of hell. In little more than an hour the Royal Navy lost three destroyers, a Fleet minesweeper and a gunboat alongside assorted other craft. Four destroyers were damaged.

The German attacks were relentless. The noise of screaming bombs and shellfire meant we had to shout at the tops of our voices – and often we still could not be heard. Everyone on deck suffered from hoarseness afterwards, a condition that was labelled 'Dunkirk Throat'.

There was the wreckage of sunken ships all around, minefields that were recently laid by enemy aircraft and burning oil tanks by the dockside.

If you weren't bombed by the Luftwaffe there were enemy submarines and motor torpedo boats at large which posed an even greater danger.

Keith came under attack at just after 7.30 a.m. Aboard *Keith* was Admiral Frederic Wake-Walker, who was in charge of beach operations. The Admiral must have seen from *Keith*'s decks the many lines of soldiers walking into the sea towards us. Her attempts to take evasive action by sailing in a tight circle were hampered by magnetic mines and recent shipwrecks clogging the channels. Then a bomb went down her funnel and exploded in the boiler room, causing clouds of smoke and steam to pour out. The ship came to a halt and someone gave the order to abandon ship. Everyone from *Keith* frantically began making for *Salamander* and *Skipjack*. Some were picked up by the tug *St Abbs*, which was almost immediately blown right out of the sea herself. She simply disappeared, leaving what remained of her surviving human cargo helpless in the water. In some ways it was too much to take in, such devastation happening so suddenly. In the near distance HMS *Basilisk* was disabled.

Salamander rescued seven ratings from *Keith*. Later we discovered the Admiral got into an MTB to continue his task – what a man!

We were anchored off the beach with *Skipjack*, only about 50 yards away. By now we had been under fire relentlessly since about 5.30 a.m., which left everybody's nerves in tatters. The sky was perpetually filled with shell bursts as the British ships tried to fend off the swarming enemy aircraft. At about 8.45 a.m. another ten German dive bombers came over and attacked *Skipjack*, scoring several hits which she initially withstood.

One of the attacking planes was shot down but *Skipjack* was hit three more times, mortally crippling her, and within two minutes she turned turtle. She floated bottom up for only a matter of moments before finally sinking. If you hadn't seen it, you wouldn't think it was possible! Rescued soldiers aboard *Skipjack* had been directed to the hold below to help with stability. The extra weight added by unscheduled passengers could have given the ship a list had they stayed in the deck areas. Soldiers were also at risk from murderous machine-gun fire on deck. But that proved disastrous for this poor bunch directed below during the rescue operation.

Most of those killed were trapped in the hull but those survivors floundering in the water were subsequently machine-gunned by low-flying aircraft. Those of us on *Salamander* who saw everything were outraged, but at the same time feeling almost helpless. *Skipjack* had had about 275 men on board. There were floating corpses and parts of bodies everywhere. It was the worst moment of my life, standing among the dead and dying. I had to say 'God, help us,' to gather whatever mental fortitude I had left. I always find it helps to say that and I believe to this day that He did. Although we were fully expecting the same medicine – we stayed afloat.

I got hold of a .303 Lee-Enfield rifle and took some desperate pot shots at low-flying German aircraft – in a vain attempt to strike back. One wanted to just be involved and try to defend the ship from these overwhelming odds. *Salamander* herself got hit several times by aircraft and shellfire. One underwater blast was so huge it lifted the ship about 2 ft out of the water. She landed back in the sea then lurched downwards so she was so much lower than she should have been, with a list to port. Many of the wounded who were lying on their stretchers were flung violently across the mess decks. (About 20 of the men we had aboard were serious casualties.) The lights went out and no one knew for sure whether we would make it. For a moment there was a collective hesitation as we all waited to see what would happen next, hardly daring to breathe. When it seemed as if we were sinking the captain ordered confidential paperwork aboard to be thrown over the side in a weighted bag. The engines were cut as the damage was assessed. In fact, we weren't sinking although the cold and cool rooms, gunners' stores and the canteen store were flooded.

On deck we were agonising about how little practice we'd had at rescuing men from the water. It just wasn't something we had prepared for during peacetime. On one occasion – on the second trip I think – I had a rope around a badly injured soldier who had bones sticking out of his trousers. Just as I tried to pull him in, the ship went ahead trying to shake off enemy gunfire and I lost him. I don't know what happened to him and I don't like to dwell on that. As a matter of fact, at the beginning of the war, none of us in the Royal Navy were

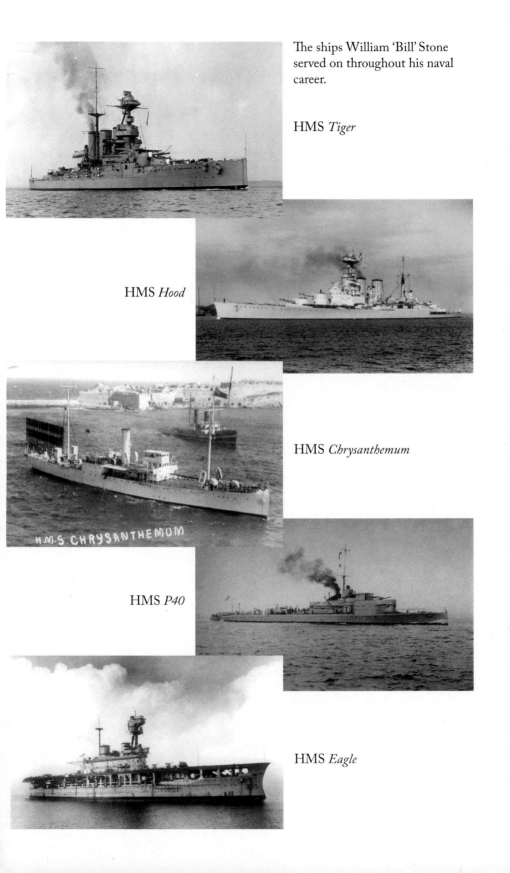

The ships William 'Bill' Stone served on throughout his naval career.

HMS *Tiger*

HMS *Hood*

HMS *Chrysanthemum*

HMS *P40*

HMS *Eagle*

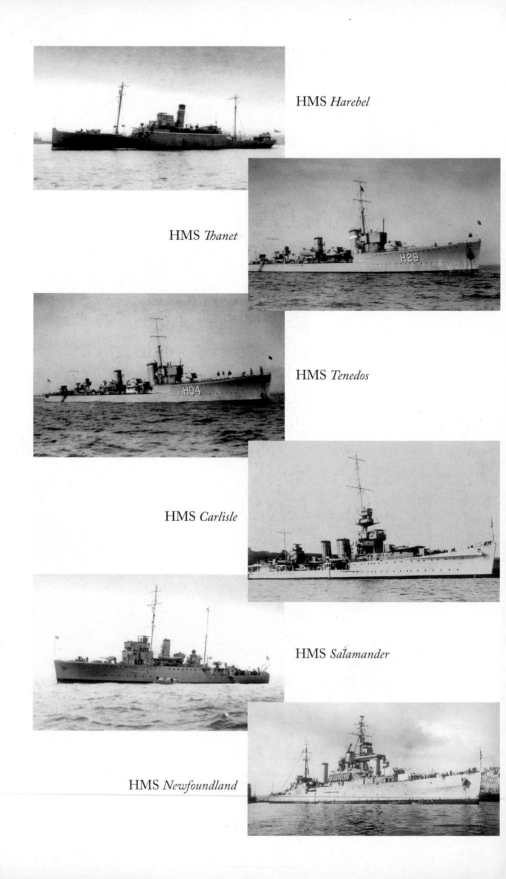

HMS *Harebel*

HMS *Thanet*

HMS *Tenedos*

HMS *Carlisle*

HMS *Salamander*

HMS *Newfoundland*

HMS *Salamander*, 1938: The ship Bill would serve with distinction at Dunkirk in Operation 'Dynamo' in 1940. Bill is under the shadow of the gun barrel, his arms folded.

The stern of HMS *Thetis* is sighted by rescuers as the crew desperately try to find a way to surface and save themselves. Only four managed to escape. (© Getty Images)

Into hell! The view that the crew of *Salamander*, and countless other ships from the Royal Navy, as well as those civilian boats, were met with as they sailed towards the devastated harbour of Dunkirk. (© Getty Images)

Rescuing the BEF: The legions of soldiers from the British Army, as well as their French and Belgian allies. Over 340,000 men would be taken from the beaches to fight another day. (© Getty Images)

The crew of a Royal Navy minesweeper – much like HMS *Salamander* – go about their dangerous duties of making a sweep to find German mines. The ship would later be mortally damaged by friendly-fire in 1944. (© Getty Images)

Operation 'Husky' in 1941 was the Allies first supply convoy to Russia. The conditions sailors and ships had to endure in the Arctic weather are evident here. (© Getty Images)

Operation 'Torch', the invasion of Sicily: Bill's ship, HMS *Newfoundland*, gave valuable support to the landings in 1943. (© Getty Images)

By the KING'S Order the name of
Chief Stoker William Frederick Stone,
H.M.S. Newfoundland,
was published in the London Gazette on
21 December, 1943,
as mentioned in a Despatch for distinguished service.
I am charged to record
His Majesty's high appreciation.

First Lord of the Admiralty

'Mentioned in Dispatches': Bill Stone's successful efforts in serving his ship in the invasion of Sicily were recognised officially by the Admiralty.

Valleta Harbour, Malta, 1941. Amid the chaos of the daily aerial attacks by Axis forces, the Royal Navy still maintained the lifeline of support to the stricken island. Bill would see the devastation close up when he moored there in 1943. (© Getty Images)

Under siege: The massive destruction wrought upon the valiant Maltese led to the British government bestowing upon the whole island the order of the George Cross – Britain's highest civilian honour for bravery. (© Getty Images)

Bill, Lily and their daughter Anne had a successful method of staying in contact once his ship had docked in a home port. The initial of his wife's name would alter depending on which port he was heading for – in this case 'G' for Greenock.

Much like this generic picture, HMS *Newfoundland* too would head off into the middle of the Atlantic War as she made her way to the USA for repairs in dry dock, 1943.
(© Getty Images)

Hello USA! The crew of the *Newfoundland* find themselves with an extended stay of ten months, waiting for their ship to be given the all-clear. Here, Bill (far left) and some friends take in the view from the Empire State Building in New York.

The prison guard: Bill found himself land-locked in post-war Europe in 1945, guarding German POWs on the island of Sylt in northern Germany. It would be his last posting until he was demobbed.

Bill's new career as a barber would be very successful, and a well-deserved peaceful occupation for a man who had seen so much death and destruction in the Second World War.

very experienced at either using lifebelts or launching the 'Carley' floats, which could have saved our lives if we were hit.

Carley floats originally came from America. After 1915 the British government officially adopted the Carley float as its favoured lifeboat design and it was fitted to most warships. Production was at Nott's Industries (Frome) in Somerset. In a Nott's catalogue the Carley floats are described like this:

> The float comprises a rolled copper tube into which are soldered at intervals of 12 in. and 19 in. divisional plates which strengthen the tube and form watertight bulkheads. Each section is sealed down only after it has been checked as airtight and three stiffeners are fixed outside of the tube which adds immensely to the longitudinal strength. After coating the tube with preservation paint it is encased in cork 1.5 in. thick, wrapped in cotton cloth and treated with marine glue to render it waterproof. Finally it is wrapped spirally with an 18 oz cotton sailcloth canvas with a minimum lap of two inches, and well painted. Rope fittings of ample size are spliced into position with grab line and wood handgrips on the outside.

Floats came in various sizes and came with paddles, ladders, ropes and boat hooks, depending on their size. They were easily stowed and launched but men compelled to use them were entirely exposed to both the elements and the enemy so they were replaced after the Second World War.

From the decks there still came fire from small anti-aircraft guns, a Lewis gun, Bren gun and assorted rifles that were intended to keep the still-marauding Luftwaffe at bay. Below stokers formed a chain to spray oil on the sump of the after fan, to stop it seizing up. After about 15 minutes we got up steam again. We managed to limp back with one boiler, at a speed of about seven knots. Below decks it was so packed with soldiers and stretchers that it was difficult to move between the engine room and the boiler rooms. We arrived at Dover by mid-afternoon. However, the damage *Salamander* had suffered meant it was to be our last voyage to Dunkirk. Our role in Operation 'Dynamo' had finished.

Unknown to me, on our way back on the final trip, we were attacked by a submarine that fired a 'tin fish', or torpedo, at us. When we got back to Dover the coxswain and the able seaman on the wheel said to me: 'Chief, we held our ears today and waited for the explosion. Jerry fired this torpedo that was coming straight for us amidships.' *Salamander* had been saved by her shallow draft – the torpedo had passed straight underneath us. The only explanation that we could think of for our lucky escape was that the German submarine had mistaken us for a destroyer and had set the torpedo to run at a greater depth than the *Salamander*'s draft.

Five crew of the *Salamander* died on 1 June, including two stokers. One of them, Henry Thompson, aged 20, was awarded the DSO [Distinguished Service Medal]. But they weren't on board when they were killed. They had volunteered to man boats that were picking up men from the shore. Those of us aboard all knew things could have been much worse for us. One soldier who had escaped the beaches with almost nothing grabbed my coat from the deck as he went up the gangplank. I said, 'Good luck to him'.

Those were awful days but one just tried to quickly get over what one had experienced, and carried on as if nothing had happened – there was little else that you could do but get on with the task at hand. The whole country felt under siege, but at the same time we believed in our cause, the fight against Hitler, as well as self-preservation!

At the end of May 1940 the all-conquering Wehrmacht was squeezing the BEF [British Expeditionary Force] out of France.

The better part of the British Army – and its equipment – had been dispatched to Europe following the outbreak of war in 1939. French and English forces had been reasonably confident that the Maginot Line, a series of defences designed to keep the Germans behind their borders, would stem any invasion. They had not figured that Hitler's forces would simply bypass the fortifications with ease.

Those who then believed the trench warfare of the First World War would be repeated were also in for a shock. Hitler was about to do what the Kaiser had singularly failed to achieve two decades earlier: to kick British forces off the continent.

The German onslaught was forcing Allied soldiers up to the coast where a rescue operation was the only hope. Without it most of the fighting men in Europe opposed to Hitler would have been taken prisoner. Britain's capacity to fight invasion would have been at an end. Curiously, Hitler called a halt to the advance of key Panzer units. No one is sure why. Perhaps he was concerned they would be exposed to British counter-attack. There's speculation that he promised the final glory to Hermann Goering's Luftwaffe or possibly he felt a softly-softly approach would lure Britain to the negotiating table. It gave the Allied soldiers two days' grace to make good their escape.

Every man involved in the retreat had a story to tell. In the confusion many men were split from their units. Given the speed at which the Germans travelled, British and French soldiers had no idea if they were inadvertently behind enemy lines. Hedges and trees that would later hamper the Allied invasion forces in 1944 post-D-Day, provided ideal cover for troops on the move in 1940. Most kept under cover by day, hiding in cow byres, hay lofts, stables, railway goods yards, houses and shops. They formed foraging parties – looters by another name – to find supplies but many went hungry and without sleep for several days.

The roads to Dunkirk became strewn with deserted and sabotaged vehicles. Perhaps more depressing still was the sight of the hungry, dejected horses from the French horse-drawn artillery units. And there were lines of refugees heading for the coast too, slowing the progress of the soldiers and providing target practice for the Luftwaffe. Soldiers quickly learned to march near ditches in order to duck out of any aerial attack. Those killed were covered by gas capes more readily associated with First World War soldiers and left where they fell.

Even in the absence of orders from officers, the men knew which way they were heading. Dunkirk was marked by smoke palls from burning oil storage tanks.

When they arrived at the coast men rested in the wrecks of burnt-out buildings or against the promenade wall, or dug themselves shallow 'graves' in the sand. Off shore ships emerged over the horizon, targets for submarines, mines and enemy bombers and fighters, who now focussed their firepower out to sea rather than on the sands. At first small boats were mobbed by soldiers desperate to get from shore to ship and either sunk or later abandoned without oars. Soon Naval personnel began organising the *best use of small boats. And when the tide was right men waded out to their shoulders in an effort to reach rescue ships. Conversely a high tide left them crushed on the remaining strip of sand.*

Although it was spring a cold breeze whistled over the beaches, carrying with it the smell of burning oil and discharged weapons. The talk was about the prospects of rescue and the possible presence of fifth columnists.

Hungry and tired, the majority of men were nonetheless quietly resigned to watching, waiting and hoping. Their nerves were stretched by the sound of screaming bombs and the sight of ships coming under a barrage of fire.

Norman Strother-Smith, of the Royal Horse Artillery, recalled Dunkirk under fire:

Dunkirk was a terrible sight. The road was covered with debris and all along one side were lorries, cars and motorbikes, all jettisoned. Some were in the canal. Some had been blown up. In the road two cars were burnt out, still smouldering, and in places were bodies of men covered with blankets. There was equipment, petrol and all sorts of stores destroyed. Houses were blazing furiously from recent bombings and the others were all shattered. All the time the sky was full of black smoke from oil tanks that had been blazing for some five or six days.

The air raids were something I shall never forget. The noise was something incredible. The bombers came over in waves of three generally at least a dozen strong and the Dornier at any rate had a peculiar engine noise of its own. It had a low-pitched throb which could be heard for miles so that a dozen of these made a roar something terrific. As they approached, the anti-aircraft guns would open fire. The air would be full of the cracking of heavy guns, light guns and quick-firing 'Bofors' and each one made the same noise on bursting. The sky was full of puffs of smoke. And then the bombers would start their machine guns firing on the battery positions. It was a deafening noise – the guns and automatics and all the time the throbbing of engines. All of a sudden could be heard a screaming noise. At first one wouldn't know what it was but after the first raid we all knew the sound well. It was bombs.

They took some 10 to 18 seconds to fall and all the time we could hear this screaming getting louder and louder. It always sounded as if we were sure to be hit but each one seemed to pass right overhead and the sound died away and almost as soon the ground shook as the bombs hit it and the air was full of the roar of explosions, or if they didn't burst the thudding of each bomb could be heard. Very frequently there was no burst.

Each wave of three planes loosed off the same attack and the noise would start again. All the time we would have our faces buried in the ground and our muscles taut, ready for any nearby explosion. The raid would last about five or ten minutes but it seemed like one hour from the moment that the planes could first be heard. After it we would get up to see what damages had been done; all expecting to see hundreds of dead and all the place shattered and blazing but the bombs did little damage. I never saw one man hit and at the worst I saw a few cattle killed and perhaps one house shattered and smoking.

Miner Wilfred Cowie was among the last to leave Dunkirk.

It was horrible on the beach. We were lying in bomb craters on the beach, expecting every day to get away. Every day seemed to take forever. Luftwaffe planes were firing at us and then there was the shelling. That was the worst thing of all. The shells screamed as they were going over the top of you and you never knew where they were going to land.

Once I took shelter in a bomb hole with three other lads. I was the only one who came out alive. The others were killed by a machine-gun blast from an aeroplane. There were hundreds of lads killed. We had to go and get the identity discs from the bodies and give them to our superiors. It was a bit upsetting but it was just a job that had to be done. We saw so many young men dead that in the end we didn't worry about it. I came back in a trawler. It took 36 hours to reach the east coast after the skipper diverted to avoid mines. Several men on the boat died when they were hit by machine-gun fire from Luftwaffe planes passing overhead.

Behind them men from assorted units were fighting a fierce rearguard action to stall the German advance. The unluckiest of these were the men of the Royal Warwicks, the Cheshires and the Royal Artillery captured at Wormhoudt. Taken prisoner by a crack SS squad, they were herded into a barn where guards first tossed grenades into their ranks and then took the survivors out to be shot. At the end of the grisly episode about 90 men were dead and a further 20 had escaped, although some were so badly wounded they could not survive.

The evacuation wasn't perfect. It was at times confused, there were collisions between ships and wasted opportunities. However, some 338,000 men escaped from Dunkirk on a curious armada of small ships and Naval vessels, the nucleus of Britain's army for the remainder of the war. Initially the expectation was that just 35,000 would be saved.

Dunkirk is perhaps best remembered for the armada of small ships that chugged out of British waters to scoop up survivors from the French beach. Most were, in fact, crewed by Royal Navy men or Royal Naval reservists having been requisitioned for the task in many cases without the owners' knowledge or consent. One of the little ships, however, was captained by its owner Charles Lightoller (1874–1952), the most senior officer to survive the Titanic *disaster.*

Lancashire-born Lightoller had survived a shipwreck, a ship fire and a cyclone before he celebrated his 21st birthday. Perhaps assuming the dangers at sea were too prevalent, he joined the 'Klondike Gold Rush' in 1898 and then became a cowboy in Canada before returning to Britain in 1900 – the year William was born – and a job with the White Star Line.

Much later he boarded the Titanic *at Belfast and was in his cabin having recently finished his watch when he felt the collision between ship and iceberg occur. Soon he was organising the lowering of the lifeboats on the port side and the evacuation of women and children. He did so until the* Titanic *had sunk so low that he saw a large wave roll over the boat deck, at which point he dived into the water. At that point he was sucked under as the ship lurched towards the seabed, being blown back to the surface when hot air from the turbines blew upwards. And as he bobbed in freezing seas one of the ship's funnels toppled, nearly sinking him again.*

Lightoller finally reached a canvas lifeboat and used his seamanship to save its other occupants from being swamped by waves. He was the last survivor to be taken aboard the SS Carpathia.

It was his recommendations adopted by subsequent inquiries that led to the number of lifeboats aboard ships to be determined by the number of passengers aboard rather than the tonnage and the introduction of lifeboat drills. In the ensuing war he joined the Royal Navy and was twice decorated for bravery. Later he refurbished his boat, the Sundowner, *and covertly surveyed the German coastline on behalf of the British government while posing as an elderly holidaymaker.*

When he was asked to relinquish the Sundowner *for service at Dunkirk he insisted on making the trip. On 1 June 1940, at the height of the action, 66-year-old Lightoller, with his eldest son Roger and an 18-year-old sea-scout, sailed for Dunkirk and the trapped BEF. Although the* Sundowner *had never carried more than 21 persons before, they succeeded in rescuing 130 men from the beaches of Dunkirk. In addition to the three crew members, there were two crew members who had been rescued from another small boat, the motor cruiser* Westerly. *There were another three naval ratings also rescued from waters off Dunkirk, plus one hundred and twenty-two troops taken from the stricken destroyer* Worcester. *Despite bombing and strafing by the Luftwaffe they all arrived safely back in Ramsgate just about 12 hours after they had departed.*

In all the years since Dunkirk I had never come across anyone we had rescued in the *Salamander* until the summer of 1999. It was then, at a reunion of the Henley Branch of the Dunkirk Veterans Association, a chap came up to me and inquired, 'What ship were you in at Dunkirk, Chief?'

'*Salamander*,' I replied.

'You saved my life,' he said.

Fred Roby told me that he had broken into a boat shed at La Panne with some other soldiers and pinched a rowing boat. They had started to row home when we picked them up. It is pretty unlikely that they would have made it all the way back across the Channel in the rowing boat. 'I couldn't swim then and I can't swim now,' he said. 'I would have been food for the fishes.'

Fred was later injured in the push at Arnhem, suffering a fracture to both femurs and a double fracture of the pelvis. But at least he survived to fight another day. Without the soldiers retrieved from Dunkirk England would have been defenceless. As it was, she barely had a land-based weapon to her name. It felt good to finally meet someone whose life *Salamander* had rescued. He was one of many 'Brown Jobs', as we in the Navy called soldiers, whose war was far from over.

Guardsman Frank Fletcher shared his memories of the Dunkirk evacuation and rescue by the Salamander *with the BBC History archive:*

It was a dark night when we pulled out. Orders were, 'no talking and keep spaced out'. Beyond us the mole at Dunkirk was on fire and the road was being shelled by very accurate German artillery. We were to use La Panne beach to the east of Dunkirk. One of the younger officers had acquired a vintage bicycle and was riding up and down the lines to make sure no one was left behind, wounded or otherwise.

He must have been doing 20 miles an hour in the dark when he ran into a mass of telephone wire. The bicycle still headed towards the beach but it took several guardsmen about ten minutes to disentangle him. It was the only humorous moment of the night.

About 2 a.m. the moon came out and it was possible to see where we were going at the final crossroads. The RSM – Cyril Sheather – stood checking and counting how many men had made it to the beach. He was never seen again, presumably killed carrying out the final order.

The sand dunes gave a certain amount of cover from the shelling and all we could do was wait for daylight to see if the Royal Navy was going to rescue us. The light improved, the tide came in and destroyers appeared off shore. Spirits rose among the troops in the sand dunes. Before the destroyers could collect their quota, the Germans gave them the full treatment; one received a direct hit and sank in a few minutes. The second was hit on the starboard side, blowing a large hole in its plates, but it didn't sink. The troops standing on the port side were up to their knees in water. With one of her propellers out of the water, she turned around and crept away doing about three knots.

Next two minesweepers appeared; the troops left on the beach were mainly guardsmen, Grenadiers and Coldstreams, the remains of a Scottish regiment and a few stragglers who hoped someone would get them home.

A Corporal and myself swam out and salvaged a Carley life float; it held four of us and we tried to get out to the nearest ship. With the tide coming in we didn't make a bit of progress but a lifeboat full of Scottish Troops commanded by a CSM who obviously fancied himself as a sailor threw us a line. We made it to the nearest minesweeper, the *Salamander*, the other being the *Speedwell* [probably *Skipjack*]. We later described the *Salamander* as one funnel, one gun and one hope to get back. The German planes returned to give us the full treatment; a stick of bombs dropped between the boats, nearly capsizing the *Speedwell* and causing steam to come out of the *Salamander* through holes that were never on the Admiralty drawings. However they were built of strong stuff and lived to fight another day. The hoist to the 4.5 in. gun went up in smoke and the shells had to be manhandled to the gun deck, the empties were dumped over the side burning and blistering the hands.

The morning wore on and we cruised up and down the beach taking on board any of the troops that made it to the nets slung over the sides. The 4.5 in. kept banging away helped by several Bren guns taken on board by the troops. I did ask the Petty Officer in charge of the gun whether we would get back. He said, and I quote, 'Son, I volunteered for this ship, the British Navy has never lost a *Salamander* yet through enemy action.' As it survived several Russian convoys later in the war his confidence was not misplaced.

The Germans were still trying to sink us. One ME 110 received a direct hit above us and dived into the sea. The final few shells were being manhandled to the gun deck, a few more planes flew over but for once they were ours. The troops on deck gave them a cheer and toasted them in Navy cocoa. It was thick enough to cut but as the first hot drink for several days there were no complaints.

Having loaded our quota we turned and headed to the open sea and the white cliffs of England.

Following Dunkirk *Salamander* was put in to the Royal Albert Docks in London to undergo repair to the damage that had been sustained during the evacuation.

Lily and baby Anne again came up from Devon to stay with friends at Bryanston Square, near Marble Arch, and I was able to spend nights there. I don't know if I suffered from nightmares immediately after the event but years later, after I broke my hip aged 106, my daughter told me how in hospital I was shouting about Dunkirk in my disturbed sleep. That was more than 65 years after the event. So the trauma of those days obviously never left me.

Like many other ships *Salamander* was sent on patrols up and down the English Channel, keeping an eye on the enemy coastline as Britain awaited Hitler's invasion. By now the Germans controlled everything from the North Cape to the Pyrenees. It felt like we were the front line and there wasn't much a ship the size of *Salamander* could do about German hostilities. We knew that we could blow up at any minute if we hit a mine. Most days we engaged with enemy aircraft. If we didn't, other ships close by in the flotilla did. However, with every passing week, fears of all-out invasion receded.

The role of the minesweepers in these uncertain times is rarely heralded. However, the men aboard were serving for some weeks with near certainty that they would one day soon be facing the might of the German navy. As it happened, Hitler stalled when the Luftwaffe failed to win the battle of the skies. British Naval commanders were not only concerned about an impending invasion but also the prospect of flagging spirits in the senior service in the wake of the perceived defeat at Dunkirk. The response from the Royal Navy was pivotal as the Army had been reduced in men and weapons and the Air Force was still involved in a bruising battle with the Luftwaffe. Naval commanders were agreeably surprised as men appeared as devoted to the war effort as ever.

On 12 August the flag officer in charge at Harwich where Salamander *was based wrote: 'The operations covered by these reports entailed a degree of hard work, determination and technical skill which reflects the highest credit on all concerned and showed a very fine spirit to exist in the Minesweeping force at Harwich.' Two days later Reginald Drax, Commander-in-Chief of* The Nore, *wrote: 'The zeal and devotion to duty of the minesweeping flotillas deserve the fullest recognition that can be given, particularly in view of the fact that their work is done out of sight and in the constant expectation of air attack.'*

Indeed the mood of the nation was summed up by Prime Minister Winston Churchill, in power for just 16 days when the drama of Dunkirk unfolded, who said, 'We shall fight on the beaches . . . we shall fight in the fields and in the streets . . . we shall never surrender.' Earlier, Churchill had paid tribute to the Royal Navy for its role at Dunkirk.

Meanwhile, the Royal Navy, with the willing help of countless merchant seamen, strained every nerve to embark the British and allied troops; 220 light warships and 650 other vessels were engaged. They had to operate upon the difficult coast, often in adverse weather, under an almost ceaseless hail of bombs and an increasing concentration of artillery fire. Nor were the seas, as I have said, themselves free from mines and torpedoes. It was in conditions such as these that our men carried on, with little or no rest, for days and nights on end, making trip after trip across the dangerous waters, bringing with them always men whom they had rescued. The numbers they have brought back are the measure of their devotion and their courage.

In September *Salamander* was at the forefront of a planned operation that was meant to ruffle German feathers early in their occupation of France. Codenamed 'Lucid' [originally 'Lucifer'] she was going to escort one of two old merchant ships filled with fuel oil and high explosives that would be set alight and let loose at Calais among ships thought to be gathering for the invasion of Britain. The idea of 'fire ships' wasn't new. It had been used in Elizabethan times against the Spanish Armada. But on this occasion the weather was so bad we were recalled and the plan was eventually dropped.

It was severe weather rather than enemy action that damaged *Salamander* at the beginning of December. A heavy gale left her listing but seaworthy. After repairs at Grimsby we sailed to Invergordon in north-east Scotland, where we were based whilst on duty escorting Atlantic convoys.

On *Salamander* when the lighters came alongside we had to check the fuelling. Some of the lads didn't pay too much attention sometimes and I would have to yell at them. Once, when I saw two stokers talking together and not minding what they did, I was really mad. 'Stand by your bloody hoses,' I bellowed. And the captain, who was behind me, said, 'I'd like to endorse that statement, Chief.' His cabin had once been covered in oil thanks to someone being careless with the hose.

Later the ship was transferred to Aberdeen for modifications to the minesweeping gear. At the same time 4 in. of cement was placed fore and aft along the bottom, and angle irons were welded across the frames. After that there was flooding in the lower compartments when we sailed in high seas at a rate of about 4 ft every 24 hours so we went back to Aberdeen for more repairs.

Lily and Anne were again able to join me and we all stayed locally for a short while. After we married I wrote to Lily regularly but I knew the letters were read by the censor. Still, I wanted to see her when I docked. So I would address her with different initials that would signify the port where I was docking. When I addressed the letter Mrs G Stone, for example, she knew I was coming in to Greenock so she would move there for a while to be near me. One of my officers used to ask me, 'Chief, how is it that your wife always knows where we're going?' I always said it must have been a bird that told her. They never found out how she knew.

Soon afterwards came the devastating news of the sinking of HMS *Hood* during the Battle of the Denmark Strait. I remember well the day I heard that she had been lost, along with practically all of her crew – it was a hammer blow to the country. I was on leave with my family at Wrangaton at the time. I just couldn't believe it. Like every other sailor who served in her, I'd formed a deep attachment to the

Hood. It felt like hearing a close friend had died suddenly; I was in shock. The pride of the British Navy was now lying at the bottom of the ocean; from the initial salvo to sinking with her crew took less than 11 minutes! I felt sick and was unable to eat my dinner thinking about all those men that had perished. The feeling of loss stayed with me for many days afterwards as everyone was talking about it.

Indeed, such strong emotions never go and actually resurfaced when the *Hood*'s final resting place was discovered in 2001 – at a depth of 10,000 ft. Rightly the British government quickly designated the site as a war grave in 2002 and *Hood* now falls under the Protection of Military Remains Act. My old friend Ted Briggs sailed out and, in a very emotional service, laid a wreath at the actual site of his lost ship.

Those were dark days and the only ones in the war that I really felt down. A month or so later Hitler launched his surprise attack against Russia [Operation 'Barbarossa'], which brought that country into the war. I felt that Russia coming in on our side was one of the best pieces of news I had heard in a long time. Soviet Russia had millions of men under arms and vast resources. But it wasn't that Russians would be killing a lot of Germans that gave me peace of mind. I knew they had the winter weather on their side and that would make the world of difference. Within six months America had joined the war too. I had no real doubt about the outcome after that. Together, we would beat Hitler!

10

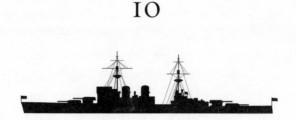

OPERATION 'DERVISH' –
THE RUSSIAN CONVOYS, 1941

One of the results of Russia becoming our ally was the start of the Russian convoys. HMS *Salamander* was one of the ships which formed the escort on the very first, codenamed Operation 'Dervish'.

The convoy was relatively small, only six merchant ships – SS *Lancastrian Prince, New Westminster City, Esneh, Trehata, Llanstephan Castle*, the fleet oiler *Aldersdale* and the Dutch freighter *Alchiba*. The Commodore was Captain J.C.K. Dowding from the Royal Naval Reserve who had won a DSO at Dunkirk. The escorts comprised the ocean minesweepers HMS *Halcyon, Salamander* and *Harrier*, the destroyers HMS *Electra, Active* and *Impulsive* and the anti-submarine trawlers HMS *Hamlet, Macbeth* and *Ophelia*.

Aboard the merchant ships were raw materials including wool, rubber and tin. There were 15 Hurricane fighter-aircraft crated in the holds of the 'Dervish' vessels.

The merchant ships left Liverpool on 12 August 1941 and formed up at Iceland on 20 August where they were joined by the escort ships, including the minesweepers. We provided escort for the passage to Archangel, where we arrived on 31 August. Unlike many of the later 'PQ' convoys, 'Dervish' proved to be an uneventful trip for us.

As a Chief Stoker I was in charge of all the other junior stokers on the ship.

Still, I once again found myself living in fear just as I was every minute at Dunkirk. Even though it was the summer it was much colder than most of us had ever experienced. We felt vulnerable to attacks by U-boats or the Luftwaffe.

When I was below decks I slept on the lockers and I always kept a torch strapped to my arm. I put two condoms on it, one at each end, so that if the ship was hit you would still be able to see, even if the ship's power was lost. Be prepared! I suppose I learned that in the scouts back in Kingsbridge.

Something that I do remember well from that trip is that *Salamander* was refuelled at sea. As I recall we took on about 50 tons of fuel oil. Being in charge of everything to do with oil and water in the ship, I was responsible for the *Salamander* end of the refuelling operation. All went smoothly from above decks although refuelling became a notoriously difficult issue for Arctic convoys when the sea was rough.

The ship stayed for some months, minesweeping in Russian waters. There was always trouble on the Russian convoys but we were lucky while we were there. Strong winds and tides proved more of a problem to us than the Germans at the time. We didn't see any submarines and no ships were lost but we always felt tense. It wasn't much different when we went ashore.

Bloody Bolsheviks! Nobody ever spoke to you there except the children, who used to say, 'Chocolate?' They were all very suspicious and unwelcoming. It was only much later that we realised they were told to behave like that by Stalin and that the secret police were everywhere. However, after *Salamander* was repaired in a floating Russian workshop in October we had to admire the workmanship, which was excellent. They resolved the problems of buckled frames, which had been caused by heavy weather back in April.

During our return from Russia the Engineer Officer told me that when we arrived back I was due to leave the *Salamander*. I asked to see the Commander, as I didn't want to leave. The Commander would not change his mind though, and said that I had been on the ship for four years and was due for a move. As it transpired he did me a favour. The ship was given ice-chipping machinery, lagging and high-pressure hoses and stayed on Arctic convoy duty for another year, witnessing some of the worst of the casualties.

I had no idea how lucky I'd been on the convoy. Later, I heard from fellow stokers how rough things got on the Arctic convoys. For a start, there was the cold. It was a court-martialling offence if you touched bare metal with your hands. The severe cold would glue your hand in place and rip skin to shreds if you tried to move it. Even your hair froze, which was horrible for older men who had hair in their noses. There was always the danger of being washed overboard from listing ships in heavy seas.

Below deck it was cramped and airless. On the Arctic convoys the food was traditionally poor but that wasn't as much of a problem as you might imagine as the rough seas meant many men suffered from seasickness.

In the Arctic Ocean ships felt like they were sitting ducks. Even if you weren't under attack, you were waiting for firing to start at any moment. The high tension alone was tiring. Danger came in the form of Luftwaffe planes, U-boats and magnetic mines.

Destroyers could often accelerate out of trouble. But they were accompanying large and heavy merchant ships who proceeded at a slow pace. The seas were often mountainous, with waves of up to 40 ft in height, and that slowed the Royal Navy down as well.

When ships were caught in a hail of shellfire and bullets it was noisy and terrifying. Sometimes the planes came in so low sailors on deck could clearly see the face of the pilot. You were really running a gauntlet of attacks on fair weather days as the Nazis had air bases in strategic positions along the length of the coast to attack at any given time – dependent on the size of the convoy [see Map 3].

Of course, Allied shipping gave as good as they got. Gunners went at it while the ships dropped countless depth charges to counter the threat of submarines. In the summertime it wasn't so uncomfortably cold but the hours of daylight were lengthened considerably and so was the window for aerial attack. It meant gunners could be at their posts for hours. They got very short on sleep and were kept going by copious mugs of extremely thick cocoa.

The responsibility of accompanying merchant ships weighed heavily with those of us in the Royal Navy. Seeing a ship hit and sunk was a horrifying experience. One moment a large ship was sailing in the water. The next there was a blinding flash and a loud bang! When the smoke cleared there was no trace of the ship at all, except perhaps for a bit of wreckage floating on the water. Many of the ships of the Arctic convoys were carrying ammunition or fuel, which is why the explosions were so intense and deadly.

If there were survivors they stood little chance in the icy waters. The cold stiffened the ropes that lashed lifeboats to accompanying ships, making them difficult to launch. And convoy ships could hardly put the brakes on during an attack. Some men from both the Royal Navy and merchant navy were picked up but they were the lucky ones.

During World War II, Arctic convoys were formed in Scottish harbours, such as Loch Awe and Scapa Flow, and in Iceland's capital Reykjavik and the naval base at Hvalfjörður. Once safely through their hazardous passage, they were subsequently unloaded in Archangel, Severodvinsk and Murmansk in Russian-held territory.

Until 1942, each convoy had between five and twelve ships, but later on, their number increased to between thirty and thirty-five. Winston Churchill pledged to Stalin that Russia would receive a continuous cycle of convoys. The aim was to keep the Eastern Front amply supplied, thus splitting Hitler's resources. However, for his part, Stalin saw the Arctic convoy losses as sabotage rather than tragedy. In all, 42 convoys or 811 ships were dispatched to Russia; and of that number, 58 merchant and 16 warships were sunk and 1,944 sailors killed.

Later in the war, *Salamander* was nearly destroyed in a 'friendly-fire' incident, which was kept from the public for decades afterwards. She was minesweeping off Le Havre on 27 August 1944, when she was mistaken for an enemy vessel by some RAF Typhoons. During that action our own aircraft sank two minesweepers, the *Britomart* and the *Hussar*, and badly damaged *Salamander* – blowing off most of her stern.

For now I was going to be land-based. It was off to barracks for me to await a new draft. You had to go where you were posted, even if it was a submarine. In peacetime submariners were volunteers but not during that time in the war. In the early part of the war we didn't have many submariners but later on there were more. I hated the idea of being on a submarine and so did my brothers.

I had not been there a fortnight when I received a chit to say that I was going to be drafted. That day another Chief whom I knew greeted me:

'Morning Chief,' he said.

'Morning be buggered!' I replied.

'What's the matter with you, you old so and so?' he said.

'I've got a draft chit,' I said.

'I know you have,' he said. 'I'm going with you. We're going to Wallsend to stand by a new ship.'

'Oh, that's a lovely job,' I said.

II

STORMING SICILY, AND SAILING TO MALTA, 1942–43

In December 1941 I arrived at Wallsend, Newcastle-upon-Tyne, as part of the advance party on a new ship, the cruiser HMS *Newfoundland*, which was still under construction. As I was to be here for some time, I was able to rent a house so that Lily and Anne could join me. It was good to be harbour-based after a year at sea.

At first I was a bit concerned about *Newfoundland* as, being a new ship, she would be fitted out with a lot of modern electrical equipment whereas I was used to older ships with reciprocating equipment. But the ship gradually grew up around me so that, by the time she was commissioned at the end of 1942, I knew every inch of her. I used to spend some of my spare time copying plans of the ship and have drawn her from stem to stern.

She was built with a double bottom for defence and buoyancy and the first time I went down into it I felt peculiar and passed out. I could have died down there – and some seamen do – if I had not come around. Someone told the Commander and he said to me afterwards, 'I've heard something about you, Chief. In future you take someone along with you.'

A pal of mine suggested the war would probably be over by the time *Newfoundland* was ready to sail. Sadly, that didn't come to pass although it seemed like a long time before she was ready for service. The captain, William Slayter, wouldn't go to sea in her until a dynamo was installed one deck below aft to the boiler room. The ship was all electric and, if the boilers failed, the lights went out. With the dynamo we had secondary lighting. He also made sure we had a battery-powered lamp to every ladder. In the Navy we had lost a lot of men after their ships were torpedoed simply because they couldn't see where they were heading after the main lights went off.

We left Wallsend on 8 January 1943 at 11 a.m. for North Shields. Enemy mines hindered our progress after that, when they were dropped into the sea during an air raid.

In early 1943 we did working-up exercises at Scapa Flow to get *Newfoundland* ready for the battles ahead, before sailing to Devonport in March. When I arrived I was so horrified to see the utter devastation of Plymouth, as a result of the German bombing, that I openly wept. The city I had grown to love was decimated due to the heavy air raids the Germans had thrown at it. But what was remarkable was the spirit of the people; they were battered, but certainly not defeated. For a short while we were on Atlantic convoy duty with the battleships *Rodney* and *Nelson* and aircraft carrier *Formidable* and two destroyers, getting a rough ride in the Bay of Biscay. But by April we were in the Mediterranean, getting ready to support the invasion of Sicily.

Places that William cherished from his youth received severe punishment. In Plymouth there was a seven-night blitz, although the nights were not consecutive. More than two hundred and ninety people died on 20 and 21 March 1941 during two sustained raids. The death toll from five nights of bombing at the end of April included ninety-six sailors at the Naval barracks alone. Only seventy-six bodies were recovered while the rest were burned beyond recognition. Fires consumed the heart of the city on both occasions. Using French airfields, German bombers preceded by pathfinders targeted Plymouth for its Naval links. They flew at such high altitudes there was little the city could do for its own defence.

When he arrived in Malta, William saw how the island that was at the heart of Royal Naval operations in the Mediterranean had also been decimated by aerial bombing. By the time HMS Newfoundland *docked the worst of the 'Siege of Malta' was over. It had begun on 12 June 1940, the day after Italy joined the war. Mussolini's aerial bombardments were soon carried out in tandem with German planes using Sicily as a base. As Britain used Malta's airfields and docks as a springboard to attack Axis forces in North Africa, Hitler and Mussolini believed it essential to obliterate the island. It was equally imperative to the Allies to keep it open. Malta's survival hopes were pinned on the success of heavily armed convoys that inevitably attracted enemy attention.*

In the first six months of 1942 there was only one 24-hour period on Malta without air raids. Indeed, German records show that between 20 March and 28 April that year, the Luftwaffe alone dispatched 11,819 sorties to it, offloading 6,557 bombs. It was in April 1942 that King George VI presented Malta with the George Cross, to underline the island's gallantry. There were hundreds of deaths and survivors were often not only homeless but starving.

Life became more tolerable on Malta when the North African campaigns came to an end in 1943. In the same year the King visited Malta and was conducted on part of his tour by an island priest, Canon Emanuel Brincat. His parishioners once had 10,000 homes but now they had only 1,707. Instead they took shelter in caves and crevasses. Like politicians at home, the King was relieved to keep the outpost of Malta, especially following the loss of the strategically vital port of Singapore in 1941.

Before the invasion I remember that we went to Bone in North Africa for a couple of spells. We were an ack-ack ship pounding the 'Mareth Line', which was being defended by the Germans in Tunisia. The Mareth Line fortifications were built by the French but fell into German and Italian hands after the Allied invasion of North Africa. The ship's guns were firing 6 in. shells from 6 p.m. until the following morning in response to the nightly aircraft attacks. The noises of the shell fire resounded down below. Somehow, though, you got used to the incessant racket.

On 8 May a Yankee merchant ship caught fire just ahead of us in the harbour. Its crew abandoned ship, leaving our men to fight the fire. It was eight hours before the flames subsided and the threat to our own safety was extinguished.

One night whilst we were there *Newfoundland* was under attack from enemy aircraft and the Chief Engine Room Artificer 'Geordie' Pearson and I were at our action stations. He was extremely jittery, and not surprisingly so, since he had been in HMS *Edinburgh* when she had been sunk in May 1942 by a torpedo strike on an Arctic convoy. She went to the bottom of the Barents Sea along with £45 million of gold bullion she was carrying, Russian payment for American armaments. Geordie was picked up by a Russian destroyer and that was sunk too! By now there were lots of men like Geordie in the Royal Navy, who literally shook with fright when the guns started pumping and the bombs were dropping. No one thought anything about it. Nobody called them names or considered them cowardly. They had seen action that was profoundly terrifying. To watch the sea coming up to meet you on a sinking ship was a shocking experience and you never forgot it. We all knew there were men at home who deliberately missed their ships' 'departure hour' or contrived to get permanent jobs in the barracks. These were the men with a question mark over their courage.

Bone, in Algeria, was a supply port so it was laden with fuel and ammunition. The ship was always at risk during air raids. Much of the town had been destroyed by enemy fire. Finally in May 1943 the Germans surrendered and French and Italian North Africa was in Allied hands. According to Churchill, it was 'one continent redeemed'. All the troops that had been fighting in North Africa could be re-directed to other trouble spots. Now Allied attention turned to Italy or, specifically, Sicily, the large island on Italy's toe.

Allied battle planners didn't want the Germans to know what was planned so they launched Operation 'Mincemeat'. A dead body in a major's uniform was 'planted' in the sea off the Spanish coast bearing false documents that made it seem the Allies' next move would be towards Sardinia and Greece rather than Sicily. The ruse worked because Axis forces were still split by the time we arrived.

However, before the main invasion of Sicily there were a few small islands that we had to capture. Our targets in Operation 'Corkscrew' were Pantelleria, Lampedusa, Lampione and Linosa.

While they were in enemy hands our shipping in the Mediterranean was at risk. Pantelleria had an airfield and plenty of sheltered coves for E-boats. We considered it as 'Mussolini's Gibraltar', a vital staging post for the Italian empire. It was also studded with gun emplacements. Plans to invade Italy were put on ice until these islands, about 50 miles east of Tunisia and 60 miles south-west of Sicily, were taken.

HMS *Newfoundland* – affectionately known by her crew as 'Newfie' – was the flagship of the British cruiser squadron in the Mediterranean. Admiral Cecil Harcourt had chosen it as his flagship due to it being new and powerful. Our first sortie to Pantelleria was on 4 June 1943 when we released some 130 salvoes from as little as 12,000 yards from the targets. Together with several other cruisers and destroyers, *Newfoundland* returned to carry out a heavy bombardment of the island on 8 June as an overture to the landings. When the ship fired its guns we didn't take much notice. The ship listed a bit and some of the stokers kept a tally in chalk on the boilers. It was about the only indication we stokers had of what was going on above. Soon we discovered that with 266 salvoes we had knocked out many gun emplacements, working in conjunction with other ships and RAF and USAAF bombers. We were able to drop back to Malta to rearm. While we were away there was a leaflet drop on Pantelleria, urging its occupants to surrender. They did not – but I bet they wished they had!

The main action came three days later when an orchestrated bombardment hit the island after two more ultimatums had been refused by island commanders. It was a combined operation between navy, army and air force units. What those Italian defenders must have gone through, I don't know. The racket was bad enough in the bowels of *Newfoundland*. Even so, one plucky (or stupid?) gun battery was still responding so firing continued.

We had pasties for our midday meals during the action, what we West Country ratings called 'Teddyoggies', brought round to us in buckets.

There was some response from enemy aircraft but nothing our guns couldn't handle. In the end a white flag appeared on Pantelleria at 11.25 a.m. on 11 June. The bombardment continued for another 20 minutes until we could ascertain whether or not it was genuine. I learned later that only 139 men had been lost out of a garrison of 11,657, so well dug were the defences. Mussolini later branded the commander of Pantelleria, Rear Admiral Gino Pavesi, a traitor.

After Pantelleria fell we turned our firepower on to Lampedusa. Our night time bombardment was soon followed by star shells and bombs delivered by Wellingtons of the North African command. We started bombardments at 11.30 p.m., then repeated them at 2.30 a.m. and at 6.30 a.m. Lampedusa shore batteries were starting to improve their aim at this time, and the waterspouts created by their shells were getting a bit close for comfort. We pulled out of the firing line.

But soon the white flags were flying on Lampedusa. One thing in particular stands out in my mind from that operation. Following the bombardment we trained our binoculars on the coast and could see on the beach one of the local women wearing a red dress and standing on the sea wall, waving a white flag. The Yanks named her the 'Lampedusa Floozie'.

Linosa fell without a shot being fired on 13 June, the third island to surrender to us in three days. Then it was back to Malta for some well earned relaxation. During all the mayhem at Pantelleria two cats aboard ship – a black one called 'The Admiral's Cat' and a tiger-striped one called Minnie – had both given birth to a total of eight kittens, which cheered the crew up no end!

If the invasion of Sicily was to succeed then Pantelleria had to fall. On the island there were Freya *radio direction finder stations able to detect Allied planes taking off from North African airfields. If Pantelleria remained in enemy hands those stations would rule out tactical surprise during the forthcoming Sicilian invasion. Further the island held an estimated 80 German and Italian fighter planes on its Marghana Airfield, along with a number of bombers. Its various coves and grottoes sheltered motor torpedo boats and submarines that would pose a serious threat to an Allied invasion convoy.*

Considered by many to be an impregnable military fortress, Pantelleria had heavy gun emplacements and well-concealed batteries. Aerial reconnaissance over the 42-square-mile rock island revealed more than 100 big guns embedded in rock or concrete. It had a garrison of some 10,000 troops.

From 7 June aerial attacks combined with a naval bombardment went on around the clock. With the weight of bombs gradually stepped up each day, the North African Air Force delivered its knockout punch on 11 June following the refusal of the island's garrison to respond to demands for surrender.

That day more bombs were dropped on Pantelleria than had been dropped during the entire month of April on all enemy targets in Tunisia, Sicily, Sardinia and Italy put together.

Out of eighty guns forty-three were damaged by the bombing, ten beyond repair. All control communications were destroyed together with ammunition stores, air-raid shelters and all the elements of the Axis's artillery system. The ground was set for the amphibious assault.

About an hour before the landing craft reached the beaches the ships opened fire. When the first of the Commandos landed the white flag was already flying. Churchill was to record later in his memoirs that the only Allied casualty was a man bitten by a mule.

In June 1943, 14,203 bombs amounting to 4,119 tons of explosive were dropped on 16 batteries. And one unfortunate consequence of the bombing of Pantelleria was that it underlined the newly-discovered principle that the dropping of a large number of bombs on highly defended locations in advance of invasions would '. . . make land movements a matter of flitting from one dazed body of enemy troops to another'. Not everyone was convinced. In a later memo Air Chief Marshall Tedder of the Royal Air Force wrote, 'Pantelleria is becoming a perfect curse.'

But for now this early manner of 'shock and awe' played well with audiences at home. After the Pantelleria and Sicily operations an account was published by Alfred Wagg, a correspondent stationed on HMS Newfoundland *throughout the action, in the July edition of a US newspaper called* Collier's. *By wireless from Malta, he told readers:*

Pantelleria's assault was a serious trial show for the masterful hands of our allied brass hats. They had to 'show the boys how you do it'. They had never before really seen all the armed services of sea and land blast and bombard together in one operation involving so many allies.

The boys . . . had cleaned up these four islands without a single casualty and had successfully driven off 25 dive-bombing sorties. The loss of aircraft was negligible. Our ships were undamaged except for a few fans shaken loose from our cruiser's ceilings and some smashed crockery in a destroyer.

It was, conceded Wagg, a straightforward strategy that had paid dividends.

The 'Pantelleria Plan' was not a maze of complicated ideas, as you might expect. It was simple. It was sensible. It worked. There were no 'channels' to clear before one force could come to another's aid. It was accomplished through synchronized waves of assault, timed so that the shore defences were overwhelmed by mass attack.

Wagg gave an account of the hectic events of 11 June, just prior to the Italian surrender.

At 11.57 our first landing craft touched the beach three minutes ahead of schedule. On the shore, several large explosions appeared; the Italians were scuttling and sabotaging stores of munitions. By 12.06 flares from one beach signified that the boys were okay on shore. At 12.15 enemy aircraft coming from Sicily jettisoned their bombs far astern when a flight of Lightnings got on their tails. At 12.35 the infantry ashore sent us a message: 'White flag flying on Mount Gelkhamar not confirmed means surrender of whole island.'

At the end of the operation Wagg discovered that the brutal bombardment of Pantelleria was gleefully seen by many as revenge for the bombing of Malta and the impending opportunity to strike back at Sicily was welcomed.

Back at Malta, everyone was feeling pretty cocky after long years of isolation and this hanging-on business which would draw the sap of life out of anyone. They cheered the ships as we returned to the harbour.

Next morning I walked to a hilltop with a Maltese shopkeeper who pointed toward Sicily across the narrows and said: '. . . those Italians have been bombing us for three years. Now it's our time for revenge.'

Soon after we returned to Malta we held a regatta and I was on the crew of a whaler. Our boat's crew was entirely Chief Petty Officers – the oldest men in the ship – so we didn't expect to win much but, to our surprise, we won four out of the five races. Afterwards General Montgomery, who happened to be in Malta at the time, came aboard the ship and said to us, 'You men are fighting fit. The oldest men in the ship and you win four races out of five.'

There was a week's trip to Suez in June before the next action began to unfold. When the time came for the main invasion of Sicily, Operation 'Husky', HMS *Newfoundland* was again sent to provide shore bombardment in support of the landings. During Husky, we spent three days off the coast of Sicily and then went back to Malta to refuel and provision the ship.

My job at the time was D.B. Chief. That put me in charge of the ship's 'double bottom' where the oil fuel was stored. I had to monitor the rate that the fuel was being used at and ensure that it was drawn evenly from the many fuel tanks.

I remained optimistic. The coxswain used to say, 'We've had it.'

'Be off with you,' I'd reply. I kept looking on the bright side.

My ship and the 15th Cruiser Squadron were part of 'Force K' under the command of Rear Admiral Harcourt, who was still flying his flag from the *Newfoundland*.

On 9 July we sailed from Malta and rendezvoused with some of the landing craft. Then we joined the largest combined operation yet mounted. It was our job to cover the landing of the Canadian and the British troops on the east coast of Sicily.

And during Operation 'Husky', launched on 10 July 1943, HMS *Newfoundland*, together with *Orion*, *Mauritius* and *Uganda* of the 15th Squadron, provided support to troops advancing up the coast road by keeping up a shore bombardment. *Newfoundland* is recorded as having provided bombardment support on four separate occasions during that day.

During the next couple of weeks this support of the landings continued. On 14 July we shelled two aerodromes setting oil dumps alight alongside the towns of Catania and Syracuse. Following a request from the army ashore we knocked out a heavy mortar battery. Later that afternoon, alerted by paratroopers via portable radio who landed behind enemy lines the night before, we targeted a machine-gun nest. Short of fuel and ammunition, we returned to Malta for stores, a swim and a sleep on 15 July. Although by this time much of Malta had been turned into rubble it still seemed a haven for a few short hours. Then we returned to do more of the same in Sicily.

At night we went back to the port of Augusta where we acted as an ack-ack ship. It was quite traumatic because, being a port, Augusta got a lot of attention from enemy aircraft. Radar told us when the planes were due and the gunners were at action stations, ready for them when they arrived. Enemy aircraft came in wave after wave. We had near misses but not everyone was so lucky. If you were on deck in the morning you could quite often see the casualties from the previous night's action floating past in the tide!

Allied planners agreed to Operation 'Husky' after deciding an invasion of France during 1943 was out of the question. It was designed to open shipping lanes in the Mediterranean, eliminate the island as an Axis base and beckon the fall of Mussolini's government. General Dwight D. Eisenhower was given overall command with British General Harold Alexander as the ground commander. The principal forces for the assault were the US 7th Army under Lt General George S. Patton and the British 8th Army under General Bernard Montgomery. At its height Husky involved 2,590 ships and 180,000 men, many of whom were suffering from seasickness due to unseasonably rough water.

During the night of 9 July, Allied airborne units began landing, while the main ground forces came ashore three hours later on the south-east and south-west coasts of the island. The glider landings were scattered and largely ineffective. However, thanks to accurate naval bombardments, the beach landings were singularly successful, not least because high winds made the Italians believe it was an unlikely night for an invasion. In fact, about 200 landing craft were put out of action by rough seas.

Sicily is an island covering an area of about 25,000 square kilometres and has three mountain ranges, from one of which protrudes Mount Etna, the oldest active volcano in mainland Europe. To defend its ports – Palermo, Messina, Catatonia and Syracuse – there were about 30 airfields.

The Allied advance initially suffered from a lack of coordination between US and British forces as Montgomery pushed north-east towards the strategic port of Messina and Patton pushed north and west. As Montgomery's army got bogged down, Alexander ordered the Americans to shift east and protect the British left flank. Seeking a more important role for his men, Patton sent a reconnaissance in force towards the island's capital, Palermo.

When Alexander radioed the Americans to stop their advance, Patton claimed the orders were 'garbled in transmission' and pushed on to take the city. The fall of Palermo helped spur Mussolini's overthrow in Rome. With Patton in position on the north coast, Alexander ordered a two-pronged assault on Messina, hoping to take the city before Axis forces could evacuate the island. Driving hard, Patton entered the city on 17 August, a few hours after the last Axis troops departed, and a few hours before Montgomery. That meant that German troops could re-group and the Allies were compelled to fight their way up Italy. The campaign taught the Allies valuable lessons that contributed to the success of D-Day the following year.

On 22 July another raid began in the early hours. Fifteen bombs dropped close to the ship, throwing up huge columns of water but causing no damage. But it turned out that *Newfoundland* had ridden her luck too far.

Just after midday on 23 July, *Newfoundland* sailed from Augusta heading for Malta. The ship had been at sea for about an hour and got up to a speed of 25 knots when, at 1.38 p.m., she was hit on the port side by a torpedo. The submarine had remained undetected when it attacked so the incident came as a bit of a shock to all of us.

During his long life, William spoke only sparely about the drama that unfolded on the Newfie *after she was torpedoed. It's thanks to shipmate John Richardson that we can include some idea of what happened below decks after the explosion. Mechanician Richardson was off duty when the submarine struck.*

I was asleep on a form alongside the Chief Stokers' and Mechanicians' mess table when the loudest of any explosions I had felt until then threw me to the deck and put out the lights. In the confusion I found myself trying to step into my lifebelt and put my shoes on over my head.

Chief Stoker Stanton, who had been 'dead' from a heavy malarial attack for a week and was lying on the lockers at the other end of the mess at the ship's side, took such a fright that from a position lying flat on his back, he shot clear over the table and form and, bouncing beside me, fled out through the door of the mess.

Through long experience, everyone rushed to their action stations, helped by the emergency lighting, and as they ran below and as the main lighting was regained, the calm voice of the Captain over the intercom told us, 'The ship has been torpedoed. We are proceeding to Malta as planned.'

There was quite a bit of damage to the ship – the rudders were blown off together with six bulkheads at the stern. It was a dramatic scene down below but we stokers weren't prone to panic. Don't forget, we had done extensive training both before and during the war in what we called 'damage control'. On many previous occasions I had been fighting imaginary fires and repairing make-believe destruction, sometimes in the dark. This time, though, it was for real. Sadly, one man, the depth charge sentry working on the quarter deck, was killed. One man was trapped in the steering compartment which had been blown open by the torpedo.

Leading Stoker James Dunn was up to his neck in water by the time he was released by the After Damage Control party, which had to wrestle open a watertight hatch. Dunn kept his cool, however. When he was released he said, 'I thought that all you buggers must have your heads down and were going to leave me to drown!' After being wiped down and changing his uniform he carried on with his work. Later he was recommended for a medal for his devotion to duty.

William was mentioned in dispatches for the bravery he showed when Newfoundland *came under fire. The award was almost certainly meant to reflect his considerable skills as Chief Stoker in getting the ship firstly to the safety of Malta despite the damage suffered and then on to America. He wore the bronze oak leaf on the ribbon of his campaign medal with pride.*

However, research carried out much later by Paul Bevand of the Hood Association revealed that William appeared to have been the victim of an injustice. Official papers linked to his case show that he was recommended for a decoration rather than a mention in dispatches.

On a form dated 26 July 1943 handwritten by the reporting officer it states clearly that William should receive a decoration:

> This rating showed great skill, courage, devotion to duty and leadership throughout the whole time the ship was taking part in Operation 'Husky' and more than bearing out my opinion of him formed in the previous three months in action off North Africa and particularly during the operation leading to the capture of Pantellaria and Lampedusa. His organisation and thoroughness have enabled his department to answer every call made upon it with promptness and efficiency, thereby materially assisting in the success of the operation.

That form was sent to the administrative authority on 9 August and the Fleet Honours Committee on 11 September. The first concurred with the initial recommendation and the second declared 'Recommended for a Decoration'. Finally, the form was sent to Admiral Andrew Browne Cunningham (1883–1963), Commander-in-Chief in the Mediterranean, known affectionately among his men as 'ABC'. On 26 September 1943 he wrote a single word – 'concur' – to endorse the original recommendation. Yet by the time the London Gazette *was published on 21 December 1943 detailing most recent awards Chief Stoker William Frederick Stone, of South Brent, Devon, was recorded as being 'Mentioned in Dispatches' rather than receiving the Distinguished Service Medal that he previously seemed destined to have.*

When William's daughter Anne contacted the government in 2000 about the mix up she was told the deadline by which all applications for wartime medals had to be made had passed.

Today it is impossible to tell if a bureaucratic bungle has resulted in William missing out on a decoration that he was due. Or perhaps someone further along the chain reduced the award on the grounds that too many elevated honours had been given. It's hard to see who would have had greater authority than Cunningham, though, who unambiguously pressed for a medal for William and left his post shortly afterwards to take up the prestigious post of First Sea Lord.

We knew Malta was about an hour away so, provided we weren't attacked by other submarines in the area, we stood a good chance of getting to safety. As *Newfoundland* limped towards Malta, a search for the submarine was immediately started by HMS *Laforey* and the other ships of the 8th Destroyer Flotilla.

The chase was on and, as always with submarines, it was a tense game of cat and mouse. At 3.41 p.m. Laforey *was herself subjected to a torpedo attack but the tables were soon turned.* Laforey *and* Eclipse *managed to force the Italian submarine,* Ascianghi, *to the surface where she was sunk by gunfire at 4:23 p.m.*

At the time the Royal Navy was certain the culprit had been punished. Today, however, there's reason to believe Germany's U–407, captained by Ernst-Ulrich Brüller, fired the torpedo at Newfie, *as it was also in the area at the time. Captain Hutton of the* Laforey *certainly believed the Italian submarine had fired on* Newfoundland. *In his report of the incident he wrote:*

> At 15.41 the U-boat [sic] had the temerity to fire two torpedoes at
> *Laforey* which missed astern. Turning up the track a good contact
> was obtained and after five depth charge attacks by *Laforey* and
> *Eclipse* the submarine surfaced and was sunk by gunfire at 16.23.

I picked up one survivor who informed me that she was the *Ascianghi* and that she had fired four torpedoes at *Newfoundland* two hours previously.

At any rate, the attack on Sicily and the holing of the ship turned out to be a bit of a swansong for Mussolini. The day after the Newfie *was hit the Fascist Grand Council met in Italy for the first time since the start of the war. A day later Mussolini was effectively fired by the Italian King Emmanuel III. Mussolini was arrested, only to be rescued by German daredevil Otto Skorzeny from a mountain prison shortly afterwards. Mussolini then set up the Salo Republic in northern Italy until his death at the hands of Italian partisans in April 1945. As for U-407, she was sunk on 19 September 1944 in the Mediterranean by depth charges from* HMS Troubridge *and* Terpischore *and the Polish destroyer* Garland. *Five of the crew died while forty-eight survived.*

When we arrived at Malta there were two tugs to help us with the last leg of the journey. *Newfoundland* was patched up in a dry dock. In fact the stern was stabilised with concrete. We were told more permanent repairs would be done elsewhere, which we all thought meant back in England. When we got to Gibraltar I was told to fill up to 99 per cent instead of the usual 95 per cent in the oil tanks, as we were going on a long trip. I still thought we were going home and, as I couldn't go ashore at Gibraltar because I was in charge of the oiling, I gave one of our stokers a ten-shilling note to buy me some oranges and bananas to take home. However after we left Gibraltar and were at sea for a few hours it was broadcast on the ship's radio that we were on our way to the US and I had to eat the fruit myself instead of taking it to my wife and daughter as I had planned.

12

ACROSS THE POND –
THE ATLANTIC CONVOYS, 1944–45

I shall never forget the journey across the Atlantic to Boston. HMS *Newfoundland* was still without rudders and we had to steer her by means of adjusting the speed to the port and starboard screws, which made life in the Engine Room hectic. Bear in mind too that we were with a convoy and we still had to zig-zag the ship in order to avoid interception by submarines. At the suggestion of Lt Maurice Head, a keen sailor in civilian life, a 'sail', made out of quarter deck awnings, was rigged up on the fo'c'sle to assist our steerage.

They ran a 4 in. wire from the main director to the bow and the fo'c'sle awning was folded over it to make a long but effective sail. The 6 in. guns on 'A' and 'B' turrets were raised to maximum elevation to support sails. This spread of canvas helped steering and improved fuel consumption. We all thought it was a stupid idea when we first heard it but it worked.

When we arrived in Boston escorted by two US *Goodyear* anti-submarine airships, the city was just about to start its first ever 'black out' exercise. All the lights were out and smoke had been released to screen the harbour. What a welcome!

A while after this came the news that I had been recommended for a 'Mention in Dispatches' for my work in *Newfoundland* during the 'Husky' campaign. My award was eventually recorded in the *London Gazette* on 30 December 1943 and I received a bronze oak leaf emblem to pin to the ribbon of my campaign medal.

We also discovered copies of *Collier's*, with an account of the action we'd just seen in Pantelleria and Sicily. *Collier's* correspondent Alfred Wagg had been aboard *Newfoundland* throughout.

We spent about eight months in Boston whilst *Newfoundland* was being repaired. The propeller shaft had to be taken out and replaced after the stern was completed, and the oil tanks were discharged and cleaned. After we got there the majority of the ship's company returned to England. Those of us who remained were offered hospitality by local people, many of whom had emigrated to America years ago. In my case, I was invited by a Mr and Mrs Pounder to visit their home in New Bedford, which was about 60 miles from Boston. Annie and her husband Bill, who was a carpenter by trade, originally came from Burnley in Lancashire. I went to their home nearly every weekend during the refit. They would never take anything to help pay for my keep but I did manage to get them a few bottles of whisky, which they found very acceptable!

I was in Boston for Christmas of 1943. It was so restful to be away from the war for those few months although I missed my family. Bill and Annie used to take me to the local music hall at the weekend and I would often end up on the stage dancing away or sometimes singing 'All the Nice Girls Love a Sailor'. Once I had a week's leave and they took me by car to New York where we visited the Empire State Building and many other places of interest. They were lovely people.

During the war America was a land of plenty compared with Britain. There was a great range of food and lots of it. The lights were on in people's houses and down the high streets. In 1943 the cinema was another popular venue for a night out. It was the year that the Hollywood films *For Whom The Bell Tolls*, *Casablanca* and *Lassie Come Home* were released.

After the war, when I lived in Paignton, Bill and Annie Pounder came over to England on holiday to visit relatives. I was able to book them into a local hotel for two weeks and pay for them to stay there as a thank you for all that they had done for me.

While William was enjoying the comparative luxury of Christmas in the US, drama of a very different kind was unfolding in his neighbourhood on the South Hams in Devon.

Since the disaster of Dunkirk, Allied strategists had been at work on plans to free Hitler's 'Fortress Europe'. Unwittingly, the people of the South Hams found themselves on the front line. D-Day rehearsals meant that the area had to be evacuated and its residents had to put their lives on hold while Allied troops primarily from the US readied themselves for battle.

In November 1943 about 3,000 residents of Slapton Sands and the surrounding area were suddenly instructed by the Admiralty to leave their homes. About 750 families living in parts of six parishes on 30,000 acres of land were uprooted with their furniture, livestock and even sheds with barely a word of explanation. It included the insular-old, the sick and the belligerent, those who rarely left their farms of the near vicinity. Few of the affected had ever moved house before and most didn't own a suitcase for life had changed little in Slapton from the days when William's parents lived there. There were young people whose schooling was interrupted and farmers and labourers whose work was suddenly at an end. Beloved pets were put down by a vet if they could not travel. Herds that had been built up over generations were sold at knockdown prices in the local markets. Meanwhile, some young people saw the extraordinary intrusion as a chance to escape the shackles of farm life.

Clergymen were alongside the unfortunate men from the Navy when the news was broken at a succession of village meetings. They were concerned that their historic churches would be wrecked by whatever plans were afoot. All they could do was leave a message for the incomers, pinned to the church doors.

This church has stood here for several hundred years. Around it has grown a community which has lived in these houses and tilled these fields ever since there was a church. This church, this churchyard in which their loved ones lie at rest, these homes, these fields are as dear to those who have left them as are the homes and graves and fields which you, our Allies, have left behind you. They hope to return one day, as you hope to return to yours, to find them waiting to welcome them home. They entrust them to your care meanwhile and pray that God's blessing may rest upon us all.

Roads that were barely more than tracks were clogged with removal lorries and trucks. Frequently the lorries and trucks were clogged with mud. Members of the Women's Voluntary Service were transported in to soothe the process.

By Christmas the residents were all relocated, some to nearby communities that were already housing evacuees from distant cities. Some went further afield to stay with relatives or friends. Nobody expected to be told what was going on. The warning 'Careless Talk Costs Lives' that appeared on posters throughout the war kept everyone discreet. But they knew their homes and gardens would become a military range. In brutal terms, houses would be targets as a deadly war game unfolded.

The requisitioning of Slapton and the surrounding area was part of Operation 'Bolero', the codename for the American build-up in Britain. Much of southern England was transformed into a canvas army camp to accommodate more than two million American soldiers and a quarter of a million Canadians.

With them they brought tons of equipment. Still, British troops had their doubts. Many soldiers had survived the assaults on North Africa, Sicily and Italy and, at first glance, the Americans and Canadians appeared top heavy with gear but light on experience. Mindful of the lack of active service among most of the transatlantic troops the architects of D-Day organised scores of amphibious exercises to help fill the gaps.

And that's what happened at Slapton. After the residents pulled out, the US Army moved in. There were lines of US military vehicles including jeeps, Dodge Weapons Carriers and Humber Staff Cars, and files of American GIs. Local people had guessed the area around Start Bay was to be used for military training. What they didn't know was that Slapton Sands had been identified as a likeness for some of the Normandy beaches which would soon be codenamed Utah and Omaha. Consequently it was imperative that amphibious training could take place here, to give the planned invasion of Europe the best possible chance of success.

Children were quick to ask soldiers for 'gum, chum' when they encountered Americans at large in nearby towns. As for the Americans, they were happy to part with cash for basics like a loaf of bread and would pay six times the going rate. GIs socialised with local people at dances held in Kingsbridge and Totnes that occasionally led to romance. Sometimes there were scraps between mutinous locals and American soldiers.

Life settled into a comfortable routine for both local people and servicemen until training for the D–Day landings, known as Operation 'Tiger', began in earnest. Then the air was alive with the rattle of gunfire and the thud of explosions. And worse was yet to come.

THE SLAPTON SANDS DISASTER

On 28 April 1944, two hours after midnight and just as the moon dropped below the horizon, 749 US servicemen were killed in Lyme Bay when stealthy German E-boats prowled among the Landing Ships, Tank (LSTs) that were in rehearsal for D–Day. Three different convoys met off Portland after setting off from Start Bay, Plymouth and Dartmouth. The slow-moving ships had just completed a 180 degree turn in order to head back to Slapton Sands for a practice landing when the attack happened.

During the previous afternoon, assault forces from the US 4th Infantry Division had gone ashore at Slapton Sands. Now the landing ships were loaded with engineers and quartermaster troops with assorted equipment, who were to rehearse the art of offloading on to a beach. They were the practice invasion's 'second wave' and did not expect to be challenged.

Of course, measures had been taken to protect the troops. A number of British ships were stationed off the south coast looking out for enemy craft. Unfortunately those facing Cherbourg had missed the German gunboats as they left harbour. Only two vessels were escorting the LSTs, however, and one of those had withdrawn to a port for repairs. A typographical error meant that the British and American ships were operating on different radio frequencies. So when a British patrol vessel spotted the German E-boats just after midnight the warning failed to reach the Americans who had no idea they were at risk.

Three out of eight LSTs in the flotilla were hit. One burst into flames that were soon fuelled by ammunition and fuel aboard the vehicles it was carrying. Another keeled over and sank within moments. A third lost its stern but managed to return to port. In the darkness and confusion men had little idea where the attack had come from and the responses from other LSTs were haphazard.

Many of the men who died were below deck and had no chance of escape. Among those who did abandon ship were a number wearing lifebelts around their waists rather than their armpits so they were tipped head first into the water where they drowned in a sea smothered by oil. Still more died of hypothermia.

Bodies were towed in from the sea or washed up on the shore for several days afterwards. Years later one British sailor who was sent to the scene in a motor launch recalled what he saw.

On arrival we found hundreds of dead US soldiers floating and bobbing around. Their body movements were being accentuated by a heavy swell. They were fully clad with steel helmets firmly fastened. A large proportion had badly burnt faces and hands and from a distance we initially mistook them for coloured troops. Having passed through burning oil-covered sea it would seem a fair number had suffocated and in their death throes had drawn their legs up to their *Mae West* life jackets, causing them to hunch up with rigor mortis. We pulled them in with boat hooks and set them on the boat sides, along the rails, with their faces facing outboard; we loaded about 50 or so per boat and returned to Portland.

The action of placing the bodies facing outwards was to avoid the crew having to look at the damaged and grotesque faces. However, this served little purpose as the next boat alongside had done the same and we could easily see the awful visage on those boats.

He and his shipmates were warned not to discuss the events of that terrible night with anyone.

THE COVER UP

The loss of men and machines was a blow to the Allied high command. Among the dead were all the trained beach marshals destined for Omaha during D-Day. Their absence certainly cost lives and created confusion in one designated part of the beach.

However, their primary concern was that ten men in the lost ships were of senior rank and security clearance and knew details about the D-Day landings. Had they been hauled out of the water and interrogated by the Germans the entire plan, now in its advanced stages, would be in jeopardy.

Eventually the men were identified among the dead. Having cracked German codes, eavesdroppers at Bletchley Park listening station also quickly reassured planners that there was no evidence of the Germans knowing that the invasion would be in Normandy. Enormous cardboard camps complete with fake tanks and even campfire smoke constructed on the Kent coast made Germany think the invasion would come at the Pas de Calais, *a view confirmed by double agents.*

The incident was hushed up, again to preserve the integrity of the D-Day plans. Victims were included in the D-Day tally while survivors were sworn to secrecy. However, the incident was related in the Stars and Stripes *newspaper distributed among US soldiers as early as July 1944. It was also mentioned in several books that appeared in the late 1940s and 1950s and lay on file without a 'Secrecy' classification in the US national archives.*

Only much later did the incident become a talking point after efforts by Slapton resident Ken Small to establish a permanent memorial to the dead men gained momentum. Using his own money he hauled a Sherman tank, lost off Slapton in a different exercise, on to the sands and made it into a memorial that publicised the events that happened at Slapton during the war. With some justification, there was a string of denials from the American hierarchy that there had been a cover-up about the E-boat attack.

But there were still more deaths among the visiting Americans at Slapton, according to local accounts. Several residents claimed there was a mass grave of men who had been killed after live ammunition was distributed during Operation 'Tiger'. So men were mistakenly shot dead by mock 'defenders' as they made their way up the beach. And there was talk that another glitch in communications meant a planned rocket attack from ships out to sea rained down on land-based troops. Other than accounts by local people, there's little to substantiate exactly what went on in Slapton Sands when it came under fire.

One day in early June, Devon residents awoke to find their streets deserted. The colony of US soldiers who had learned to call Slapton home had moved on to the Normandy beaches where they were fighting in the bitterest of the beach combats. The sudden departure caused shock waves in the community, many of whom never discovered what happened to the uniformed friends they made in those six months.

Now the uprooted folk of the South Hams could return to their homes and farms, in the wake of mine detectors who got to work eliminating unexploded ammunition scattered across the area. But to the delight of the locals the Americans had discarded tools, equipment and canned goods, all of which were put to good use. However, some South Hams people had died in the interim, others had found a new life elsewhere. The close communities that had once been a hallmark of the neighbourhood were never the same again.

The sound of birdsong, which vanished from the area during the 1944 nesting seasons, soon returned to Slapton Sands. A rampant rat, rabbit and pigeon population was quickly brought under control as were the weeds that choked fields and gardens. However, the Royal Sands Hotel that once perched proudly on the shoreline was in ruins. Ultimately it became the site of a car park.

In July 1954, the US Army presented to the people of this area a granite obelisk monument with a bronze plaque:

> Thanking the people of the South Hams area, who generously left their homes and land, to provide a secret battle practice area, for the successful assault on Normandy on 6 June 1944. Their action resulted in the saving of many hundreds of lives and contributed in no small measure to the success of the operation. The area included the villages of Blackawton, Chillington, East Allington, Slapton, Stokenham, Strete and Torcross together with many outlying farms and houses.

Indeed, many valuable lessons had been learned prior to D-Day: that large escorts were needed to safeguard amphibious landing craft; that rescue craft should remain on hand; communications systems should be standard and fire fighting equipment improved. Men were also told they should never look directly at flares because it reduced their ability to see in the dark. They were told how to correctly wear a lifejacket and that they should loosen their bootlaces if an order to abandon ship seemed likely so the heavy footwear was easier to remove in the water.

Eventually the repairs to the *Newfoundland* were completed and time came for us to leave Boston and head back home across the Atlantic. Our journey to England was completely unescorted. First we called in at St Johns, the capital of Newfoundland, to oil. Some of the chaps got a 'run ashore' but, being responsible for oiling the ship, I missed out on that one.

This was a great occasion for the people of Newfoundland. The ship had been partly financed by them, as Newfoundland was one of the colonies of the British Empire. There were great celebrations; civic ceremonies, a march through the city and crowds of locals came to visit the ship. When I went out on deck the dockyard 'mateys' would shout across to me. One said, 'Take good care of that ship, Chief – I paid half a crown towards her.' After four days there we finally sailed back home.

Afterwards I heard that we had lost radio contact with the Admiralty during the latter part of the journey and it had been feared that the ship was lost but we arrived safely in Greenock, on the River Clyde, although with very little fuel left in our tanks. This was shortly before D-Day, June 1944.

I travelled to Devon for leave by train, taking with me all the presents I had purchased for the family while I was in America. I had to borrow a trolley from the station to carry all my presents home. There was a dinner set, a tea set, lots of clothes, tins of fruit, tea, sugar and dried fruit. On my return to Greenock, Lily and Anne came with me and we rented a flat there for a few months during which time HMS *Newfoundland* was being refitted. We would regularly see the liners *Queen Elizabeth* and *Queen Mary* in the Clyde as, during the war, they were used as troop carriers.

In September 1944 I left *Newfoundland* and rejoined the barracks at Devonport where I was based until the end of the war in Europe. I was on a French ship called *Impassible* which had fled to Britain before France capitulated. She was moored at the breakwater in Plymouth Sound and I went there each day by steamboat, returning home at night to the flat we rented near Mount Gould Park in Plymouth. Anne, now five years old, was able to start school.

I remember listening to Winston Churchill's broadcast telling us that

Germany had surrendered on 7 May 1945. We were all overjoyed that at last the war was over, in Europe at least. Everyone was rejoicing and I remember Lily, Anne and I all celebrating at a local street party.

However, I was then drafted to join a Naval party which was to be sent to guard the island of Sylt, off the north-west German coast. I was given a week's training in the use of a revolver as I had little previous experience of firearms. We were issued with khaki uniforms to wear with our Naval caps. We travelled by rail to London docks, by ship to Ostend and then across Belgium and northern Germany by Army trucks. We crossed the Rhine by a bridge constructed by Allied forces. As we journeyed we passed through towns that had been completely flattened by the Allied bombing. Hamburg was especially badly hit. I remembered how I had wept as I walked through the devastation of Plymouth and was somehow glad to see it was not only the British cities that had suffered. However, seeing the effects of the Allied blitz and the many starving, homeless people lining the ruined streets was another matter. It was terrible to see such destruction, no matter which side was the victim. In the months after the war there was chaos in Europe.

The bombing of Hamburg took place almost two years prior to William's visit. The northern port was the target for Operation 'Gomorrah' in July 1943 which instituted saturation bombing by the RAF at night and the USAAF by day, almost certainly inspired by the success of the aerial bombing of Pantelleria. Planes dropped a combination of incendiary and high explosive bombs which rendered all efforts at fire fighting ineffective. Before striking they dropped tin foil strips called 'chaff' to confound German radar which, until that point, had done a fine job in defence of the city. On one night during the operation so many bombs were dropped that a firestorm was created, sparking high winds and scorching temperatures over an area of several square kilometres. By the time Operation 'Gomorrah' drew to a close at the beginning of August, some 50,000 civilians had perished and a further million people were homeless. It was, the Allies discovered later, a significant blow to the Nazi hierarchy that almost led to them pulling out of the war. Afterwards, Hamburg was cordoned off and little was done to repair the damage.

George Funnel, of the 55th Kent Regiment, was like William a witness to the long-lasting results of the destruction. He had joined up in 1939 aged 17 after lying about his age. Although he had seen the effects of the blitz in London, having been stationed at an anti-aircraft battery, he was nonetheless still shocked by what he saw as he fought his way through Europe from 1944:

> In Hamburg there was mile after mile of devastation. I lived through the London bombing but it was nothing like as bad as that over Germany. Even when we got to Hamburg, long after the air raids had taken place, there was still the stench of death coming from crumbled buildings. It took ages to find some of the burned remains. On the streets we only found a few old men and young boys. The rest of the male population had been called up into the army. The vast majority of the people we met were women struggling to survive as best they could.

Sylt is the largest of the North Frisian islands, facing a bracing North Sea breeze. It had been made a fortress for the Second World War, with bunkers extending beneath the sandy dunes. When I got to Westerland in Sylt I found that I was sharing accommodation with a Shipwright Chief Petty Officer. We had a bungalow to ourselves, and what a lovely place it was – complete with a garden and swimming pool. Whilst we were there an officer came around to inspect us and I remember that he said to me, 'I bet you didn't have billets like this in Plymouth, Chief.' I had to agree that we didn't. On Sylt I was in charge of 12 ratings. Our job was really a precautionary one – just to make sure that nothing happened that might indicate that there were pockets of German resistance. This was not amongst my favourite drafts as I was used to being at sea and did not like the land-based guard duties.

After just a few months, I was pleased to be sent home. I was overdue for discharge as I should have left the Navy in 1940, after 22 years' service, but due to the war I had to continue. Still I had been drawing my pension since 1940 and now it was definitely time to retire.

On the journey back I was in charge of several ratings who were also returning to England. We went by motorboat to Cuxhaven and by train to Ostend, then took passage to London in one of the old light cruisers. The last leg of the trip was by train to Plymouth and the Naval Barracks. That was the end of my war and, indeed, my service.

In September 1945 I was at last demobbed after 27 years. We all received a civilian suit, cap and shoes. Now I would be able to be with my wife and daughter and start a new life ashore.

Looking back over my 27 years in the Royal Navy, I must say I had a wonderful life. The places I visited, the friends I made and the comradeship of my fellow sailors were very special. We worked hard but also had some memorable times ashore. Of course, there had been some really terrible times during the final six years of my service and I feel a great sadness for all those who lost their lives. I really count my blessings and feel sure that someone 'up there' was looking after me.

I am proud to have been awarded the following medals:

British Medals:
British War Medal 1914 to 1918
1939–45 Star
The Atlantic Star (Bar on ribbon 'France and Germany')
The Africa Star
The Italy Star
1939–45 Defence Medal
1939–45 Victory Medal (Oak Leaf on ribbon signifying
    a 'Mentioned in Dispatches')
Long Service and Good Conduct Medal

Memorial Medals:
Malta Memorial Medal
Russian Convoy Medal 1945–85
Dunkirk Medal
Russian Convoy Medal 1945–95

Ships, Dates and Ranks:

Naval Barracks, Devonport 23 Sept 1918–17 Oct 1919
    Ordinary Seaman/Stoker

HMS *Tiger*, Battle cruiser 18 Oct 1919–17 Oct 1921
    Stoker 1st Class

HMS *Hood*, Battle cruiser 6 Jan 1923–4 Dec 1924
    Stoker 1st Class

(Sailed on Empire Cruise, 1923–24)

HMS *Chrysanthemum*, Sloop 15 June 1925–25 Nov 1927
    Leading Stoker

(Stationed Malta)

HMS *P40*, Submarine Chaser 7 Feb 1928–13 Sept 1928
    Leading Stoker

HMS *Eagle*, Aircraft Carrier 29 May 1929–12 July 1931
    Stoker Petty Officer (Stationed Malta)

HMS *Harebell*, Sloop 29 Aug 1931–12 Jan 1934
    Stoker Petty Officer

HMS *Thanet/Tenedos*, Destroyers 24 Jan 1934–30 Aug 1934
    Stoker Petty Officer

HMS *Carlisle*, Light Cruiser 5 Sept 1934–28 April 1937
    Stoker Petty Officer

(Stationed Simonstown S. Africa)

HMS *Salamander*, Minesweeper 23 Nov 1937–30 Oct 1941
    Chief Stoker PO

HMS *Newfoundland*, Light Cruiser 17 Dec 1941–4 Sept 1944
    Chief Stoker PO

(Mentioned in Dispatches – Sicily Landings 1943)

Naval Barracks, Devonport 4 Sept 1944–8 May 1945
    Chief Stoker PO

Naval Party No. 1744 9 May 1945–2 July 1945

(Based Sylt, Northern Germany)

Naval Barracks, Devonport 3 July 1945–18 Sept 1945

13

DROPPING ANCHOR –
POST-WAR LIFE BEGINS, 1945–2000

Before I left the Navy I had decided to use my barbering skills in civilian life. There looked to be opportunities in Plymouth where we were living but firstly we all went for a holiday at my brother-in-law's home in Yorkshire. On my return I found a job in a ladies' and gentlemen's hairdressing business but unfortunately I soon received my notice as the owner had decided to specialise in ladies' hairdressing only. I was unemployed for a few weeks but, during that time, Lily's cousin, who owned a chemist's shop in Plymouth, told me about a gentlemen's hairdressing and tobacconists' business for sale in Winner Street in the old part of Paignton. Lily and I immediately went to have a look at it and decided it would suit us just fine. The price of the business was a little over a thousand pounds. So I put down a deposit of £10 from my demob bounty and by Christmas 1945 we had sealed the deal so now I was captain of my own ship.

It was quite a small shop with two haircutting chairs, basins and mirrors. On the first floor there was a kitchen/dining room and a separate sitting room. On the second floor there were two bedrooms. Outside there was the lavatory and for bathing we used a tin bath taken inside for the purpose. However I now had a garden of my own, in which I mostly grew flowers, especially gladioli and chrysanthemums. I loved to get out into the garden in the evenings after supper. I found it very restful after a busy day haircutting.

My Navy routine meant that I was used to being an early riser so I would be up at about 6 a.m. Each morning after washing and shaving I would take a walk down to Paignton seafront and back and then open up the shop at 7 a.m. to catch men on their way to work. As there was usually a bit of a lull before the rest of the population was up and about I would close the shop for a short while to have breakfast. I would normally finish the working day about 6.30 p.m. If I was especially busy Lily would come down to help by taking the money for haircutting and for sales of other items sold in the shop. We did a really good business in cigarettes, tobacco, hair creams, razors, blades, toothpaste and a variety of toiletries. And of course I would ask customers if they needed 'something for the weekend, sir?'

I would charge 1s for a cut and 9d for a shave. I always used a cut-throat razor on my customers and also to shave myself – something I continued to do until I was in my nineties when I was persuaded by my family to start using a safety razor. It was certainly a busy shop, so much so that I soon needed to take on an assistant.

The summer visitors, many of whom would return year after year, provided an important part of our income since they would often arrive without flannels or soap or without having found the time to have a haircut.

William, Lily and Anne lived in a popular holiday resort that was part of the 'English Riviera'. Paignton, Torquay and the port of Brixham cluster around Torbay where grand hotels and holiday camps vied for the favours of holidaymakers. The area was blessed with a balmy climate and the palm trees that proliferated in the resorts gave them a tropical feel.

Resort holidays were popular in Britain from the late 18th century when the key to holiday happiness was fresh air, bathing and some well-manicured gardens. Although it was a privilege open to the monied few in Edwardian times the numbers taking an annual holiday exceeded 15 million by the end of the 1930s. Resorts with rail links were particularly popular.

After William settled in Paignton the holiday industry was in the throes of upheaval with the arrival of holiday camps. The popularity of holiday camps was increasing until the war brought it to a sudden halt. However, in the wake of Billy Butlin's success with camps at Skegness and other sites, businessman Fred Pontin (1906–2000) saw the possibilities of the leisure industry and began to establish holiday camps of his own, including one at Paignton. Instinctively he steered away from the sprawling, almost militaristic, Butlins camps and instead marketed 'small unit holiday camps for the connoisseur'. Devon and Cornwall were once considered too remote to reap the benefits of an influx of holidaymakers. But this was the age of the car. While the roads were never straight or fast, drivers were happy to make the south-west trek for what was generally perceived to be better weather. Paignton enjoyed the heyday of holiday camps during the '50s and '60s which brought throngs of people into the resort – and frequently into William's barber's shop.

However, there was growing competition for the British holidaymakers' pound. In Spain, where the weather was undeniably sunnier, coastal resorts were mushrooming. With the cost of air travel heading inexorably down, the 'Costas' were suddenly providing an alluring alternative to the likes of Torbay. As the 1960s progressed the Spanish holiday trade expanded, leaving resorts like Paignton on the sidelines.

Nevertheless there were still a number of people who visited hotels in the Torbay area. No one is entirely sure whether that aspect of the holiday industry was hindered or helped by the production of Fawlty Towers, the comedy show featuring John Cleese who allegedly based the character of Basil Fawlty on a hotelier in Torquay. Cleese allegedly stayed in Torquay's Gleneagles Hotel in the early 1970s with other members of the Monty Python comedy team. Its proprietor was, he said, 'the most marvellously rude man I've ever met'. The hotelier in question put one of the team's suitcases outside in the garden when he heard it ticking, fearing it contained a bomb. In fact, it had an alarm clock inside. And he criticised the table manners of another. Fawlty Towers ran for 12 episodes and was shown from 1975.

Wednesday was my half-day and I closed all day Sunday, when we took the opportunity to either visit friends or family or quite often in the summer go on a day trip by coach onto the moors or to another part of the West Country. We also enjoyed going to the local theatres to see plays, operatic productions, pantomimes and band concerts.

After a while, and with the business well established, we bought a semi-detached house high up on the hill behind the town with glorious views over Torbay. It came with a bigger garden both front and back and I cultivated every square inch to grow flowers and many vegetables. Lily and Anne would complain that the lawn was getting smaller with every season.

Over the years I had continued to be a member of my Masonic Lodge at Portland, although I had rarely been able to attend meetings. In the early 1960s I transferred to Courtland Lodge in Paignton which I enjoyed for more than 20 years before leaving Devon.

I always had it in mind to work until I was 70 but in 1968 my assistant decided to leave as he wanted a change. By this time our daughter Anne had been working in London for some years and had been married at St Mary Abbots Church in Kensington the previous year to husband Michael. This seemed to be a good time to retire so after 22 years I sold the business and then the house, and we moved to a detached house at Broadsands, between Paignton and Brixham. This too had great views over Torbay and there were only two fields between us and the beach at Broadsands. The old railway line connecting Paignton to Kingswear at the mouth of the River Dart ran along an embankment nearby and had been taken over by a private company operating a steam engine and carriages, mainly for visitors. We enjoyed watching it pass by and, in later years, it was a great attraction to our grandchildren who would run into the garden to wave to the passengers. The driver would respond by sounding the engine's whistle.

Our new house was a lovely home with a beautiful garden in which I spent most of my time. I grew many flowers and a variety of vegetables, some of which I would sell to a local shop and some I would share with my neighbours. In return they often gave Lily and I a lift into Paignton as we didn't have a car of our own. My garden was well fed with both seaweed, which I collected from the beach, and manure delivered by a local farmer. I used to talk to the birds and once a little robin perched on my fork allowed me to smooth his breast with my hand trowel. I kept the lawns immaculate, with not a weed in sight, and trimmed the privet hedges every week. I got interested in topiary, much to the amusement of passers by. I used to fashion the hedges into the shapes of all sorts of animals like horses, elephants, foxes and hedgehogs. I collected mushrooms from the nearby fields and in the autumn I picked blackberries and hazelnuts from the hedgerows. I think I worked harder in my retirement than I ever did before!

Lily's health gradually deteriorated over the years, with the onset of arthritis eventually making everyday chores very difficult for her. But she wouldn't entertain the idea of having some home help. However, by 1985 it was becoming a matter of concern to Anne and I as to what we should do for the best. Anne and Michael suggested that we considered moving closer to them and our grandchildren, Christopher and Susan, at Beaconsfield in Buckinghamshire and, although I was sad at the prospect of moving from Devon, I could see it would be better for both of us.

After much searching Anne and Michael found a new house still under construction on a small estate in the lovely old town of Watlington, nestling at the foot of the Chiltern Hills in the Oxfordshire countryside. The properties were specifically designed for older people and had a warden and communal gardens, and were only a few minutes from the shops. Michael videoed the house and the surrounding area and brought all the details to us in Devon. We thought it would suit us well and it was less than half an hour from their home. So the decision was made and our house was put on the market. It sold very quickly and now we had a problem because the new house was not finished. Our furniture was put into storage and Lily and I moved temporarily into Primley House, a local residential home set in extensive grounds on the outskirts of Paignton. Anne and Michael dealt with all the arrangements and we eventually moved into our new home in December 1986.

We soon settled in and made friends with the neighbours and the many people we met at numerous local functions or during shopping trips in the town. Quite a number of them served during the war or knew service life. Everyone was very friendly and welcoming. We enjoyed attending St Leonard's Church each Sunday and after a while the Rector asked me, 'Why don't you come up to Communion, William?' 'Well,' I said, 'I've not been confirmed. Being in the Navy for so many years, I never got around to it.' So it was that a few months later I came to be confirmed at the age of 88. In the same year Lily and I celebrated our golden wedding anniversary and Anne drove us back to Devon where we were thrilled to stay in Kingsbridge for a week, visiting relatives and old friends. It really was a trip down memory lane.

By the time I was nearly 90 Lily was becoming seriously disabled with arthritis although mentally she was always bright. Fortunately I was fit and able enough to help her around the home and I would take her out in the gardens in a wheelchair. Anne did our laundry and also prepared meals which she brought down to us regularly. Even so I was glad of the additional help given by our friends locally. We had a stair lift installed to help Lily and carers came in morning and evening to assist her. After a while the local cottage hospital was able to provide respite care for her one week every month to give me a rest. I liked that although I missed Lily. But I was happy that she was mostly able to stay at home and that I could look after her. Eventually, Lily's bed had to be moved into our sitting room and a hoist installed but the last few months of her life were spent in Watlington hospital where I visited her almost every day. Then one day in hospital it was clear that the end was near and I put my arms around her and I said, 'Lily, you're going to have a long sleep now and God will look after you.' She died later that evening. She was 87. I really missed her.

Following Lily's death in November 1995, I received a lot of support from friends and neighbours. On my first Sunday back at St Leonard's, General Sir John Mogg and his wife Margaret, whom we had become friendly with over the years through that church and the Royal British Legion, said to me, 'William, you are to sit with us now.' As I got to know them better I found out that Lady Mogg's sister, Sarah Mackinnon, had been married to a Naval officer who was flag-lieutenant to Admiral Evans (famous as 'Evans of the *Broke*' and a former customer of mine). He was on HMS *Carlisle* at the same time as I had served in that ship on the Africa station back in 1936.

Once again, William found that rank and class was no barrier for him and he was entirely comfortable rubbing shoulders with one of Britain's most eminent generals. Sports-loving General Sir John Mogg began military life as a cadet in the Coldstream Guards. Although he was commissioned in 1937 into the Oxfordshire and Buckinghamshire Light Infantry he didn't see active service until August 1944 when he was chosen to command the 9th Battalion of the Durham Light Infantry. In operations from Normandy to Hamburg, he was twice 'Mentioned in Dispatches', and twice awarded the Distinguished Service Order.

After the end of the war he became a keen parachutist after commanding the 10th Battalion of the Parachute Regiment in the Territorial Army. In 1958 he was promoted to brigadier and went to Malaya where Commonwealth soldiers were fighting communist rebels. Following a stint as commandant at Sandhurst he became deputy to General Alexander Haig at Supreme Allied Command of the North Atlantic Treaty Organisation [NATO] in Belgium.

After Sir John's death in 2001 an obituary published by the Royal Green Jacket Regimental Association paid the following tribute:

> General Sir John Mogg, who died aged 88, was, in his time, probably the British army's most popular general, and finished his career in one of NATO's most influential posts. His large frame was combined with an exceptionally genial, warm and sympathetic character, which appealed not only to soldiers of all ranks, but to people in every walk of life, whatever their nationality.

I found life lonely without Lily but I kept myself busy, went to bed early, was usually up shortly after 6 a.m. and often down at the shops before 9 a.m. That's Naval training for you. However thanks to the additional help of my family, I coped well living on my own. The only thing I never really got the hang of was bed making, which is hardly surprising as I had spent so many years sleeping in a hammock!

In my early days at Watlington I met my good friend Rupert Gandy who had also been at Dunkirk and was on the committee of the Dunkirk Veterans Association. He suggested that I should join and I was delighted to go with him to meetings at both High

Wycombe and Henley-on-Thames, where I made many more friends. It was through one of these groups that I also joined the Royal Naval Association at High Wycombe.

In Watlington I became a member of the local branch of the Royal British Legion whose meetings were held only a short walk from my home. Here I made another good friend, Don Read, who had been in the Army. He invited me to go with him to meetings of the Thames Valley branch of the Western Front Association near Reading, which he thought I would find interesting. Although I had no connection with the Army, I was made very welcome by the members and enjoyed the talks given by the various speakers. Don also took me to the 'Ox & Bucks' branch at Chalfont St Giles and eventually I was made an honorary member at both branches!

Strangely, although I was now into my 90s, I seemed to be finding more and more things to occupy me. Each week I received the *Kingsbridge Gazette* by post and one day I was astonished to see a letter from Tom Roxby on behalf of the HMS *Newfoundland* Association looking for ex-shipmates. Anne made contact with him and shortly after, she and Michael took me to my first reunion. This was the start of many years of enjoyable gatherings in different parts of the country where I made many good friends amongst whom were a few who had actually served at the same time as me although they were about 20 years younger!

Through reading the *Navy News* I was surprised and delighted to discover that HMS *Hood* – the ship on which I had served more than 70 years ago – also had an association. When I first started attending their annual reunions at Portsmouth, I was amazed to find that there were still one or two members who had also sailed on the Empire Cruise with me back in 1923–24. One of these was Harry Cutler, who lived in Plymouth, but was too frail to get to Portsmouth. However it was wonderful to meet up with him a couple of times during visits to Devon and to reminisce about the old days in the Navy. Like me, he stayed in the Navy and served throughout the Second World War. He died in 2003 aged 98.

I became good friends with Ted Briggs, who was President of the Association and the last of only three men out of a crew of 1,421 who survived when *Hood* was sunk in 1941. Although I had moved into a care home by the time Ted died in 2008, I was so glad I was able to attend his funeral at HMS *Collingwood* at Fareham to say my goodbyes.

At the reunion dinners I was usually asked to sing my favourite song, 'All the Nice Girls Love a Sailor'. What I hadn't expected was to be asked by the Chaplain, Revd Ron Paterson, to sing the same song the following morning at church! However, I did follow this with my favourite hymn, 'Abide With Me', and continued to do it each year.

Something I missed since moving from Devon were my Masonic meetings and there wasn't a lodge nearby. So I was surprised one day to be visited by my local chemist, Frank Pate, who had been contacted by a fellow freemason who knew I had moved to Watlington. He invited me to visit his lodge at Thame. I had a wonderful welcome and was soon able to join, with Frank very kindly taking me to the meetings. A few years later I was honoured to be invited to join another lodge which was in Oxford.

As I approached my 100th birthday I reflected on how much my life had changed, especially in recent years. I seemed to be getting busier as time progressed – and I must admit I enjoyed it all. By now I was being asked to some rather grand places. In 1997, through the Dunkirk Veterans Association, I was invited, together with my friend and branch secretary, Rupert Gandy, to my first garden party at Buckingham Palace, hosted by the 'Not Forgotten' Association. I was introduced to Prince Andrew, Duke of York and he asked me about the ships I had served on. We met lots of celebrities and had a wonderful afternoon. In December that year I met the Duke of York again at St James's Palace where I had been invited to attend a Christmas Party, again organised by the 'Not Forgotten' Association. This time I was thrilled to also meet Her Majesty the Queen Mother. She recognised my First World War medal and we had a lovely chat. I had always admired her and sent her a birthday card each year. She was just over a month older than me.

14

A Century Not Out, 2000–2009

The year 2000 was, of course, very special for me. I would reach my 100th birthday, something I never dreamed of achieving, and I was having the time of my life. Much to my amusement, my friends told me that I was a familiar face in newspapers and on television. What's more, I didn't have an enemy in the world – I had outlived them all. Someone once asked me if I drank a lot. 'I had plenty of rum in the navy,' I admitted. To which they replied, 'That's why you've lived so long, William, you're pickled.'

That year the Dunkirk veterans celebrated the 60th anniversary of the evacuation and held their final reunion at the Imperial War Museum. About 55 of us members attended and there was a tremendous sense of camaraderie and much media coverage by press and television. There was even a rowing dinghy, *Tamzine*, which had been used to ferry troops from the beaches.

To celebrate my birthday, I was delighted to be guest of honour at the HMS *Newfoundland* Association reunion where I was surprised to be presented with a framed congratulatory certificate by the then President, Admiral Sir Julian Oswald. A short time after I was also guest of honour at the HMS *Hood* Association reunion at which I received an inscribed ship's bell. The High Wycombe branch of the Royal Naval Association threw a party for me; the Western Front

Association at Reading presented me with a painting of *Hood* and my family organised a party in Watlington. I thought they might arrange something but I had no idea that it would be a tea party for 140 family, friends and neighbours held in the local school hall decorated with streamers and balloons. Of course, I entertained them with a selection of my favourite old time songs. At home there were over 200 birthday cards and I was thrilled to receive a very special card from Her Majesty the Queen.

I remember shortly before my birthday I had a visit by a man from the Pensions Service who said he had come to check on my name and age and to see if I was OK. I had a laugh with him and said, 'You've just come to see if I am still alive!'

At this point William was part of the fastest growing section of UK society, according to the Office of National Statistics. He was one of about 9,000 British people to reach 100, a 90 per cent increase since 1911. And the figures for the 100-plus club continue to rise, particularly among men. In the recent past there was one man for every seven women aged more than 100 years. But the balance is changing, with more men reaching that golden age than ever before.

People are living longer thanks to improved medical treatment and better homes, hygiene and sanitation. The population at large eats better than it ever has before. Forecasters believe the number of people living to become centenarians in the UK will top 40,000 by 2031. In America the figure for centenarian population at the moment stands at about 72,000. Meanwhile in Japan the total is 30,000.

Some studies have sought to make links between centenarians to discover their secret for longevity. There may well be a genetic link and certainly older people tend to be tall and thin. Few, if any, are obese. Most will have escaped the usual symptoms of old age and show no sign of dementia before the age of 92. It seems most have never drunk or smoked to excess. William falls outside this category, freely admitting how much he liked a tipple in the Navy at a time when he – and most other servicemen – were heavy smokers. Longevity is also linked to living in a non-industrial area. After his retirement, William returned to Devon and spent years enjoying the sea air that sweeps across Torbay. However, during his 27-year Naval life he was subjected to the filthy atmosphere of ships' boiler rooms. But, he in common with many other centenarians dealt well with stress and was actively religious.

Everyone who reaches the age of 100 in Britain automatically gets a birthday card from the Queen. Those who reach 105 will receive a card from her on this and every subsequent birthday. Buckingham Palace has an anniversaries office to ensure no one misses out. Those aged above 110 are known as 'Supercentenarians'.

Couples who are married for 60 years will have a telegram from the Queen if the office is notified about a diamond wedding celebration beforehand, a task usually done by relatives or friends.

In 2001 I acquired my first passport – something I complained about as I had already been all around the world without one. But times have changed and I needed it because I had been invited by the organisers of a World War One battlefield tour group to join them on a visit to Northern France. I had no connection with those battles but apparently they liked to take First World War veterans with them and there were not many left able to make the journey. In fact, there were three of us – Arthur Halestrap, 103, ex-Royal Engineers, Fred Bunday, 101, ex-Royal Navy and myself. We were well looked after and I thoroughly enjoyed the trip. Later in November, I joined another of these trips, this time to Flanders, where I had the honour of delivering the exhortation and laying a wreath at the Menin Gate on 11 November, Remembrance Day. However, I rather overdid the 'socialising' this time and when I emerged from the coach on my return Anne and Michael thought I looked tired and ill. In spite of their instructions that I should get plenty of rest, of course I had taken no notice and had had a great time leading the sing-a-longs in the hotel bar until the early hours of each morning.

In between these trips, my family took me to Devon on a visit down 'memory lane'. We celebrated my 101st birthday in Kingsbridge with a lunch party for family and local friends. There are names on the war memorial that I recognise, men that I grew up with but who didn't survive the First World War. I remember once talking to one woman locally who lost her son. He was two months younger than me and she told me that she had cried and cried and cried. It's a reminder of just how lucky I've been in my life. Anything I can do to honour the memory of those men who've gone before me is a privilege.

Again, through the kindness of the 'Not Forgotten' Association, other World War One veterans and I were invited to their Buckingham Palace garden party in the summer where we met His Royal Highness Prince Michael of Kent, had a grand tea and enjoyed listening to the bands. Later in December, I joined 104-year-old 'Smiler' Marshall at their St James's Palace Christmas party where we met the Princess Royal and were wonderfully entertained by a variety of celebrities. It was during this period that I first met Dennis Goodwin MBE, chairman of the World War One Veterans Association, who became a friend and who had worked hard to increase recognition of the dwindling band of these men.

Throughout my life I have been lucky to enjoy good health, although in November 1992 I had been rushed to hospital with a strangulated right hernia. Ten years later in March 2002 I needed another hernia operation to the left side and was booked into the Ackland Hospital in Oxford. However, a few days beforehand I had a bad fall and was taken to the John Radcliffe Hospital, also in Oxford, where I spent some days being thoroughly checked over. Pronounced fit and well I was discharged but the same day Anne and Michael took me straight to the other hospital for my second hernia op.

The following month I was delighted to visit Wells in Somerset for a ceremony, held in the Mayor's Parlour, for First World War veteran Harry Patch to receive a certificate to go with his *Légion d'Honneur* medal. A number of other veterans were invited but sadly at the time they were not well enough to travel.

That summer I met Princess Anne again at a Buckingham Palace garden party. I mentioned to her that I knew she would be coming to Watlington, where I lived, on 23 September, my 102nd birthday, to officially open a new community centre. Of course, with her many engagements she didn't know the details. I was in the habit of asking ladies for a kiss but following my request to the Princess she laughed and declined saying, 'It's not your birthday yet.' However she obviously remembered our conversation because in due course I was invited to

Bill with his prized roses in his garden in Winner Hill Road, Paignton, Devon, 1960.

Bill with Lily (far right) at the wedding of their daughter Anne, who married Michael Davidson in 1967.

Bill and Lily with their grandchildren, Christopher and Susie, in their garden at Broadsands, Devon, in 1980.

The 'Old Salts': Bill with HMS *Hood* survivor Ted Briggs at the annual service for the commemoration of the ship, in Boldre, Hampshire, 1999.

One hundred not out! Bill attends a lavish birthday in his honour at Watlington school on 23 September 2000.

Vets in a car: Henry Allingham (107 years old), Norman Robinson (102 years) and Bill (103 years) at the Remembrance Sunday Parade, the Cenotaph, 9 November 2003.

The miniature portrait Bill Mundy created of William Stone in September 2002.

Pleased to meet you! Bill would meet many members of the Royal Family over the years, as seen here with HRH Princess Anne at the 'Not Forgotten' garden party at Buckingham Palace in 2002.

William meets HRH Prince Charles at the National Archives, Kew, at a gathering of First World War veterans in April 2003.

Bill celebrating his 104th birthday aboard HMS *Gloucester* with Commander Cree, Portsmouth, 2004.

Veterans Henry Allingham, Fred Lloyd and Bill at a presentation of Veterans Badges, Eastbourne, June 2004.

Bill on the stage at the Royal Albert Hall with fellow veterans of both World Wars at the Royal British Legion Service, November 2004.

HRH Prince Andrew shares a joke with Bill at the Trafalgar 200 celebrations, Portsmouth, June 2005.

Bill with *Bismark* survivor Heinrich Kuhnt, HMS *Hood* reunion, Portsmouth, May 2005.

Bill selling poppies in Watlington High Street, November 2005.

The then prime minister Tony Blair greets Bill (with Anne and Michael) at a function at 10 Downing Street during Veterans Day, June 2006.

Attending the unveiling of the name plate *Remembrance* with Southeastern Trains at Victoria Station in November 2005.

Bill, outside St Leonards Church, Watlington, 2005

Meeting the Queen at the Buckingham Palace garden party in July 2007.

Bill with his great-granddaughters, Sophie and Annabel, Lord Harris Court, April 2008.

Falklands War veteran Simon Weston interviews Bill at Lord Harris Court, October 2008, prior to Remembrance Day.

The old friends: Bill, with Henry Allingham and Harry Patch, at the 90th anniversary of the ending of the Great War, held at the Cenotaph in London in 2008. With the death of Henry, and then Harry a week later in July 2009, all three veterans have now sadly passed into history. (© Getty Images)

Bill's great-granddaughters, Sophie and Annabel, place posies on his coffin during his funeral service, Watlington, 29 January 2009.

Final commemoration: Bill's ashes were laid to rest with his beloved wife in the village of Buckland-Tout-Saints, Devon. The plaque bearing his name was placed on his parents' grave.

attend the ceremony in Watlington and meet her. How very kind and thoughtful of her and it was a wonderful treat for my birthday. We chatted for some time about life in the Navy and she wished me happy birthday before leaving.

One of my great pleasures was joining fellow Dunkirk veterans at the annual gathering of the 'Dunkirk Little Ships' as part of the Henley-on-Thames Traditional Boat Rally. Raymond Baxter, the famous Second World War fighter pilot and broadcaster, was the Honorary Admiral and he used to invite me onto his boat, *L'Orage*, where we enjoyed a glass of wine and a lot of laughter. It was through Raymond that I met Bill Mundy, the renowned miniature portrait artist, who said he would like to paint my picture. Anne took me to his riverside studio and some time later he invited us to London to an exhibition of miniatures where he had a display of his work, including the one of me. In 2004 Bill entered the miniature in The Miniature Art Society of Florida annual show. He and I were delighted that it won an award. We became good friends and he would visit me regularly.

Someone else who painted my picture was Jack Russell, the former England Test cricketer, who had become a respected artist. He brought his easel and paints to my house at Watlington and we spent an enjoyable day together.

Each year around Remembrance Day I helped my Royal British Legion friends sell poppies to raise funds for serving and ex-serving members of the armed forces and their dependents. We would also visit the local schools and talk to the children about our war experiences and the importance of remembering those who had sacrificed their lives for their country. On Remembrance Sunday we would march down Watlington High Street for a service at the War Memorial after which we would go to a nearby pub for lunch where we swapped stories and sang a few songs.

I was again delighted to attend the Christmas party at St James's Palace organised by the 'Not Forgotten' Association and where I met the Duke of Gloucester. Each year, just before Christmas, Icknield Community College give a tea party for all senior citizens in the surrounding area, arranging coaches for those who can't get there on their own. The children provide the entertainment, finishing with a sing-a-long for everyone.

In April 2003, I attended the final gathering of World War One Veterans held at the National Archives, Kew, Surrey. About eight of us attended and we met Prince Charles who spent some time chatting with each veteran. There were a number of children there who interviewed us and the event was broadcast via computers to schools around the country. Press and TV were also there to record this historic moment.

Later that month Anne and Michael took me to Blackpool for the HMS *Newfoundland* reunion which was, as usual, a happy occasion including a trip to Lake Windermere for a two-hour boat cruise. On our way home from Lancashire I was so pleased that we were able to visit relations in Yorkshire whom we had not seen for many years.

The following month we went to the village of Boldre, near Lymington, for the HMS *Hood* annual service of commemoration. The widow of Vice Admiral Holland, who was lost when the ship was sunk, established the '*Hood* Commemoration' at St John the Baptist church as a memorial to all those who died.

I met up with my friend Ivy Bowers who was two months younger than me and who had lost her 18-year-old son on the ship. A week later I was taken to the *Hood* reunion at Portsmouth where I was honoured to take the salute at the Sunday church parade.

In recent years I have been surprised at the increasing interest in the First World War and particularly, by the media, in those veterans who still survive. As a result, a few of us have been asked to participate in various acts of remembrance at the Cenotaph in Whitehall. On 1 July I was proud to be asked to lay a wreath there on behalf of The War Memorials Trust commemorating the start of the Battle of the Somme. In the past this honour had been carried out by the First World War veteran Fred Bunday, but, sadly, he had died the previous year. I had to inspect a guard of honour before joining the group of people at the Cenotaph. The police stopped the traffic, I laid a laurel wreath, supported by Winston S. Churchill, grandson of the wartime leader, and 'The Last Post' was sounded. Afterwards we were entertained to lunch in the office of Lord Cope at the House of Lords.

Later that month Anne and Michael took me again to the 'Not Forgotten' Association garden party at Buckingham Palace, attended by Her Majesty The Queen and His Royal Highness Prince Philip. As usual there was a special table for First World War veterans and each of us was thrilled to be able to chat to the royal couple.

I had a quieter 103rd birthday celebration with a lunch at a nearby pub for about 20 family and local friends. Michael presented me with a video, which he had obtained from the Imperial War Museum, of a black and white film taken during the Empire Cruise in 1923 when I was serving in HMS *Hood*. Sydney Harbour looked like a fishing port compared to how it is today!

I had a real thrill when I was asked to join fellow veterans Henry Allingham and Norman Robinson in participating in the Remembrance Sunday parade at the Cenotaph in November 2003. We led the parade in a 1911 open-top Austin tourer, which had never happened before. The crowds on either side cheered and clapped. It was a very moving experience especially when we passed the Cenotaph. However, while we three travelled in style, Anne and Michael and the other veterans' helpers had to walk behind the car. Officially they were there to be on hand if we needed help but actually I think their job really was to push if the car stalled! After the event we all went to a hotel for a delicious lunch and then gathered around a piano for a good old sing-song.

Henry Allingham, Fred Lloyd and I once more enjoyed the hospitality of the 'Not Forgotten' Association at their St James's Palace Christmas party and had the pleasure of meeting Princess Anne yet again before being entertained with a concert.

In early 2004, I had a fall and cut my head. My doctor said, 'William, you need something better than your walking stick as a support when you are out.' So I acquired a three-wheeled walker which I named HMS *Neversink*!

In June I met up with Henry Allingham and Fred Lloyd once again, this time at the town hall in Eastbourne where we were presented with the new lapel 'Veteran Badges' by the present Lord Kitchener. This badge was to be available to all who served in HM Armed Forces. The Lady Mayor hosted a reception and we were interviewed and photographed by press and television.

Once again I laid a wreath on behalf of the War Memorials Trust at the Cenotaph on 1 July commemorating those lost in the Battle of the Somme. This time I was accompanied by Winston S. Churchill and Sara Jones – widow of Colonel 'H' Jones, who won a VC during the Falklands conflict. As previously we had lunch at the House of Lords, after which Anne, Michael and I went into the Chamber of the House and listened to a debate, which I found fascinating, before setting off for home.

In 2004, 4 August was always going to be a special day for First World War veterans as it marked the 90th anniversary of the start of the First World War. In the days running up to this date there was a lot of media interest and I was interviewed at home by ITV, the BBC and the general media. On the morning of 4 August I was up at 5 a.m. and by 7.30 a.m. I had done a live interview on radio, singing 'All the Nice Girls Love a Sailor'. Later that morning, Michael and Anne drove me to the Foreign and Commonwealth Office in Whitehall where I met up with three other veterans, Henry Allingham, Norman Robinson and John Oborne, as we were to lay wreaths at the Cenotaph commemorating the event.

Each of the veterans had an escort selected from the armed services. Mine was serving CPO Richard Blake from HMS *Gloucester*. At the appointed time we were led out into Whitehall, where there were crowds of spectators, and we lined up facing the Cenotaph. I already knew that I was to deliver the exhortation once the wreaths had been laid, and I had practised the words. However at the last minute I was also asked to read the poem *In Flanders Fields*. Fortunately, I had recently had a cataract removed from my eye so I was able to do it without any problem.

The poem In Flanders Fields *was written by a Canadian doctor, Lt Colonel John McCrae, in April 1915. He had just seen thousands of young men slaughtered in the Second Battle of Ypres in a bombardment that lasted for days and included the use of poison gas. Among the dead was a close friend. It was in memory of his friend that this poem was written, on a scrap of paper and using a fellow officer's back as a pad.*

Apparently, McCrae was so unhappy with the verse that he ripped it from his notebook and threw it away. It was rescued by a fellow officer and eventually published in Punch *magazine in December 1915, to great acclaim.*

One of its later readers was poet Moina Michael, who in 1918 was American War Secretary of the YMCA (Young Men's Christian Association). She suggested that American ex-servicemen adopted the poppy as their emblem. Later the British Legion began to sell artificial poppies to raise funds for disabled ex-servicemen. The first poppy day was held on 11 November 1921.

As for McCrae, he was emotionally scarred by his time at the Western Front. Although he continued to serve as an army doctor he appeared to his friends diminished by the constant exposure to death and grievous injury. Poised to take a job with the British Army he fell ill with pneumonia and meningitis and died in January 1918.

> In Flanders fields the poppies blow
> Between the crosses, row on row,
> That mark our place; and in the sky
> The larks, still bravely singing, fly
> Scarce heard amid the guns below.
> We are the dead. Short days ago
> We lived, felt dawn, saw sunset glow,
> Loved, and were loved, and now we lie
> In Flanders fields.
> Take up our quarrel with the foe:
> To you from failing hands we throw
> The torch; be yours to hold it high.
> If ye break faith with us who die
> We shall not sleep, though poppies grow
> In Flanders fields.

After the ceremony we were all entertained to a splendid lunch at the Ministry of Defence. It was here that I was asked when I was last on board a warship. When I replied that it was some 60 years previously my escort replied mysteriously, 'We will have to see if something can be arranged'. What I didn't know at the time was that

Michael had quietly mentioned to him that it would be my 104th birthday the following month.

It was a bombshell, therefore, on my birthday when Anne and Michael announced they were taking me to Portsmouth and even more of a surprise when I was piped aboard HMS *Gloucester* to be greeted by the captain, Commander Cree. We celebrated with champagne on the bridge, where I discovered that one of the lieutenants on board used to be my paperboy in Watlington. I was given a tour of the ship where I saw to my astonishment how the captain now takes control of action stations below decks, assisted by banks of computers, and I was amused to discover they no longer have boiler rooms these days. We were entertained to lunch in the Commander's cabin where I commented, 'You don't have rum tots on board any more, do you?' He replied that he had a special store and asked if I wanted to splice the mainbrace. I declared, 'No thank you, sir.' But I did. It was a great day, one of the best in my civilian life.

The day before Remembrance Sunday I sat outside our local post office for two hours in the morning selling poppies. In the afternoon Anne and Michael drove me to London to meet up with Henry Allingham. That evening we all attended the Royal British Legion Festival of Remembrance at the Royal Albert Hall. I had always watched this on television so it was wonderful to be there. And before the performance started, Henry and I were introduced to HM The Queen, Prince Philip and Prince Charles. Huw Edwards, the compere from the BBC, talked about the First World War and introduced Henry and myself as Dennis Goodwin and Anne wheeled us onto the stage to much applause. It was an extraordinary evening, and one which I always remember. In spite of a very late night, I was at church next morning and took part in our local Remembrance parade.

In December, my granddaughter, Susie, was married in New York State to her American fiancé, Seth. I wanted to attend but I realised the journey would have been too much for me. Of course Anne and Michael were there and able to video it all for me. Although they were away, I was still able to go to the Christmas Party at St James's Palace due to the kindness of Graham Stark, who helped with the First World War veterans. I met Prince Charles again and I remember the lovely Tiller Girls making a great fuss of me.

When Anne and Michael took me to church on Christmas morning, to my complete amazement, I found Susie and husband Seth waiting there. They had returned from their honeymoon in Jamaica and flown over for Christmas. We were joined by grandson Christopher and his fiancée, Seena. So it was a lovely family gathering.

In January 2005 I was astonished to be told I had been voted *Personality of the Year 2004* by viewers of ITV Central South! We drove to their Birmingham studios for a wonderful reception and awards ceremony.

On a glorious sunny Easter Saturday Christopher and Seena were married and held their reception in a lovely old barn at the village of Bentley near Farnham. It was a very happy day and I enjoyed meeting all their young friends and Seena's family.

Through a shipmate at the HMS *Hood* Association, I was invited to be guest of honour at the HMS *Cossack* Association reunion in Eastbourne in April. Although I had never served in the ship I was made very welcome. Following my speech, I entertained them with a few of my signature tunes. I discovered that their President, Admiral Sir James Eberle, a great character, had lived in Devon and knew many of my farming friends there. The following day, after the church parade, I was honoured to join the Admiral in taking the salute at the march past on the seafront.

In May it was both the 'Newfie' and *Hood* reunions, which I enjoyed as usual. At the 2005 *Hood* reunion I met Heinrich Kuhnt, who was serving on the *Bismarck* when she sank the *Hood* in 1941. When *Bismarck* was eventually sunk by the Royal Navy, Heinrich was one of 115 survivors fortunate to be picked up and he became a POW in England and Canada for the rest of the war. We agreed it had been a terrible waste of young lives on both sides. He sent me several miniature bottles of schnapps for my 105th birthday. The President of the Association at the time was Ted Briggs, who was one of three crewmen who escaped alive. The other two had since died. Ted became a great friend. He always used to ask me how I kept so bloody young!

It was quickly followed by a very special celebration at Portsmouth in June. That year was the 200th anniversary of the Battle of Trafalgar and it was to be marked by an international fleet review, *Son et Lumière* and Drumhead Ceremony. Myself, my daughter and my son-in-law were invited as guests of the Royal Navy to attend the event spread over several days. There were also many other veterans from different conflicts including George Cross and Victoria Cross holders. More than 100 warships from 35 nations were moored in the Solent ready to be reviewed by Her Majesty The Queen. We were lucky enough to spend the day on a boat sailing around the entire fleet. What a magnificent sight they were.

The following day, I took part in the Drumhead Ceremony at Southsea attended by Prince Andrew, Prince Michael and all the senior officers of the assembled fleet. I was interviewed by Kate Adie on the centre stage, and at the reception afterwards. I was delighted to meet up with Prince Andrew again and share a joke, something I was to repeat the following month when we met once more at the 'Not Forgotten' Association garden party at Buckingham Palace. Also participating in the ceremony was a group of children that I knew from my visits to the Icknield Community College in Watlington.

A number of warships were open to the public at Portsmouth dockyard and I went on board one of them, HMS *Nottingham*, where I was invited into the Chiefs' Mess. It looked very different to my days in the Navy. It had been a wonderful few days bringing back many memories of my time at sea.

Later in October we attended a service at St Paul's Cathedral commemorating the Battle of Trafalgar. We had marvellous seats, right at the front and adjacent to where Prince Philip, Prince Charles and many other members of the Royal Family were sitting. After the service we enjoyed a reception at The Guildhall.

This year also saw the 60th anniversary of the end of the Second World War and there were many services and parades around the country to mark the event. I was greatly honoured to be invited in July by the Lord Lieutenant of Oxfordshire, Hugo Brunner, to join him in taking the salute at the parade following a service in Christ Church Cathedral, Oxford. The following month, I took the salute at a similar parade at Reading.

It was another milestone in my life when I reached my 105th birthday. My family had arranged a splendid birthday party in the local Memorial

Hall and had invited about 100 guests. Amongst them were my many friends and neighbours who do so much to help me. There were also council representatives, church members and in a surprise visit my granddaughter and her husband flew in from America. After tea I led the singing of old time songs. I had a huge number of wonderful cards and of course the very special one from the Queen.

The Western Front Association had been approached by South East Trains to name one of their trains *Remembrance*. I was bowled over to be asked by Bruce Simpson, National Chairman of the WFA, to unveil the nameplate at Victoria Station. There was a good crowd assembled on the day and, after the unveiling ceremony, a bugler sounded 'The 'Last Post' and there was a two-minute silence to remember railwaymen who gave their lives for their country.

It was soon Christmas again and time to enjoy the usual round of parties – the local school, my lunch club, Masonic, Western Front, Dunkirk Veterans and of course St James's Palace where I met and chatted with Princess Anne once more. I appreciate how lucky I am to have so many good friends, as well as my family, to help me get to these and other occasions.

Early in 2006 I had wonderful news. My grandson Christopher and his wife Seena had presented me with my first great-granddaughter, Sophie. Shortly after I learned that Susie and Seth in America would be giving me my second great-grandchild later in the same year.

During March, while Anne and Michael were on holiday in China, I experienced severe pain in my shoulder and the doctor was also concerned about my heart. I was admitted to hospital for a week where I was thoroughly tested and my heart was pronounced fine but I did have a 'frozen shoulder', something I had never heard of before. Luckily my grandson, warden Beryl and the neighbours all rallied round to help me. For the first time in my life I found myself sufficiently incapacitated to need help even to wash and dress. Unfortunately I then contracted a bad chest infection which lasted some time and sadly prevented me attending the next HMS *Newfoundland* reunion.

By the end of May, though, I was fit enough to be taken to the HMS *Hood* reunion at Portsmouth. Much to my amusement, we were accompanied by a film crew who were making a documentary about the lives of surviving First World War veterans. We had a wonderful evening with old friends but, unfortunately, the Sunday parade had to be cancelled because of the pouring rain. However, I still got to sing 'All the Nice Girls', and 'Abide With Me' at the church service as usual.

The following weekend we were back in Hampshire attending the *Hood* commemoration service at Boldre. Here I met Dorothy Wright whose uncle, George Dimond, I remembered was a stoker with me on the ship back in 1923.

A few days later I was on board HMS *Belfast*, moored near Tower Bridge, on the River Thames, for the 'Ghosts of Jutland' exhibition, opened by the Duchess of Gloucester and commemorating the 90th anniversary of that battle. My friend Henry Allingham, as the last survivor, was guest of honour.

The government announced that 27 June would become the annual 'Veterans Day'. I attended a reception and exhibition in the grounds of the Imperial War Museum after which we went on to Ten Downing Street for another reception for veterans where I chatted with the then Prime Minister, Tony Blair, his wife Cherie, the Deputy Prime Minister John Prescott, and Chancellor (now Prime Minister) Gordon Brown. At one point six-year-old Leo Blair came in and I sang my favourite song to him.

July was one of the hottest months on record. I had laid a wreath on behalf of War Memorials Trust at the Cenotaph for victims of the Somme and later in the month went to Buckingham Palace for the 'Not Forgotten' Association garden party where the temperature that day reached 95 degrees. Henry Allingham and I shared a table and Rear Admiral Tim Laurence – Princess Anne's husband – came and chatted with us, as did a number of celebrities. We enjoyed a cream tea and listening to the band.

I was always pleased to return to my beloved Devon and so I was thrilled when I discovered that this year I was to celebrate my 106th birthday there. Anne and Michael had arranged a lunch party in Kingsbridge for about 30 family and very old friends. Among the guests were two of my nieces, one of whom was nearly ninety-four.

On Sunday we attended the church at Buckland Tout Saints where I was married in 1938 and the congregation sang 'Happy Birthday' to me. During five very happy days spent in Devon, we visited many friends and all my old haunts.

Shortly after returning home, I learned with sadness that my friend, Raymond Baxter, had died and I went to his funeral in the lovely old church at Ewelme, near Henley-on-Thames. Being such a well-known personality, it wasn't surprising that the church, beautifully decorated for Harvest Festival, was full.

Over the years, I have become accustomed to visits by television and film crews, but I was particularly surprised and pleased to be filmed in early October for one of my favourite programmes, *Songs of Praise*, to be shown on Remembrance Sunday in November.

For some time I knew that I was becoming increasingly unsteady on my feet and I now had carers on a daily basis to help me. I wanted to stay in my own home and be independent for as long as I could. However, in mid-October my world changed. I had been to church as usual, returned home and prepared my lunch, put it on the table, turned round and without warning fell down. Fortunately, I had my alarm pendant around my neck so I was able to summon help and was soon in hospital where a broken hip was diagnosed.

Anne writes, 'After I got the call to say William had had a fall I drove to Watlington where I found him already in the ambulance about to depart. I picked up some belongings from his home and followed to the John Radcliffe Hospital in Oxford where he had already been X-rayed showing that the hip was broken. The following morning he was operated on to repair the break and we were able to visit him later in the day. We continued to visit him daily but often found him confused, probably due to the effects of the anaesthetic and painkillers on a 106-year-old man. At some point he was moved to a room on his own as he had been distressed and shouting out, appearing to think he was back at Dunkirk – something which never seemed to have worried him before.

'After about a week we received the good news that our daughter, Susie, in America, had given birth to a baby girl, Annabel, William's second great-granddaughter. He was delighted and it helped cheer him up. Two days later,

Michael and I attended the funeral of Michael's 98-year-old stepmother who had died a few days earlier. However, almost immediately we had some shocking news from America. It was discovered that baby Annabel had a life-threatening heart condition which required urgent surgery.'

When Anne gave me the devastating news about Annabel, I was very upset. Michael was able to make a short video recording of me sending a message to Susie and, of course, Annabel. I told Susie to be strong and said that I was asking God to take care of Annabel.

'Annabel's story as a fighter and a survivor is as remarkable as William's,' agrees Susie.

'She was born at St Peter's Hospital in Albany on 24 October 2006 and initially appeared healthy. But three days after delivery tests detected a heart murmur. After further screening we learned the devastating news that our tiny, 6 lb daughter had a life-threatening congenital heart defect called "Hypoplastic Left Heart Syndrome".

'The condition would require immediate stabilisation at Albany Medical Centre Neonatal Intensive Care Unit and the first in a series of three open-heart surgeries.

'Hypoplastic Left Heart Syndrome (HLHS) means the left side of the heart is chronically underdeveloped. As a result it is unable to maintain blood circulation and its workload falls on the right side. Eventually that will lead to heart failure. Surgical intervention is the only option for survival, with either three open-heart operations or a heart transplant. Recent advances in surgical technique have hiked the survival rates of three-stage surgery to more than 90 per cent.

'In the hours after Annabel's diagnosis we placed numerous urgent phone calls seeking advice to determine where Annabel should undergo surgery and who should perform the procedures.

'We fully expected Annabel to be transferred to Boston Children's Hospital or the Children's Hospital of Philadelphia. But up and down the east coast medical directors agreed that the cardiothoracic paediatric surgeon at Albany, Dr Neil Devejian, was one of the best in the field. It was a tangible relief to realise we could remain close to home and the support of family and friends throughout the uncertain weeks ahead.

'Annabel underwent the first-stage operation at just seven days old. The procedure involves rebuilding the underdeveloped narrow aorta – Annabel's was just 2 mm in diameter – and inserting an artificial shunt to maintain blood flow to the lungs. After eight hours in surgery and almost three hours more for post-operative stabilisation we had the surreal experience of visiting Annabel in a paediatric intensive care unit managed by a nursing staff dressed entirely in Hallowe'en costume. Snow White, one of the Blues Brothers and Mrs Claus were each on hand to advise us about Annabel's status and prepare us for the intensity of her post op appearance.

'We stayed on site for three weeks in a windowless room near to the PICU, initially permitted to visit Annabel for just five minutes at a time. Over the next few days they lessened her sedation and she grew stronger, showing her fighting spirit from the start.

'The first month of Annabel's life was a blur. Hours spent on a ward, rarely seeing through windows to know weather or night from day. Annabel surprised the doctors with her feisty spirit, often kicking away her wires and tubes – and proved extremely responsive to her treatment and care. Her surgeon used her as a textbook case study in a surgical presentation and, in time for my parents' arrival from England, we were given the all clear to bring Annabel home before Thanksgiving.

'After the first surgery Annabel needed two further heart catheterisation procedures. The second resulted in emergency open-heart surgery to remove a coarctation – a constricted section of her aorta.

'At just under five months of age and 10 lbs in weight, Annabel was in surgery again for eleven hours. In the following 24 hours Annabel did not present any of the anticipated complications from her diminutive size and she awoke to find the PICU staff all dressed in green for her first St Patrick's Day.'

At the beginning of November, I moved to the Wallingford Community Hospital to continue my recovery. I found walking very difficult and painful and spent a lot of time using a wheelchair. Unfortunately I wasn't allowed to travel by car at this stage so was confined to hospital. However as Remembrance Day approached I was delighted when two of the nurses volunteered to wheel me to the local church and War Memorial, where I was made welcome by the congregation. In the afternoon I was interviewed by local television and then watched the *Songs of Praise* programme for which I had been filmed at my home back in early October.

All the staff at the hospital made a great fuss of me and were very kind. They stuck the many 'get well' cards I had received all over the walls of my bedroom. Of course, I also had visits from my family and friends to cheer me up. Anne and Michael went to America for the last two weeks of November to visit Susie and family and especially to see their new granddaughter, Annabel. Whilst they were away a nurse took me back to my home at Watlington to assess whether I would be able to return once my hip was healed. With sadness I realised that I was not going to be able to cope on my own again.

Anne writes, 'Even before William's assessment, we had come to this conclusion and we had already started to look for suitable care homes. On our return from America this became a priority as the hospital now confirmed he was ready for discharge. After many weeks of searching we were lucky to find a space for William at Lord Harris Court Masonic care home, near Wokingham. It was not an area William knew but in the past he had expressed a wish to live in a Masonic home should the need arise. William was able to enjoy Christmas in the hospital, especially joining in with a visiting choir, but eventually on 1 February 2007, we moved him to Lord Harris Court.'

It took me a while to settle into Lord Harris Court. The care home was large – I was told there were about 90 residents. I had a comfortable ground-floor room overlooking the circular drive which leads up to the entrance, so I had a good view of everyone coming and going. Michael soon brought many pictures from my old home and hung them in my room. They were a wonderful reminder of past events and caused great interest amongst staff and visitors. There were four lovely lounges, one of which was often used for activities and entertainment. I especially enjoyed those occasions when we had sing-a-longs or concerts where I would often give the residents a rendition of my favourite songs. It was good to have so many friendly people around me, especially the kind and caring staff.

There was a chapel within the building, which I started attending each Sunday. My voice was still strong and, of course, I knew most hymns off by heart so the Chaplain would have me sitting near the front and referred to me as his 'choir'. Anne and Michael would visit regularly and often old friends would call in. I also enjoyed seeing my great-granddaughter, Sophie, when she came with her parents. She was a very lively little girl and always running around much to everyone's amusement. If the weather was fine the family would often wheel me around the lovely gardens which gave me much pleasure.

Although I was now in a care home I was still able to attend special occasions, the first of which was to return to Watlington for a Royal British Legion lunch party celebrating the 80th anniversary of the branch. It was good to meet up with old friends.

My first big outing was to the HMS *Hood* Association reunion at Portsmouth where I met up with old shipmates and enjoyed their company at the gala dinner. Sadly, yet again, Sunday parade was rained off but in spite of this I enjoyed the church service as usual.

In June I had a wonderful surprise when Susie, Seth and my new great-granddaughter, Annabel, suddenly arrived in my room from America. This was just a few months after Annabel's second open-heart surgery and as soon as they had been given the 'green light' to travel they had flown over to see us all. A few days later, at Anne and Michael's home, we had a family gathering where for the first time I was able to enjoy the company of my two great-granddaughters together.

July was a busy month. First was a visit to the Ministry of Defence in London where Henry Allingham and I met the heads of the Armed Forces, together with the Minister for Veterans. After a light lunch there we were taken to Buckingham Palace for the Queen's Garden Party before which we were introduced to Prince Charles and Camilla, the Duke of Kent, Princess Alexandra, Prince Edward and his wife Sophie and then the Queen and Prince Philip. Less than a week later we were back at Buckingham Palace for the 'Not Forgotten' Association garden party where we met the Duke and Duchess of Gloucester. The Duchess, as Patron of the World War One Veterans Association, kindly came and sat with Henry and me for some photographs.

Also in July I went to Henley-on-Thames for the annual gathering of the Dunkirk 'Little Ships'. It was a lovely sunny day but it was following a time of heavy rain and floods and the River Thames was very swollen. I met up with veterans and hoped to watch the sail past of the boats but suddenly a broadcast warned that a river surge was imminent and the area in which we were gathered was shortly expected to flood. So the day was cut short and I understand that the boats were not allowed to move from their moorings for nearly a week.

At the end of August it was a pleasure to have fellow veterans, Henry Allingham and Harry Patch, come for the day to my care home. The home had organised for us to have lunch together in a private room where we enjoyed each other's company over a glass of wine.

For my 107th birthday the care home had organised a lovely party and a pianist to provide musical entertainment. The residents and I, together with my family and some local friends, thoroughly enjoyed an afternoon of old time songs followed by birthday cake and a glass of 'bubbly'.

I spent another enjoyable afternoon at the Phyllis Court Club in Henley listening to a music concert arranged by the 'Not Forgotten' Association. Shortly afterwards I returned to Watlington on Remembrance Sunday for the Royal British Legion service at the town war memorial. It was lovely to be remembered by so many local people whom I had not seen since I left the town.

This year, en route to the 'Not Forgotten' Christmas party at St James's Palace, the Royal Hospital Chelsea kindly allowed us to break our journey there. I met and chatted to a number of the pensioners who were a lively bunch and if I had been an Army man I am sure I would have loved to live there. Later at the party I met up with some of them again.

Within a few days I was back at Watlington for another Christmas party with my friends at the local Icknield Community College before enjoying all the usual festivities at Lord Harris Court.

By now I had become used to receiving constant requests for my autograph, not just in this country but also from around the world. However, in early 2008 I was bemused to be asked to sign a fuel tank from an American Army Harley Davidson motorcycle. It had taken part in the Normandy landings and continued all the way to Berlin. Its English owner was a Second World War enthusiast and had already obtained the signatures of Vera Lynn and the nephew of Glenn Miller. So he brought it to my care home and I duly signed it. As I knew that my friends Henry Allingham and Harry Patch were to visit me for lunch again the following week we kept the tank and they also signed it, much to the owner's delight. During that day we talked about the forthcoming 90th anniversary of the end of the First World War and the suggestion that we three veterans should take part in a remembrance service. We agreed this would be a good idea and hoped we would all be fit enough to attend.

In April I was overjoyed that my granddaughter and family came on holiday from America again. They made several visits to see me together with my grandson and his family. It was wonderful to see my two great-granddaughters, Sophie and Annabel.

On a sunny day in June I was honoured to be visited by a group of Masonic friends led by the Provincial Grand Master of Oxfordshire and at a small ceremony, attended by the residents, I was presented with a certificate in recognition of my 75 years' service to Freemasonry. We had a lovely cake and a celebration drink.

I was pleased to be able to go to the 'Not Forgotten' Association garden party at Buckingham Palace in July but was sorry that this time my friend Henry Allingham was unwell and not able to join me. Nevertheless, I had an enjoyable afternoon, meeting many old friends, and was pleased to chat with Princess Anne's husband, Vice Admiral Tim Laurence.

Anne writes: 'During this year William had a number of falls and suffered an increasing number of chest infections which, from time to time, gave us cause for concern. But on each occasion, after a course of medication, he managed to recover. However at the beginning of September these infections became more serious and required hospitalisation. There was some doubt that this time he would recover, but once more he confounded everyone by rallying and eventually we were able to return him to his care home just a few days before his 108th birthday. He had been very much looking forward to this occasion and there was already mounting media interest.'

What a wonderful day I had. All the residents and carers were wishing me 'Happy Birthday' and showing me my picture in the newspapers. I had received a huge pile of cards including, of course, the very special one from the Queen. After lunch, as Anne and Michael wheeled me into the lounge, I was greeted by a crowd of family, friends and residents and television and press cameras. With much hilarity all round, I was interviewed and photographed before spending the afternoon in my favourite way – leading a sing-a-long of old time tunes. Sometimes I didn't sing the words they expected. 'Daisy, Daisy' was one of my favourites.

> Daisy, Daisy, give me your answer do,
> I'm half crazy
> All for the love of you.
> It won't be a stylish marriage
> For I can't afford a carriage,
> But you'll look sweet
> Between the sheets,
> Of a feather bed made for two!

Then something very special happened. I was taken to the nearby Masonic centre where over 450 brethren stood and welcomed me and sang 'Happy Birthday'. It was a wonderful end to my birthday.

Not long afterwards I was saddened to hear that my friend Ted Briggs from the *Hood* Association had died. I was pleased that I was able to attend his funeral, held in the chapel on the shore base, HMS *Collingwood*, Fareham, to pay my respects along with my colleagues from the HMS *Hood* Association.

As Remembrance Day approached, which I knew was to be a special occasion commemorating the 90th anniversary of the end of the First World War, I learned that we three remaining veterans would be taking part in a ceremony at the Cenotaph. As part of the plans for coverage of the event I was interviewed by television and press including Simon Weston, the well-known veteran of the Falklands campaign, whose presence in the care home caused quite a stir as everyone wanted to talk to him.

As we needed to be in London early, it was decided that we should travel up beforehand and stay overnight. It poured with rain throughout the journey and I wondered how on earth we would manage at the ceremony. Thankfully it was a clear sunny morning, although cold. After breakfast Anne and Michael took me to meet up with Henry Allingham, now 112, Harry Patch, 110, and our Service helpers. In my case Leading Writer Jon Ryder of the Royal Navy was to push my wheelchair and Marine Mkhuseli Jones, MC, would lay my wreath. We assembled and waited in the MOD building. We three veterans, now all in wheelchairs and united by great age, were all very different people with contrasting experiences behind us, a far cry from the young men that we were when the guns fell silent at the end of the First World War.

The music for the service was being played by bands from the Royal Marines, the RAF and the Grenadier Guards. The London Welsh choir was singing and my heart lifted when they played 'It's a Long Way to Tipperary', 'If You Were the Only Girl in the World' and 'Pack Up Your Troubles'. These were all songs I've sung countless times down the years and to hear them again brought back so many memories.

The first hymn was 'Eternal Father', one of my favourites and close to every Navy man's heart. Then, as 11 a.m. approached – led by WO1 Pipe Major N. Hall, from the Royal Regiment of Scotland and carrying our wreaths – we were wheeled into Whitehall to much applause from the crowds of people and the massed ranks of the Armed Services gathered there. We moved to our places facing the Cenotaph where the Prime Minister, Gordon Brown, Duchess of Gloucester and other VIPs were already waiting nearby. I had to screw up my eyes against the glare of the low-lying winter sun.

Already the Cenotaph was surrounded with poppies and wreaths. We were there to mark the anniversary of the ceasefire on Armistice Day but the Queen and other members of the Royal Family had paid their respects on Remembrance Sunday, a few days previously.

Marine Mkhuseli Jones took my wreath and placed it at the foot of the Cenotaph on my behalf. When he came back to my side he briefly rested his hand on my shoulder. It was an almost overwhelming moment for me and I really appreciated that gesture. He and I both knew it wasn't just about the men who died in the First World War but all those who had perished since. Then Harry and Henry's wreaths were laid on their behalf.

Marine Mkhuseli Jones was awarded the Military Cross after being under fire in Afghanistan on numerous occasions during a six-month stint. Once he was on foot patrol when he and his comrades were attacked.

'I was at the flank of the patrol and immediately identified the attacking position and took it out,' he said. 'Nobody else spotted the position so I opened fire while my colleagues got to cover. I was completely focussed. At the end of the day it is what I am trained to do.'

In another incident he and his patrol were ambushed from the front and rear but in fire-fights lasting 20 minutes the Marines would better them each time. South African-born Mkhuseli – known to his friends as 'Cousie' – had been a Royal Marines Commando for three years when he received the MC from the Queen. The MC is awarded in recognition of distinguished and meritorious service in battle.

A keen rugby player, he now lives in Wales. After accompanying William at the Cenotaph he said, 'It was a truly amazing and moving moment for me – something I will never forget.'

As Big Ben struck the 11th hour, Royal Marine buglers sounded 'The Last Post' and a two-minute silence was observed. I was tucked beneath a tartan blanket and wrapped in a warm coat, but even without them I doubt I would have felt the chilly breeze that was making the Standards flutter. I looked down at the red poppies and then up at the pale blue winter sky and could hardly believe that I was still here, representing all my comrades who'd gone before.

Following reveille, I was delighted to join in the singing of the final hymn, 'The Day Thou Gavest', another of my favourites. I knew the words well. Prayers and the National Anthem ended a very moving service and another incredible episode of my life.

After the ceremony, we were pushed past the crowds and into Downing Street – Gordon Brown chatting to me along the way. Inside that famous address we met numerous politicians, senior officers of the armed services and, of course, television and press. We veterans were the centre of attention and happily chatted with them all. I even sang to Haydn James, director of the London Welsh choir, who promptly invited me to choir practice!

On the way home I was surprised when we stopped at Tate Britain art gallery where three photographs of Henry, Harry and I were being exhibited. The MOD had commissioned Don McCullin, the famous war photographer, to take these pictures of the veterans to commemorate the day.

I finally arrived back at my care home tired, but thrilled to have taken part in a unique and marvellous occasion.

The focus of Armistice Day is usually a local war memorial. The war claimed so many lives and few of the victims were returned to Britain for burial. Thousands of families devastated by the effects of the war had no grave to visit and no place in which to contemplate their loss. As a consequence, villages, towns and cities across Britain began building war memorials, which were communal initiatives paid for by local people and sponsored by councils. Most of the country's 37,000 war memorials were put in place between 1919 and 1922.

Nationally it's the Cenotaph in London that attracts most attention. Initially it was made from wood and plaster and put up in 1919 for the Allied Victory Parade held that year. But its design was so popular that it was reproduced the following year in Portland Stone. Cenotaph is derived from the Greek meaning 'empty tomb'. It is devoid of religious symbolism and adorned only with the words The Glorious Dead. *The Cenotaph was unveiled on the same day as the funeral of the 'Unknown Warrior' in Westminster Abbey.*

The two-minute silence – another hallmark of Armistice Day – was originally the idea of Australian journalist Edward George Honey, who put it forward on the pages of the London Evening News *in the spring of 1919. When he heard about it King George V felt it an ideal way to show respect among the population at large as well as offering a window of reflection for the bereaved. 'All locomotion should cease so that, in perfect stillness, the thoughts of everyone may be concentrated on reverent remembrance of the glorious dead,' he declared. For many years traffic as well as people came to a halt for those two minutes on Remembrance Sunday, the one that falls nearest to Armistice Day itself.*

I feel sure that someone has been taking care of me over all these years. I only have to think back to Dunkirk when, with ships sinking all around me, I said, 'God help us' – and He did. Experiences like that give you faith. Sometimes I can hardly believe that me, a farmer's boy from Devon and now well over a hundred, should have been to so many important events and met such wonderful people. I have been lucky but I have always worked hard, both in the Navy and on Civvy Street and it hasn't done me any harm.

My motto has always been 'Keep going!'

People often ask me to what I attribute my long and healthy life. I tell them – 'Clean living. Contented mind. Trust in God.'

My wife, Lily, taught me a prayer that has also been an important part of my life. 'Lord keep us safe this night, secure from all our fears. May Angels guard us while we sleep till morning light appears.'

Anne writes: 'Over the next few weeks William increasingly suffered periods of chest infection and was not well enough to go to his usual seasonal parties but at Christmas he had recovered sufficiently to enjoy the festivities held in the care home. On Christmas Day we went with him to the chapel service after which we all joined residents and their families for a celebratory drink. Later, when watching the Queen's speech on TV, William was delighted to see it included pictures of the three veterans at the Cenotaph the previous November.

'By early January William was not well again and now seemed unable to shake off a very heavy chest cold. Gradually his condition worsened and gave rise for concern. He was under constant care and attention and we visited and sat with him each day. We tried to encourage him to eat but with little success and for the most part he slept. On the morning of 10 January we were joined by our son Christopher at his bedside. William was sleeping, with a recording of his favourite Royal Marine Band music

playing softly. Around mid-day he slipped away, his life ending very quietly and peacefully as he always hoped it would.

'At 108 we knew 'The Ancient Mariner' couldn't go on forever – although there were times it seemed he might! He had had a truly remarkable life, which he enjoyed to the full. He was always cheerful and smiling, ready to chat and joke with everyone. He had a good voice and loved singing. William loved people and he loved life. He had a strong faith and was a very determined character, which undoubtedly helped sustain him throughout the years. The hundreds of condolence cards, letters and messages we received showed that he was much loved and would be missed, not just by his family, but also by his many friends.

'The three weeks leading up to William's funeral were an intense period of preparation. We were most appreciative of all the assistance and support from the MOD, the Royal Navy Ceremonial Team and the Clergy at St Leonard's church, Watlington. Without them we could not have given William such a fitting send off and celebration of his life.'

15

Testimonials

O ne of the most eloquent testimonials to William has come from the man who knew him best, son-in-law Michael Davidson, who spoke these words as a tribute to William at his funeral.

'William had a truly wonderful life. He was born during Queen Victoria's reign, in quite humble circumstances in the hamlet of Ledstone, near Kingsbridge, Devon.

'His subsequent entry to the Armed Services was hastened by the First World War – although in my own mind I am sure he would have enlisted anyway, since his family had a tradition of sending its sons into the services, in particular the Royal Navy.

'His first days at Devonport were rather inauspicious, since he very quickly succumbed to the flu pandemic sweeping the world. But William survived – unlike millions who didn't. This early sign of a strong constitution was something that would continue to dominate the rest of his life.

'But it was the Royal Navy which did so much to shape and develop William's character to make him the person we all came to know. And, of course, it was the Navy which carried him to so many different parts of the world.

'How exciting it must have been for a young man of 23, who had spent his early years in a quiet farming community, to find himself on the deck

of that icon of the Royal Navy – the Battlecruiser HMS Hood *– inching her way through the Panama Canal whilst leading a squadron of ships as part of an 11-month world cruise!*

'And it was whilst in Hood *that William began to develop an off-duty skill in hair cutting. He must have become quite adept because, later on, he would be called upon to visit other ships whilst in port to cut officers' hair. Amongst his "customers" were Admiral Evans – famously known for his exploits as "Evans of the* Broke*" in 1917, and General Franco's brother, Major Franco, who was rescued from the sea by William's ship after his plane had ditched.*

'Hair cutting was obviously quite lucrative, since in 1927, William bought a car whilst stationed at Portland, Dorset, so that he could more easily get home to Devon when he had weekend leave. He seems to have had quite a few weekends off – possibly helped by the fact that more than one officer on board had a home in the West Country and would seek a lift from William!*

'Car ownership was unusual in rural areas in those days – usually limited to the local Squire, Doctor, Vicar etc so William's became a well-known sight as he toured the local pubs with his friends. Its familiarity possibly enhanced by the addition of – what I can best describe as – items of ladies' underwear in the appropriate colours of red and green and fixed each side of the windscreen to signify port and starboard!*

'William always assured me that these were properly purchased from a shop, although he did admit it was in Malta!*

'In 1938 William settled down and married his long-time – and I suspect long-suffering – girlfriend, Lily. And in 1939 their only child, daughter Anne, was born.*

'In 1940, having completed 22 years' service, William should have left the Navy but as World War Two had commenced he had to stay on. He did, however, have the consolation of being able to start drawing his Naval Pension – something he would take much delight in reminding every Admiral he was to meet in later years. As one remarked, "No wonder the Navy's finances are in the state they are today!"*

'By now Chief Stoker on board the minesweeper HMS *Salamander, William was soon thrown into the conflict with the evacuation of troops from Dunkirk.*

'The luck, which had followed William so far in his life was to be severely tested. As William used to recall, whilst other ships around him disappeared, together with their crews, in flame and explosion, Salamander, although damaged from the constant aerial bombardment, survived to make a number of trips taking on board hundreds of soldiers from the beaches.

'William's luck continued whilst serving in the light cruiser HMS Newfoundland, when she was hit by a torpedo during the Sicily landings and he, like the others, was fortunate to survive. For his actions during this time, William was "Mentioned in Dispatches".

'After the war, William settled into civilian life, running his hairdresser's and tobacconist's business in Paignton, Devon. He retired in 1968 to nearby Churston to devote his time to his beloved garden. And there William's story might have gently rolled on to its conclusion.

'Except in 1986, with Lily's health beginning to deteriorate, we persuaded them to move nearer to us at Beaconsfield. Neither of us knew anything about Watlington at the time, but it was near enough to us and had the accommodation we were looking for.

'And what an inspired decision it turned out to be! If you don't know Watlington, it is a small town – almost a village – but as we were to find out, and come to appreciate, it has a tremendous sense of social community.

'William, being William, soon became a familiar figure around the town. He and Lily became regular attendees of this church and at the age of 88 he was persuaded by the Revd Christopher Evans to be confirmed.

'As Lily's health began to fail, we were thankful for the wide circle of friends they had established. Although by now we had become very involved in the running of William and Lily's lives and monitoring their welfare, it would have been so much more difficult without the help of the many friends in and around Watlington. Eventually William became Lily's full time carer – a role I think he quite enjoyed as he was once again in charge! Often, despite her protestations, William would put Lily into her wheelchair and insist on taking her for "a trip round the bay" as he would call it.

'After her death in 1995 William continued to live in his own home. By now he was beginning to be a regular of many organisations and associations, attending local meetings and with us taking him to his reunions around the country. Something else was also beginning to happen. The media and the wider public were waking up to the fact that there was a dwindling group of men who had survived World War One. As a result we suddenly found ourselves, by now in established roles of personal assistant and driver-minder, ferrying William to some extraordinary places and meeting many interesting people – Buckingham Palace garden parties; Christmas parties at St James's Palace; receptions at Ten Downing Street; wreath laying at the Cenotaph; taking part in the Trafalgar 200 celebrations; and even unveiling a train – to name but a few!

'William took to all this like the proverbial duck to water! It only needed a journalist's recorder to appear, or a TV camera to be aimed, and without waiting for the question, he was off! I once calculated that within 90 seconds, he could deliver a brief account of the key points in his life.

'As William approached and passed his century we began to speculate how long he would keep going and so we tried to arrange something rather special for each new birthday. As the years began to pass this became more of a challenge, not helped by the fact that William, when asked after each event if he had enjoyed it, would reply: "Yes, but what are you going to do for next year?"

'It is worth mentioning one birthday in particular. In 2004 William and three other First World War veterans laid wreaths at the Cenotaph commemorating the start of the First World War. His escort was a serving Chief Petty Officer who, later at lunch in the MOD, asked William when he was last on board a warship. He learned that it was 1945. Sensing an opportunity I mentioned to him that William's 104th birthday was due the following month and, thanks to some behind-the-scenes work, William was invited to celebrate his birthday aboard ship.

'And so on 23 September we drove William to Portsmouth where he was piped aboard the destroyer HMS Gloucester, had champagne on the bridge with the Commander and the crew soon had him up and down gangway ladders, with some pushing and pulling, as they took him on a tour of the ship. We finished the day being entertained to lunch in the Commander's quarters where William, of course, was delighted to have a glass of Pusser's rum.

'As we know, William loved the ladies – and as many here will testify, he invariably sought a kiss! Even the royal ladies were not immune to *this approach in spite of firm prior instructions to behave! I have to say they all dealt with his request charmingly. Fortunately they were usually wearing wide-brimmed hats, which gave them the perfect excuse that it was a practical impossibility. He never, however, included Her Majesty The Queen, perhaps realising this would be a step too far! Although, on one occasion when they met she asked him how he was feeling. From experience we knew what the answer would be and sure enough he replied, "With both hands!" I think, judging from her expression, she was just a bit bemused by the reply. But, at 100-plus you can get away with almost anything!*

'But there was another side to William's character which we as close family were probably the only ones to see. He was a very determined person – wanted everything done immediately, preferably yesterday – no doubt all down to his Navy training – and frequently Anne would remind him that (a) he was no longer in the Navy and (b) she certainly wasn't one of his men! However, it was this determination and drive which undoubtedly contributed to his quality of life and longevity.

'There were occasions when we would, in a moment of exasperation, remind him of all the effort and organisation that went into the running of his life. To which he would reply with that mischievous smile he always wore, "But you couldn't be doing it for a nicer person, could you?" And we would have to agree with him.

'William loved children. He was always delighted to meet the children from the local schools in Watlington. And they seemed to warm to him.

'Around the time of the Poppy Appeal, William would accompany his British Legion friends to the schools to talk to the pupils about the war and the importance of remembering the sacrifices made by so many. He would have been especially pleased to see the schools represented here today and the children taking a role in the service.

'He was, of course, delighted when he was presented with two great-grandchildren of his own in recent years. He already knew that this year he would be doubling that number but, sadly, he won't get to see them now.

'In 2006 William finally had to give up his independent living after falling and breaking his hip and we were fortunate to be able to find him a place at Lord Harris Court, the Masonic Care Home at Sindlesham.

William had been a Freemason since 1933 and only last year had been presented with a certificate acknowledging his 75 years of loyal service. He soon settled into life at the home and of course was quickly entertaining his newfound audience with his repertoire of old time songs – some with alternative words! We could not have wished for better care and attention than that which he received there.

'Although his mobility was now much impaired, it didn't stop us taking William to the Cenotaph last Remembrance Day. He was honoured to be able to join with Harry Patch and Henry Allingham in the wreath-laying service to commemorate the 90th anniversary of the First World War Armistice. It was a very moving occasion and, although we didn't know it at the time, it was to be William's last. But what a fitting finale to his life.

'Finally William's luck ran out and on Saturday, 10 January we were sitting with him in his room, together with our son Christopher, when, at about 1 p.m., the story of William's life ended, very quietly and peacefully, as he always hoped it would.

'A couple of days later Anne and I were interviewed on local television and one of the questions we were asked was what were our lasting memories of William. For a moment we were both stumped. My first reaction was where do we start and how long have you got! But I think if I had to find a single word to sum up my memories of William it would have to be "cheerfulness". I don't recall, at least in public, he was ever less than enjoying life to the full and with a constant smile on his face.'

Artist Bill Mundy was in Bill's wide circle of friends. His speciality is painting miniatures and he is known for this all over the world.

'William Stone was 102 years old when I first met him at the Traditional Boat Rally in Henley. With a chest full of medals, many badges wending their way down his lapels, and a beret jauntily perched on his head, William looked no more than 70 years old. I immediately resolved to paint his portrait some time.

'His mind was razor sharp, his hair was plentiful – and darker than mine.

'He came out to pose for me with his daughter, Anne, and I made a nice little miniature of him wearing all his decorations. Later in the year

he came to the RMS Miniature Show in London and asked what would I be doing with the miniature after the exhibition.

'"I'm leaving it to you in my will," I said. In fact I exhibited in America that year where everything has to have a price tag. But I made sure the price was so high that nobody bought it. And when I got back I gave it to him and I know he always loved it.'

Afterwards, artist Bill became a regular visitor, revelling in the company of a man he knew as 'the ancient mariner'.

'When people asked him why he had lived such a long life, he said it was because he'd sold his ticket for the Titanic. *Once I asked him if his teeth were his own. "Yes," he replied. "Really?" I said, delighted that once again he was proving so remarkable and durable. "Yes," he replied, "I know they are mine. I paid for them!"*

'You wouldn't think he was 30 years older than me. I found him such an interesting guy who always had a story to tell. If I ever took a friend to meet him there was surprise at the strength of Bill's handshake. He would squeeze your hand so tightly. He did hand exercises first thing in the morning so, when you shook his hand, you would think it belonged to a man aged 30 or 40. He was such a lively character who loved singing shanties. He was a peaceful man, a gentleman.'

William quickly made an impression on people. Kevin Winter was just one of hundreds of people who wrote to Anne after William's death.

I had the honour and privilege of escorting Bill and yourself, along with Henry Allingham and Charles Henry Walker, to sea on the day of the Trafalgar 200 celebrations.

My abiding memory of that day is of Bill attempting to lead a sing-song whilst we sheltered below decks during a heavy thunderstorm on our trip back up Southampton Water.

To me Bill was the Royal Navy's ambassador. Bill epitomised all that an old 'matelot' should be; full of life, always ready to share a 'dit' and to be at the heart of any sing-song going.

I spent 34 years in the RN before retiring in August 2008 and will always remember the day I spent in your father's company as one of the proudest of my career. I only hope I can live up to the standards set by people like Bill during my post-service life.

Vice Admiral Sir Adrian James Johns KCB, CBE, ADC, is a senior officer in the Royal Navy and was until recently the Second Sea Lord, as well as the Commander-in-Chief of Naval Home Command. In this capacity he had met with, and talked to, William several times at various naval functions. He was keen to pay his own personal tribute.

William Stone was the very epitome of a Royal Navy man. He was cheerful, conscientious and he cared – not just for his family and friends, but for the well-being of fellow sailors and for his ship. He was well-drilled in his duty but when wartime disasters struck it was sheer determination that underpinned his courageous actions.

Born in rural Devon, he represented a special breed of sailor when he joined the Royal Navy in 1918. He was broad-minded, relished the opportunities ahead of him and he wasn't afraid of hard work. A lover of sports, he was a team player in all senses of the word. During the Second World War his personal contribution ensured that many soldiers from Dunkirk and sailors from the Sicily landings lived to fight another day.

William will remain a beacon for every Royal Navy serviceman or veteran as a man who served his country during two world wars. Remarkably, he also claimed his Naval pension for nearly 70 years – a feat we all aspire to but few will attain. Perhaps only William himself could pull off this achievement with such charm and decency.

When William lived in Watlington, before his death he became friendly with a regular visitor of a neighbour. She wrote the following poem based on the stories he told her about his childhood, which was read out at William's memorial service held in St Peter's Church, Buckland Tout Saints, against the distant sound of new lambs bleating from a next-door field.

HAVE YOU HEARD THE CIDER SINGING?

Oh, I spent many years in the Navy
Sailed the seas far and wide in each war
But whenever I'm quietly sitting
I remember my young days on shore.

In September the year nineteen hundred
Busy farmers were harvesting corn
In a cottage in Ledstone in Devon
The tenth child (of fourteen) I was born.

In the Pound House upstairs were our quarters
Down below us: the stable, the sty
And the cider press, poultry and rooster
Whose loud crowing would not let us lie.

Oh we threatened to chop his b***** head off
And to make us a good hearty pie
'Cause at five with his loud 'cock-a-doo-doo'
He would rival the hounds at full cry.

You could hear the pigs grunting and squealing
As their feeding would turn to a brawl
Or the horse's head knock on the ceiling
As he pulled at his hay in the stall.

The back kitchen was where we stored apples
And their ripeness was chosen with skill
Then at last down the chute they would rattle
To the stone crushing trough in the mill.

The old pony was put in the harness
That hung down from the big oaken bar
Hauling round the stone wheel made for crushing
Working steady – he'd have to walk far.

With a big wooden shovel we'd stir it
For no metal should touch acid fruit
You must always be watchful and careful –
Just a shovel or knife could pollute.

He would plod round for hours, that pony
'Til all apples were crushed to a mess
Skins and pips, juicy flesh, all together
Then we'd shovel the pulp in the press.

On a thick mat of reeds went the pummace
And more layers of each 'til 'twas done
Then the heavy board placed as a cover
And the great wooden screw set to run.

The big screw was turned tight and then tighter
'Til the flow of juice came to a stop
And we'd dip from the tub, fill each hogshead
But no bung was yet put in the top.

It would work, it would seethe and would bubble –
Two deep breaths and you'd feel like a king
If you stood with your ear near the hogshead
That was when you could hear cider sing.

We mixed meal with the pummace next morning
Which the pigs gobbled up with delight
And the hens and the rooster came pecking
And would clear ev'ry bit, ev'ry mite.

Four huge hogsheads of cider we'd keep there
Fifty gallons in each – that's a lot
We would draw a big jug every ev'ning
Then we'd stick in a poker, red hot.

We would take a deep draught of that cider
And would savour the drink without haste
This time there was magic in metal
And it changed it, improving the taste.

Tuppence ha'penny a pint was the cider
And 'twas part of the wages back then
Men would come out from town ev'ry evening
To do work and drink cider again.

They would help in the field for the harvest
While a reaper would cut the corn right
Then they'd twist a straw rope round an armful
Really tucked round the sheaf good and tight.

A bit later they got a real binder
That could cut, roll and tie all in one
With some binder twine. Oh, what a marvel
Then the stooking of sheaves was soon done.

We'd be sweating and hot, getting thirsty
And at four we'd be looking to see
When the Missus would come with a basket
Full of cake, lovely buns – and the tea.

Some days later, the corn dried, we'd cart it
To the mowhay and build up a rick
Then we'd thatch it to keep out the weather
And it's better to get it done quick.

In late autumn or winter we'd thresh it
But each night first poked round with a stick
And the rats would run out in a hurry
Which the dogs would kill off good and quick.

Yes a penny a rat farmer'd give me
And I kept up a constant supply
I would bring them round twice to the farmer
And a third time I might even try.

But the farmer put paid to the racket
When I put some up twice, past their prime:
'Oh I've seen these same rats once before, boy.'
And he cut each rat's tail off first time.

Only rats with their tails got the pennies
So I had to get round all of that
And I set up some traps for the catching
But quite often we caught the old cat.

I would also place snares to trap rabbits
In the runs round the fields on the flat
You'd get sixpence a skin (I got fourpence)
Still, much more than I got for a rat.

We 'ad eggs, we 'ad pork, we 'ad rabbits
Carrots, turnips and 'teddies in store
Very 'appy we was. They was good days.
And for food 'ardly knew there was war.

Ev'ry day of my life I've been busy
I was born to be busy you know
Yes my motto is always 'Keep going'
That's the way to avoid feeling low.

Oh ... so many memories ... so many years ... so many ... so many

As I ponder on years that are over –
Navy days and my times spent ashore
I would rather that rooster was crowing
Than be hearing the racket of war.

As I'm looking the rabbits are running
Through the fields of a rich, rippling gold
And so sweetly the cider is singing
In those mem'ries that never grow old.

(Jo Mary Connelly, 2008)

WILLIAM'S SHIPS

HMS TIGER

The *Tiger* that William served on was the 11th Royal Naval ship to bear the name. She was built at Clydebank, launched in 1913 at a cost of £2.5 million and entered the First World War as the most heavily armoured battlecruiser in the Royal Navy.

Tiger found herself at the forefront of the Battle of Dogger Bank in 1915 when Royal Naval ships surprised a German raiding party off the British coast. Although victory belonged to the Royal Navy there were ten sailors killed on *Tiger*.

The following year *Tiger* took part in the Battle of Jutland. Here she was hit by no fewer than fifteen 11 in. German shells and suffered twenty-four dead and forty-six wounded. After some repairs she was passed fit to take part in the 2nd Battle of Heligoland Bight in November 1917, an action designed to pen the German navy in its home ports.

In 1918, just before William joined the ship, it underwent a major refit and its new profile was not altogether admired. In the 1919 edition of *Jane's Fighting Ships* a contributor wrote that *Tiger* had been 'a remarkably handsome ship until the present hideous rig was adopted in 1918'.

After William left *Tiger* it became a sea-going training ship until it was sacrificed as part of the 2nd London Naval Conference of 1930 which sought to further reduce battle fleet size among the leading nations.

Although she stepped into the hole in the Home Fleet left when *Hood* went into dock for a refit she was broken up in the early 1930s.

HMS *HOOD*

Hood was a product of the First World War when bigger was felt to be better. Her keel was laid down in September 1916 at a time when Britain still felt naval superiority was pivotal for victory in warfare. The loss of three battlecruisers at Jutland in the same year meant *Hood's* blueprint was revised to include better protection. Disastrously, plans to further protect the gunnery magazines were rejected.

When she was launched at Clydebank on 22 August 1918 *Hood* was the longest ship ever built by the Royal Navy. The ceremony was conducted by Lady Hood, whose Vice Admiral husband died at Jutland when HMS *Invincible* exploded.

She underwent perpetual modifications before putting to sea as tests revealed the weakness of her armoury. Her cost mounted to more than £6 million. But to those joining the ship she was nothing short of magnificent. Many were veterans of coal burners so *Hood* was not only new but clean. For stokers there was less shovelling, more switching on and off. Moreover, there was a barber's shop, cinema, canteen, bookshop, chapel and a soda bar. Fish and chips were readily available. Every Friday there were Cornish pasties for supper. Never mind that she was a wet ship. Water rushed over her rails and turrets even in moderate seas.

Hood went to Scandinavia in 1920 then began a tradition of spring cruises to Spain and the Mediterranean. In 1922 *Hood* visited Brazil and later the West Indies. The voyage around the Empire's outposts in 1923, which William helped to crew, was nonetheless its most significant engagement to date. Thanks to that, her silhouette became known worldwide as a symbol of Britain's sea power.

In 1925 *Hood* went to Portugal before becoming the lynchpin of the Home and Atlantic Fleets for a decade. She moved to protect British interests during the Spanish Civil War between 1936 and 1939.

And, unsurprisingly, she was the target for one of the early air attacks of the Second World War just weeks after the outbreak of hostilities. *Hood* was later dispatched to put the ships of the French navy out of action after its 1940 capitulation.

Even as hostilities erupted there was a suspicion among some in the Admiralty that *Hood* was outmoded. *Bismarck*, a German battleship, was 20 years younger, had armoury that was in places at least twice as thick as that of *Hood* and was equally fast and powerful although smaller in her overall dimensions.

In May 1941, when *Bismarck* broke out into the Atlantic, the stage was set for a naval clash of epic proportions. *Hood* set out from Scapa Flow to pursue the *Bismarck* in the company of the new battleship HMS *Prince of Wales*, still carrying civilian workers who were giving the battleship its finishing touches. Meanwhile, *Bismarck* was travelling with the cruiser *Prinz Eugen*. None of the ships had the protection of air cover.

Bismarck was hoping to cause havoc among the ships of the Atlantic convoys. For a while the ships skirted one another off the Greenland icepack. Eventually, the opposing forces met in the Denmark Strait, west of Iceland, on 24 May. *Hood* and *Prince of Wales*, travelling in close formation, charged at their quarry. Firing began when they were about 13 miles from *Bismarck*, whose captain Gunther Lutjens was only reluctantly drawn into a duel. He would rather have stuck to his primary purpose, picking off convoy support vessels. If he knew how relatively simple his task with *Hood* would be, he might have embraced it more eagerly.

Hood was turning to achieve a better line of fire when she was hit by characteristically accurate German shelling. Initially there was speculation that a shell fell down *Hood*'s funnel, splitting the ship beneath the waterline. However, it was later thought that an explosion amidships in the 4 in. gun ammunition was the cause of its demise. An ominous plume of smoke belched from the centre of *Hood*. Within moments she headed to the seabed, taking most of her crew with her. There were three survivors who found themselves shivering on life rafts amid oil slicks, unsure how long it would be before rescuers arrived.

For her part, *Bismarck* had suffered damage from two British shells and was compelled to head for France for repairs. A full-scale search by British ships for *Bismarck* was thwarted for two days until Swordfish planes from HMS *Ark Royal* located her. The following day a cluster of British ships turned their gunnery towards *Bismarck* until the mighty ship was wrecked. When German sailors began streaming into the water the British withdrew. HMS *Dorsetshire* was left to fire the killer torpedo. However, it seems likely that before the torpedo was triggered, German sailors opened the stopcocks to ensure the *Bismarck* sank.

HMS CHRYSANTHEMUM

Launched in 1917 *Chrysanthemum* – one of the 'Flower Class' sloops – was immediately sent on convoy duty before joining the Mediterranean fleet. Before his death *Chrysanthemum* would have been a familiar sight to Sir Walter Congreve at the port side in Malta. During the Spanish Civil War she was used to rescue British nationals from Valencia and transferred them to a liner at Barcelona. In 1938 she was docked permanently in the River Thames, initially for use by the Royal Naval Reserve. During the Second World War the ship, still moored, became a Royal Navy boot camp for new recruits. She was finally sold in 1988 and scrapped seven years later.

HMS P40

Built in 1914 she was used for patrolling the coast looking for German submarines and E-boats. During conversion in the early 1920s the torpedo tubes were removed and an underwater dome fitted to the hull containing echo-sounding gear.

The ship was attached to the anti-submarine training school, HMS *Osprey*, at Portland.

HMS EAGLE

Eagle was launched in 1918 although she wasn't converted to an aircraft carrier until 1924. Ultimately, she was capable of carrying 40 aircraft. The ship's motto was 'Soaring to the Sun'. At the outbreak of the Second World War *Eagle* was in Singapore and became involved in the hunt for the German pocket battleship *Admiral Graf Spee*. An internal explosion which killed 13 put the ship out of commission in March 1940 while she was escorting troop transports in the Indian Ocean. As soon as repairs were completed *Eagle* joined the Mediterranean fleet and soon her aircraft were involved in a devastating attack on Italian ships at Tobruk, the start of a successful campaign against Italian shipping that included the attacks on Taranto.

After refitting in the UK she returned to the Mediterranean in 1942, helping to keep the supply lines open for beleaguered Malta. On 11 August 1942, while guarding a convoy bound for Malta, *Eagle* was holed by four torpedoes fired by the German submarine *U–73* and sank in eight minutes. Although 160 men were lost, some nine hundred were saved by two destroyers and a tug, HMS *Jaunty*. *Eagle* sank about 70 nautical miles off the coast of Majorca. For its part, *U–73* was sunk in December 1943 by depth charges and gunfire from two US ships. Sixteen of its crew died and thirty-four were saved.

HMS *HAREBELL*

Another 'Flower Class' sloop launched at the end of the First World War *Harebell* is perhaps best remembered as the ship that evacuated the island of St Kilda in 1930. Island residents grew increasingly concerned as emigration increased, visitor numbers dwindled and trawler visits lessened. During the First World War St Kilda was used as a Naval post. But feelings of isolation grew when the Navy pulled out at the end of the conflict. Increasingly short of food, islanders were reduced to eating seabirds to survive. When a pregnant woman and her unborn child died because they were unable to reach a hospital the remaining St Kilda residents lobbied the British parliament for help. *Harebell* was sent in to transport them to mainland Scotland in an evacuation that took place at the end of August. The Surgeon of HMS *Harebell*, A. Pomfret, recorded the death of the community:

> . . . all the houses were locked and the people taken on board. Shortly afterward they were looking their last at St Kilda as the *Harebell*, quickly increasing speed, left the island a blur on the horizon. Contrary to expectations they had been very cheerful

throughout, though obviously very tired, but with the first actual separation came the first signs of emotion, and men, women and children wept unrestrainedly as the last farewells were said.

Harebell was scrapped in 1939.

HMS THANET

Launched in 1918, *Thanet* went to Britain's China station to begin her inter-war service. In October 1939 she was converted to a minelayer and was based at Hong Kong. Three years later, trying to stem the Japanese invasion of Singapore, *Thanet* was sunk by Japanese shells. Confusion surrounds the fate of her crew. Many escaped and tried to make their way overland to Singapore shortly before its fall. However, a number were captured during the sinking and were executed almost immediately in reprisal for Japanese losses in a combined British and Australian operation that had taken place shortly before.

HMS TENEDOS

Also launched at the end of the First World War, the destroyer *Tenedos* was undergoing repairs in dry dock at Colombo, Ceylon [Sri Lanka] when she was destroyed by Japanese bombers.

HMS CARLISLE

Completed on Armistice Day, the light cruiser HMS *Carlisle* began active life on Britain's China station before being sent to South Africa where she was often in dry dock. In 1937 she was relieved by HMS *Neptune* and returned to Britain with William aboard. During the early years of the war she saw action off Norway and in the Red Sea, evacuating Britons from British Somaliland before Mussolini's invasion. As part of the Mediterranean fleet *Carlisle* was involved in the Battle of Cape Matapan, the Battle of Crete and, in 1943, Operation 'Husky' – the invasion of Sicily. In October 1943 an attack by German Junkers caused such extensive damage she was unable to head to sea again. Towed into Alexandria, she remained there as a hulk, used as a base ship. Too expensive to repair, she was finally broken up in 1949. *Carlisle*'s badge can still be seen on the dockyard wall in Simonstown.

HMS *SALAMANDER*

Launched in 1936, *Salamander* was a Devonport-based ship that patrolled primarily in home waters before William joined her crew. After he left *Salamander* she spent months on duty with Arctic convoys before travelling to Gibraltar to accompany tank landing craft in the Mediterranean.

Prior to D-Day she and other minesweepers were hard at work clearing the English Channel of hidden explosives, providing a safe platform for the Normandy landings. *Salamander* was wrecked and two other minesweepers were sunk in a friendly-fire incident on 27 August 1944 off the coast of France. The ultimate demise of *Salamander* was kept under wraps by the Navy for 50 years.

The ships, part of the 1st Minesweeping Flotilla, had been moved from an agreed position to a different part of the Channel by their commander. But a message about this change of plan failed to reach Naval headquarters.

As a result, RAF Typhoons came out of the sun and unleashed their deadly rockets against the Royal Naval contingent. It took just 15 minutes for *Hussar* and *Britomart* to be destroyed and for *Salamander* to suffer severe and irreparable damage. Among the wreckage of the ships 117 sailors and officers lay dead in the water. A further 153 were injured.

After the disaster the surviving sailors were dispersed among different ships and ordered not to discuss the tragedy. A 100-year-long secrecy order was placed on the incident. Only when *The Daily Telegraph* investigated papers released under an 'Accelerated Opening' policy at the Public Record Office in Kew did news of what had occurred become known.

Retired Church of England vicar Bert Hughes, who was on *Britomart* at the time, told *The Daily Telegraph*, 'It was a beautiful day without a cloud in the sky and I think I was stripped off to the waist.

'I was helping another seaman make a wire splice and suddenly there was a tremendous explosion and there was water everywhere. I assumed we had struck a mine ourselves.'

However, when he and other terrified sailors looked up they recognised RAF markings and the outline of the Typhoons.

> I jumped to my feet and everything was confusion. When we looked towards the bridge it was in a terrible mess. The ship started to circle and to settle quite quickly. Eventually an order was given to abandon ship, not from an officer because they were all dead or dying. We all went into the water.
>
> I was with a mate called Booth . . . and he couldn't swim. We survived by picking the buoyancy aids off the bodies of our dead mates as they floated by. Then we saw a big cork raft and we tried to get on but it was very full. I cursed the guys on it but then I realised they were badly hurt. There was one chap there who was very still but apparently unmarked. I gave him mouth-to-mouth resuscitation but he was already dead, hit in the base of the spine and killed at once.
>
> I will never forget the thunder of that attack. There can't be anything like the noise and the shaking of it. By this time we were floating in range of the German 9.2 in. coastal guns and they opened up on us. We didn't have any bad feelings towards the RAF. We were more interested in survival.

Immediately there was a board of enquiry set up in an attempt to discover what had gone wrong. It discovered the problem lay with lack of communication between officers in charge of minesweeping off the Normandy coast and Naval headquarters.

The ships were picked up by shore-based radar and a Spitfire was sent on a reconnaissance mission. Although the pilot thought they looked like minesweepers there was no evidence to suggest a Royal Naval contingent was in the area. Accordingly, Naval headquarters requested a Typhoon strike. Wing Commander Johnny Baldwin, in charge of the sortie, was immediately suspicious and made four separate enquiries about the identity of the ships. Each time he was told to proceed as planned.

Below, panic-stricken sailors fired recognition rockets and draped Union flags and the White Ensign over what remained of the ships to alert the pilots. In their defence, Naval headquarters – kept in the dark about minesweeper movements – had been monitoring nightly attacks by German motor boats in the area.

Three officers were court-martialled but only one was reprimanded while the other two were acquitted. The RAF was swiftly exonerated from blame. *Salamander* was beyond economic repair and in 1947 she was finally scrapped.

HMS NEWFOUNDLAND

Newfoundland was a 'Colony Class' cruiser launched in December 1941 by the wife of Ernest Bevin, the eminent West Country politician who was at that time Minister for Labour. About £100,000 of its cost was paid for by the public subscription of the people of Newfoundland.

After sailing with the Home Fleet she became the flagship of the 15th Cruiser Squadron in the Mediterranean, with her engines under William's watchful eye. After repairs in the US were carried out *Newfoundland* was dispatched to the Far East and became part of the newly formed British Pacific Fleet.

In May 1945 *Newfoundland* was supporting the Australian landing at Wewak in occupied New Guinea. Then it was on to attack the Japanese naval base of Truk in the Caroline Islands. She was then prepared for an invasion of mainland Japan that was superseded by the dropping of two atomic bombs on Hiroshima and Nagasaki. Following a prolonged spell at sea, *Newfoundland* came to land at Yokosuka where Royal Marines joined seamen in taking over the Naval base there. *Newfoundland* was in Tokyo when the Japanese surrender was finally signed aboard USS *Missouri* on 2 September 1945. By now *Newfoundland* had sailed for some 122,490 miles in wartime service. The next task was to repatriate Japanese prisoners of war.

There followed a tour of New Zealand then it was on to Australia where the crew spent Christmas 1945. In March 1946 one of the ship's commanders was killed on deck when a typhoon struck in the Malacca Strait.

The *Newfoundland* sailed up the Yangtze to Nanking in politically unstable China during May 1946, running aground on a mud bank.

There were further exercises in Japanese waters before finally returning to Devonport in December 1946.

Following a spell as a stoker training ship at Torpoint, Cornwall, *Newfoundland* was re-commissioned and headed off for extended service on the Far East station. Not until April 1959 did HMS *Newfoundland* finally leave the Far East returning to the UK via the Seychelles, East and South Africa and Freetown, arriving in Portsmouth in June.

On 2 November 1959, after 17 years of service, she was sold to Peru and re-named *Almirante Grau*. In 1973 she was re-named *Capitan Quinones* and survived another six years before being withdrawn from service.

Timeline of Maritime Events in William Stone's Life

1902 First Royal Naval submarine comes into service.

1905 Japanese torpedo boats cripple the Russian fleet at Port Arthur, sparking the Russo-Japanese war – which Japan would go on to win.

1905 Royal Naval College, Dartmouth, opens.

1906 'Dreadnought Class' of battleships developed. With its greater speed and weight of fire, the Dreadnought rendered almost all existing battleships obsolete.

1906 The Paddlesteamer *General Slocum* is destroyed by fire in New York Harbour, killing more than 1,000 people – mostly women and children on a church outing.

1906 First German submarine *U–1* enters service.

1911 Winston Churchill is named as the new First Lord of the Admiralty.

1912 *Titanic* sinks with the loss of 1,529 lives after a collision with an iceberg.

1912 First flight of an aircraft from a ship's deck.

1914   Enemy submarine sunk by HMS *Birmingham* in the first
        week of WWI.

1915   HMS *Tiger* is among the ships damaged in a running battle
        that unfolded after ships of the British Grand Fleet surprised
        a raiding party from the German High Seas Fleet at Dogger
        Bank. German ships were also hit and, following cipher mix-
        ups among the British ships, there was no clear victor in the
        battle.

1915   RMS *Lusitania* is torpedoed by a German U-boat in the
        waters off the Old Head of Kinsale, Ireland. The ship sank
        in 18 minutes claiming the lives of over 1,200 people.
        Although there were ample lifeboats aboard the *Lusitania*
        there was not sufficient time to launch them.

1915   German light cruiser *Königsberg* destroyed.

1915   More than 400 are killed when HMS *Natal* explodes and
        sinks during a Hogmanay party at Cromarty Firth. The dead
        include children and guests as well as crew. Although sabotage
        was initially suspected, a later report blamed unstable cordite
        aboard for the tragedy. It went unreported due to wartime
        restrictions but, until the end of the Second World War, Royal
        Naval crew are called to salute every time they passed her
        upturned hull.

1916   First depth charge is issued to the Royal Navy. Depth charges
        are effectively barrels full of high explosive that are triggered
        by water pressure, especially developed for action against the
        U-boat. They can be dropped from the air or by ships.

1916   Lowestoft and Great Yarmouth are raided by a German cruiser
        squadron.

1916   Battle of Jutland: The most notable naval battle of the First
        World War, it was fought between 31 May and 1 June 1916
        in the North Sea near Denmark's Jutland peninsula.
        The Imperial German Navy's High Seas Fleet was
        commanded by Reinhard Scheer while Britain's Grand Fleet
        was under the command of Admiral Sir John Jellicoe.

The British fleet was superior in number and ship size so the Germans could not hope for outright victory. Instead it was Scheer's intention to lure a substantial part of it into battle and destroy it. At the time the Royal Navy was dominating the seas and starting to strangle German supply lines.

Meanwhile, the Grand Fleet's hope was to destroy enough of the German fleet to keep it in home ports for the duration of the conflict.

The German plan was to use Vice Admiral Franz Hipper's fast scouting group of five modern battlecruisers to lure Vice Admiral Sir David Beatty's battlecruiser squadrons through a submarine picket line and into the path of the main German fleet.

Via signal intercepts, Jellicoe realised a trap was in the offing and sailed with the Grand Fleet to rendezvous with Beatty, passing the intended positions of the German U-boats before they reached their proposed positions.

Consequently Beatty encountered Hipper's battlecruiser force long before the Germans had expected it to. In the subsequent battle Hipper successfully drew the British vanguard into the path of the High Seas Fleet. By the time Beatty turned towards the British main fleet he had lost two battlecruisers along with his numerical advantage over Hipper. However, the German fleet in pursuit of Beatty to finish him off was lured towards the main thrust of the British fleet. At sundown the two huge fleets totalling 250 ships between them were pumping one-ton shells at one another through drifting mist.

Before the battle had ended 14 British and 11 German ships were sunk with great loss of life. The Royal Navy came off far worse, losing 6,094 sailors against the 2,551 lost by Germany. Jellicoe was still trying to out-manoeuvre the remainder of the German force when it slipped back into port.

Both sides claimed victory. Church bells tolled throughout Britain, implying a triumph of Trafalgar dimensions. Only upon later inspection of battle statistics were question marks laid against Naval achievements. More British than German ships had been lost, some proving to have had inadequate protection against German firepower, and tactics were open to criticism. However, the German navy was no longer equipped to contest control of the high seas. Instead, Germany focussed its resources on U-boat warfare, investing heavily in the single most effective weapon against British dominance of the waves. It was successful in some respects. In April 1917 more than 500,000 tons of shipping was sunk by U-boat action. But predatory action by German submarines brought America into the war on the side of Britain and unbalanced the stalemate that had persisted in the trenches along the Western Front.

1916   HMS *Hampshire* sinks off Orkney, killing Lord Kitchener.

1917   President Wilson breaks off relations with Germany after the US ship *Housatonic* is sunk off Sicily.

1917   More than 2,000 people die in a mighty blast at Halifax, Nova Scotia, after a ship carrying munitions collides with an aid-bearing boat in the mouth of the harbour. The explosion causes a mushroom cloud over the city, a tsunami in the harbour and a ten-minute-long shower of burning soot. When the last onshore fire was extinguished 326 acres of the Canadian city had been laid to waste and 9,000 people were nursing injuries caused by fire, shattering windows and, later, exposure in freezing weather.

1917   Women's Royal Naval Service (WRNS) is formed.

1917   First experiments with ASDIC, the secret device that navy chiefs believe will counter the submarine threat. The Allied Submarine Detection Investigation Committee lends its acronym to this underwater detection system. It sends out sound waves and the proximity of a vessel is discerned by any returning echo. For ships the timing and pitch of the echo helps to determine how far away the submarine lies or in which direction it is travelling. ASDIC was further developed during the 1920s and was a major asset in the Battle of the Atlantic during the Second World War.

1918   Royal Air Force is formed out of the Royal Navy Air Service and the Royal Army Flying Corps.

1918   The German High Seas Fleet sails into British ports after the Kaiser's surrender. Ten days after the armistice the British fleet – armed and prepared for trickery – rendezvoused with the German ships sailing under a white flag and escorted them back to the Firth of Forth. There were battleships, cruisers and destroyers in the defeated task force. Meanwhile 39 U-boats sail into Harwich.

1919   The German High Seas Fleet is scuttled at Scapa Flow.

1921   For the first time aircraft are used to sink a ship. American planes sink the former German battleship *Ostfriesland* off the coast of Virginia with six 2,000 lb bombs in just twenty-five minutes. Until now naval chiefs have been convinced only big guns attached to armoured ships would be capable of sinking a major vessel.

1922   Washington Naval Treaty is signed, limiting the naval aspirations of the US, Great Britain, Japan, France and Italy. Japan feels slighted, having been given a lower number of ships than either the US or Britain. France and Italy are held at the same number, which France deems unfair given that it has two coastlines to protect – the Mediterranean and the Atlantic – while the Italians have only one. Meanwhile the German fleet size is restricted by the Treaty of Versailles, drawn up at the end of the First World War. It is permitted no submarines or naval aviation and only six heavy cruisers, six light cruisers, twelve destroyers and twelve torpedo boats. As far as Britain is concerned, the agreement has merits and significant disadvantages as Frank C. Bowen points out in his 1925 book *The King's Navy*.

The Washington Treaty, which was signed in February 1922, in some respects simplifies naval policy, and in others complicates it. Under its provisions two battleships were laid down for the Royal Navy in 1923 and no more can be laid down until 1931. This clears the air, so far as the political aspect of building programmes is concerned. But it adds very greatly to the responsibility of the technical experts designing these two ships, since it is imperative that they should possess the very utmost qualities of offence and defence while not exceeding the size limits imposed by Washington. Long after the commencement of the *Nelson* and *Rodney* great secrecy is being maintained about their design.

1927 President Coolidge invites British, Japanese, French and Italian representatives to a conference in Geneva centring on naval capacities. No agreement is reached.

1930 The government and the Admiralty are at odds over spending on increasingly large and costly warships prior to the treaty. In a memo in February 1930 Prime Minister Ramsay McDonald says, 'In the opinion of His Majesty's government in this United Kingdom the battleship, in view of its tremendous size and cost, is of doubtful utility and the government would wish to see an agreement by which the battleship would in due time disappear from the fleets of the world.' Three months later the London Naval Treaty is agreed, limiting the size and number of warships and submarines of the major powers. Britain, the US, Japan, France and Italy take part in the talks. However, France and Italy bow out of the specific terms binding their naval ambitions. The conference results in a three-power pact that leads to the scrapping of HMS *Emperor of India*, *Malborough*, *Benbow* and *Tiger*. Battleship construction is suspended by Britain, the US and Japan for five years. Moreover, Britain recognises the right of the US to possess a fleet equal to that of the Royal Navy. Although there is scant advantage for the UK in the pact it strengthens the bond with America.

1931 A mutiny at Invergordon breaks out after rumours about pay cuts anger sailors. The government's Committee on National Expenditure had decided on a 10 per cent cut for

Naval personnel. However, for those who joined the service after 1925 who were already poorly paid this represented a 25 per cent salary cut.

Problems began after ten warships of the Atlantic Fleet arrived in the Cromarty Firth on 11 September 1931. These were HMS *Hood* (the Navy's flagship), *Adventure, Dorsetshire, Malaya, Norfolk, Repulse, Rodney, Valiant, Warspite* and the *York*.

Angry sailors gathered on a football field to debate their action after rumours of pay cuts circulated. Many left singing 'The Red Flag'. There was further trouble centred on the base's canteen.

Within four days a number of battleships were unable to put to sea as sailors refused orders. They gathered on the forecastles of their ships to cheer and jeer as officers tried to establish control. On HMS *Rodney* a piano was taken to the fo'c'sle and accompanied the singing sailors.

It was clear to officers that it would be difficult to regain control while the vagaries of the pay issue were still at large. For their part, sailors never showed aggressive behaviour towards their officers, which stood them in good stead during ensuing negotiations. Indeed, sailors didn't consider it to be a mutiny, more a justified protest although other high-ranking establishment figures felt it a sure sign of communist infiltration.

Finally, the Cabinet accepted a Naval recommendation that ratings on the old rate of pay remain on that rate, with a 10 per cent cut in line with the rest of the Service. It was made clear that further acts of insurrection would be severely punished. Admiral John Kelly was appointed to restore morale in the Atlantic Fleet, later known as the Home Fleet.

There was retribution, though. A number of the organisers of the strike were jailed, while a total of 200 sailors from the Atlantic Fleet were discharged. Several hundred other sailors were purged from elsewhere in the Navy, accused of attempting to incite similar incidents.

Meanwhile, the careers of some officers conspicuously stagnated. After all, one officer who had tried to talk below deck sailors out of militant action pointed out he himself was suffering and had written to his wife, telling her to sack one of the maids. Another advised activists to send their wives out to work. Even the most concerned officers had to concede that they had lost touch with the men who served beneath them. There was a lack of common purpose that divided ratings and officers so much that communication between the two sides was negligible. The shame felt by Navy top brass about letting the country down was reflected in the country as a whole. Curiously, ratings at foreign stations like William were virtually immune to this wave of unrest.

And there were repercussions across public life. 'The Invergordon Mutiny' caused a panic on the London Stock Exchange and a run on the pound, bringing Britain's economic troubles to a head that forced it off the Gold Standard on 20 September 1931.

1931   Rank of 'Mate' abolished.

1935   The Abyssinian crisis, in which Italy invades the African state, results in the fleet base changing from Malta – considered vulnerable to air strikes – to Alexandria in Egypt.

1935   Anglo-German Naval Treaty is agreed, restricting *Kriegsmarine* expansion to 35 per cent of Royal Naval capacity.

1936   Royal Navy stands by to rescue Britons and other refugees caught up in the Spanish Civil War.

1936   Super liner *Queen Mary* sets off from Southampton on her maiden voyage, heading for New York via Cherbourg. Passengers can stake a place on the luxury 80,000 ton vessel from as little as £37 5s, which includes meals.

1936   A ferry link transporting rail carriages between Dover and Dunkirk is launched so that passengers going from London to Paris can travel without being disturbed on the 11-hour journey.

1937   Britain's latest aircraft carrier, the *Ark Royal*, which cost £3 million is launched at Birkenhead.

1938   HMS *Sheffield* is first ship fitted with RN radar.

1938   Royal Naval expenditure estimated at £93,707,000, the highest figure since 1919.

1939   Outbreak of war brings back the convoy system to protect British shipping. More than 800 people are believed dead after HMS *Royal Oak* was sunk by a torpedo in Scapa Flow, previously believed impenetrable to German U-boats.

1940   Operation 'Dynamo' rescues 338,000 Allied troops from the beach at Dunkirk. At a cost of seven thousand men, six destroyers and other craft, the Royal Navy helps to snatch victory from the jaws of defeat in one of the most successful combined operations ever staged.

1940   More than 1,000 sailors die after Britain attacks French navy ships in Algeria following the fall of France. Churchill made the fateful decision to prevent the ships being used by the Vichy government.

1941   *Hood*, and Germany's newest and swiftest battleship *Bismarck*, are sunk. Arctic convoys to Russia begin. Japanese planes attack the US fleet at Pearl Harbor.

1942   Remnants of the Japanese navy are on the run after US victory in the Battle of Midway.

1943   U-boats are defeated in the Atlantic as the Allies break German security codes.

1944   Between September 1939 and January 1944 the number of Navy personnel increases more than fourfold, from 161,000 to 750,000. Naval treaties made between the wars had put Britain on a back foot, but the necessary fleet expansion brought about by conflict meant there was plenty of opportunity for promotion.

1944   Operation 'Neptune' gets under way in June, shipping troops and supplies to the Normandy beaches at the start of the Allied invasion. Formation of the British Pacific Fleet is finalised.

1949   HMS *Amethyst* escapes through a flooded Yangtze River after being trapped by Chinese communists.

1950   Royal Naval ships posted off Korean coast after the outbreak of war.

1958   First 'Cod War' with Iceland.

1967   The *Torrey Canyon* strikes Pollard's Rock, causing the world's first major oil spill. Her cargo of 120,000 tons of crude oil devastates the Cornish coastline.

1967   Britain's first Polaris submarine, HMS *Resolution*, is completed.

1969   Sir Robin Knox-Johnston becomes the first man to circumnavigate the globe non-stop and single-handedly, winning the *Sunday Times* Golden Globe Race.

1972   Iceland unilaterally declares an 'Exclusive Economic Zone' extending beyond its territorial waters, before announcing plans to reduce over-fishing. It polices its quota system with the coastguard, leading to a series of net-cutting incidents with British trawlers that fish the areas. As a result, a fleet of Royal Naval warships and tug-boats are employed to act as a deterrent against any future harassment of British fishing crews by the Icelandic craft.

1979   The last fleet carrier, HMS *Ark Royal*, is scrapped.

1982   The most important operation conducted predominantly by the Royal Navy after the Second World War is the defeat in 1982 of Argentina in the Falkland Islands War. Despite losing four naval ships and other civilian and RFA ships the Royal Navy proved it was still able to fight a battle 8,345 miles (12,800 km) from Great Britain. HMS *Conqueror* is the only nuclear-powered submarine to have engaged an enemy ship with torpedoes, sinking the Argentine cruiser ARA *General Belgrano*.

1985   A crewman dies when the Greenpeace ship *Rainbow Warrior* is blown up by French agents in New Zealand.

1991 Nineteen Royal Navy units take part in Operation 'Desert Storm' to oust Iraqi forces from Kuwait.

2000 Russian 'Oscar II Class' submarine *Kursk* – pride of the Russian Northern Fleet – is trapped on the seabed after an internal explosion. Despite an international rescue attempt, she is lost with all hands.

2003 The invasion of Iraq. Royal Navy units take part in the amphibious assault on the oil wells situated on the Al-Faw peninsula.

2005 Dame Ellen MacArthur breaks the world record for the fastest solo circumnavigation of the world. Her time of 71 days, 14 hours, 18 minutes, 33 seconds is a world record for the 27,354 nautical miles (50,660 km) covered – an average speed of 15.9 knots (29.4 km/h).

2009 The Royal Navy is currently deployed in many areas of the world, including a number of standing Royal Navy deployments. These include several home tasks as well as overseas deployments. The Royal Navy is deployed in the Mediterranean as part of standing NATO deployments including mine countermeasures and NATO Maritime Group 2 and also has the Royal Navy Cyprus Squadron. In both the North and South Atlantic Royal Naval vessels are patrolling. There is always a Falkland Islands Patrol Vessel on deployment; currently the new vessel is HMS *Clyde*. The Royal Navy is also deployed in the Middle East to provide maritime security and surveillance in the Northern Persian Gulf.

ACKNOWLEDGEMENTS

We would like to thank the many organisations and individuals who helped William, in so many ways, to enjoy his life to the full.

The members of Watlington Royal British Legion; Dunkirk Veterans Association at High Wycombe and Henley-on-Thames; Association of Dunkirk Little Ships; Royal Naval Association, High Wycombe; HMS *Hood* Association; HMS *Newfoundland* Association; George Cross Island Association; Western Front Association, Thames Valley and 'Ox & Bucks' branches – whose company William so much enjoyed at their meetings and reunions.

Thanks also to Dennis Goodwin, Chairman of the World War Veterans Association; Mrs Rosie Thompson, Events Organiser, The 'Not Forgotten' Association; Frances Moreton, War Memorials Trust; Wing Commander Chris Pickthall and Lieutenant Commander 'Ollie' Almond of the MOD Ceremonial, Events and Commemorations Team; the clergy and members of St Leonard's Church Watlington and St Peter's Church, Buckland Tout Saints, Kingsbridge; the pupils and staff of the Primary School and Icknield Community College, Watlington. Not least, William's neighbours and many friends within the Watlington community.

We acknowledge the friendship and support given to William by his fellow Brethren within Freemasonry, the Royal Masonic Benevolent Institution and especially the care and attention provided during his last few years at Lord Harris Court.

Over the years we have been helped by many people who have contributed their time to enhance William's quality of life, amongst whom we particularly thank Ken Cook; Sheila Foster; Bridgeen Fox; Rupert & Renee Gandy; Carole King; Lady Mogg; Bill Mundy; Peter Norman; Beryl and Alban Parkinson; Frank Pate; Don & Daphne Read; Graham Stark; Jenny Stillwell; Tony and Brenda Toms.

Finally, special thanks to Paul Bevand MBE, webmaster, HMS *Hood* Association, for his early investigations into William's naval career; to Karen Farrington for her diligence and perseverance in combining William's notes and our sources of information together with her own research, and to Iain Macgregor and all the team at Mainstream Publishing, who collectively inspired us to publish this book.

Anne and Michael Davidson

BIBLIOGRAPHY

The Oxford Illustrated History of the Royal Navy; The Public Records Office, Kew; the Imperial War Museum; www.naval-history.net; www.halcyon-class.co.uk; *Buckland Tout Saints The Parish, Its People and Their Homes*, by Patricia Cove; www.bbc.co.uk/ww2peopleswar; www.seayourhistory.org.uk; *Domesday To D-Day, A History of a Devon Parish*, by D.A. McCoy; *The Land Changed Its Face – The Evacuation of the South Hams 1943–44*, by Grace Bradbeer.

EPILOGUE

THE FIRST SEA LORD –
ADMIRAL SIR JONATHON BAND GCB, ADC

I first had the pleasure of meeting Chief Petty Officer Bill Stone when he came to the Ministry of Defence in 2007 to be honoured at a reception marking his service in the Royal Navy between 1918 and 1945. At the age of 107, he was then one of only three Great War veterans still with us, and the recollections he shared of his service, particularly in the Second World War, were a vivid and humbling testament to his courage.

Reading his memoirs, I am struck by three things. Firstly, he was a remarkably self-possessed young man whose conviction that the Royal Navy was where he belonged never waivered. I imagine that spectacular global deployment in HMS *Hood* in the inter-war years confirmed his belief that the Naval Service provided adventure and opportunity in equal measure, something he was later to cling to in the dark days of Dunkirk, the Russian and Atlantic convoys and the Sicily campaign. His loyalty to the service, and the comradeship it provided throughout his life, is a constant feature.

Secondly, I think Bill in most respects typified jolly 'Jack Tar', the archetypal British sailor. This is why we so readily identify with him; and there is plenty in these lively pages underscoring the enduring qualities of sailors and marines, who are as much the life blood of the Navy today as they ever were. Humour, a love of travel, a complete absence of prejudice and a lust for life were characteristic of Bill. Above all, there was his bravery. Bill Stone felt fear under fire, as mortal men do, but carried on with his duty regardless. He blithely faced down the spectre of being torpedoed in icy, gale-swept waters with apparent indifference. That is courage.

Most of all, while I am struck by what has changed about the Royal Navy, I am reassured by how much remains the same. Conditions and pay have changed beyond recognition; nobody would nowadays begrudge senior ratings their ability to buy 'motor bicycles' as the Naval Personnel Committee did in 1919! Although the Ship Control centres of today's warships would be unrecognisable to Bill, stokers (now Marine Engineering Technicians) still work their way through professional qualifications across different classes of ship. Mess deck life is undoubtedly more comfortable and ships much less crowded but 'Uckers' is still the board game of choice, once watching DVDs loses its appeal. And, despite the cut backs in the size of the Fleet that are the inevitable conclusion of post-war policies, as they always have been, the Royal Navy, Royal Marines and Royal Fleet Auxiliary are still globally deployed across many theatres, including fighting in Afghanistan and protecting vital infrastructure in Iraq. Courage under fire is as much in evidence today as it was then.

Bill's was a life lived in remarkable circumstances. These memoirs will be part of his legacy, to his family, those with an interest in naval history and to the generations of sailors to come. At the same time as reminding us that courage, humour and compassion need not be the preserve of the few, William Stone sets an example for us all.

Jonathon Band